TEACHING WALKTHRUs 2

FIVE-STEP GUIDES TO INSTRUCTIONAL COACHING

TOM SHERRINGTON
&
OLIVER CAVIGLIOLI

First published 2021

by John Catt Educational Ltd,
15 Riduna Park, Station Road,
Melton, Woodbridge IP12 1QT

Tel: +44 (0) 1394 389850
Email: enquiries@johncatt.com
Website: www.johncatt.com

ISBN: 978 1 913622 47 3

Typeset by John Catt Educational Limited

TESTIMONIALS

NEIL ALMOND

Assistant Headteacher of Teaching and Learning, Woodland Academy Trust

WalkThrus have taken front and centre and been the foundation of our CPD offer at our multi-academy trust. The book and related subscriber materials have enabled staff to take ownership of their own professional learning, while the shared language of the techniques has given staff at all levels a shared understanding and starting point to engage in rich conversations on how to improve their practice.

NICOLE BLACKFORD

Assistant Headteacher, Teaching and Learning, Telford Priory School

Volume 1 arrived and within a few hours it looked as though WalkThrus had exploded all over my office! The plethora of possibilities to use such evidence-informed techniques for curriculum, teaching and learning, CPD and instructional coaching were limitless.

CLAIRE HILL

Trust Vice Principal and Secondary Improvement Lead, Turner Schools

Great CPD should be actionable, iterative and focused on our *best bets* for teaching. WalkThrus offers all of this and more by offering a framework for teaching development that provides the what, why and how of great teaching, whatever your career stage.

CHRISTIAN MBA

Teacher, Speaker and Digital Content Creator (aka IamMisterMba)

Tom Sherrington and Oliver Caviglioli have crafted an absolute gem of a book. Wherever you are in your teaching career, WalkThrus has codified the very best educational research in this aesthetically pleasing, mercifully practical guide to elicit best practice.

DAVID SAMMELS

Executive Headteacher, Mayflower and Mount Wise Primary Schools, Learning Academies Trust, Plymouth

The WalkThrus really are exceptionally well put together. They give staff a focus point for professional exploration and debate. Concise descriptions and bold images make this a tool of joy. And unlike set programmes, the WalkThrus are immeasurably flexible, allowing us to tailor them to suit our development plans.

MARTINE ELLIS

Professional Development Manager and Scholarly Activity Lead, Guernsey College of Further Education

The WalkThru toolkit has helped underpin Guernsey College's teacher-led, evidence-based approach to professional development. The resources are beautifully presented and highly accessible. Our teachers love the WalkThrus, and our students are feeling the benefit – this makes me a very happy professional development manager!

ABOUT THE AUTHORS

TOM SHERRINGTON

Tom started out as a physics and maths teacher in the 1980s and has since worked in numerous schools of different kinds as a teacher and leader, gathering ideas and working with a fabulous range of teachers and students.

He began writing the popular blog teacherhead.com as a way of sharing ideas and, encouraged by the engagement from teachers, went on to publish *The Learning Rainforest: Great Teaching in Real Classrooms* and *Rosenshine's Principles in Action*, working with Oliver and John Catt Educational in both cases.

He works with schools and colleges providing support on curriculum, assessment and improving the quality of teaching and is a regular speaker and contributor to conferences and education festivals. Tom and Oliver are big fans of the researchED movement.

OLIVER CAVIGLIOLI

Oliver's childhood was steeped in design, thanks to his architect father's daily sermons on 'good taste'. His adulthood was immersed in the world of special schools, culminating in a decade of headship.

During that time, both backgrounds merged in the development of effective visual communication – firstly for children, then increasingly for colleagues.

Then, after a decade of training and writing about visual learning strategies, Oliver started illustrating other people's education books. In turn, that moved on to designing the structure, look and layout of the pages themselves.

His work with the Learning Scientists (*Understanding How We Learn*) was his first fully-designed creation, soon followed by his own *Dual Coding With Teachers*. Previous collaboration with Tom Sherrington (both *Rainforest* books and *Rosenshine's Principles in Action*) meant that *Teaching WalkThrus* was a natural development.

GUEST AUTHORS

SIMON BREAKSPEAR

Research Fellow, University of New South Wales

BRONWYN RYRIE JONES

Teacher educator, Melbourne Graduate School of Education, University of Melbourne

ZOE ENSER

Lead Specialist English Advisor for The Education People

MARK ENSER

Head of Geography at Heathfield Community College

BENNIE KARA

Deputy Headteacher, Teaching & Learning, The Bemrose School

OLLIE LOVELL

Teacher, instructional coach, host of ERRR podcast

ALEX QUIGLEY

Author, former teacher, evidence-seeker

CLAIRE STONEMAN

Director of the Exemplary Leadership Programme

JOHN TOMSETT

Headteacher, Huntington School, York

MARTIN ROBINSON

Author and Education Consultant

Guest author pages are denoted by portraits with blue backgrounds.

Welcome to Volume 2 of Teaching WalkThrus, featuring our new teacher models, Jenny and Joe. This book is a follow-up to Volume 1 (the Yellow book) and the precursor to Volume 3 (the Green book). We are over the moon with the response to the first volume, which has been sold around the world and embraced with great enthusiasm by teachers and leaders in schools and colleges of all kinds.

The books are now part of a wider set of materials that we have developed for supporting professional learning via www.walkthrus.co.uk and we're thrilled that over 1000 schools have joined our growing community. Instructional coaching is growing in popularity as a central mechanism for supporting teachers' professional learning and we are delighted to be playing our part by providing the tools to support this powerful process. We've enlisted the support of a number of specialist contributing authors in this volume, harnessing the wonderful depth of knowledge and experience that exists in the field of education.

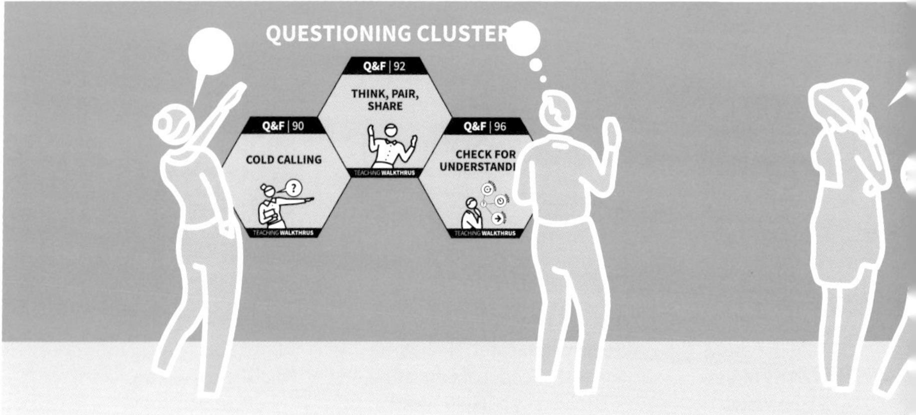

DESIGN

Our WalkThrus are written to be deliberately generic and context free. We are committed to the idea that a WalkThru is not a rigid recipe or checklist that must be adhered to. It is only ever a reference point for reflection or to support coaching and feedback discussions. At the bottom right of every WalkThru page, you will find the same message repeated: 'Attempt, Develop, Adapt, Practise, Test', spelling out ADAPT.

It is essential that teachers ADAPT the WalkThrus so that they take form in their very specific contexts – with their subject; their students; their classroom.

WHY?

It is important that everyone involved in sharing ideas about teaching understands the underlying rationale and evidence base, where one exists. This applies to all of the ideas we explore in this book, including the use of WalkThrus themselves.

The Why? section in this volume includes an overview of the all-important memory model that underpins so many of the strategies, alongside a selection of the key ideas from influential educational thinkers and researchers such as Nuthall, Sweller, Fiorella and Mayer.

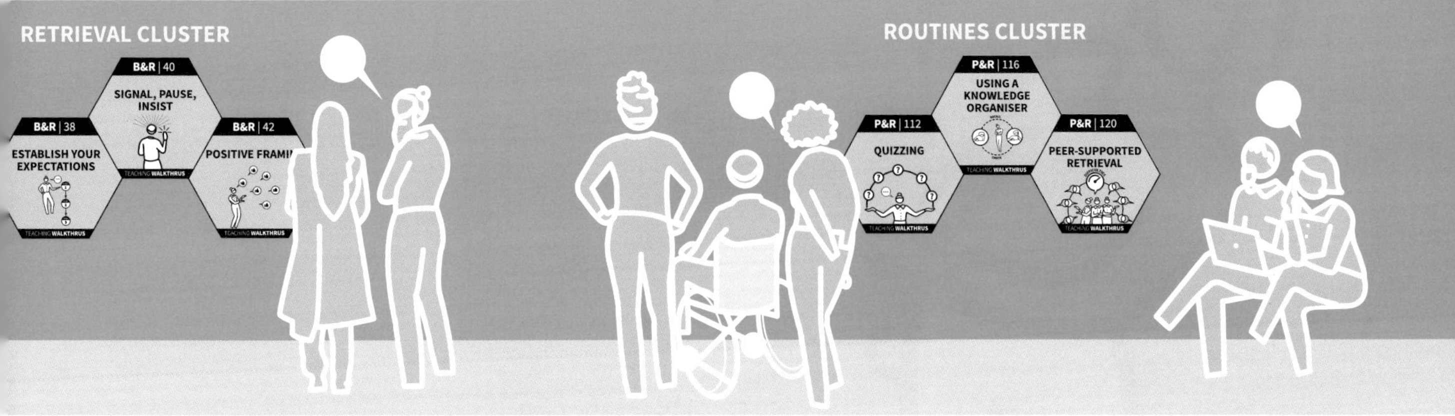

WHAT?

In this second volume, we have selected another 50+ ideas presented by Jenny and Joe as WalkThrus. The strategies are organised into the same six sections as in Volume 1, covering the range of activities that teachers need to explore with any class. It is our intention that, put together, the books should be regarded as forming one coherent curated set. There is no hierarchy between the books in terms of importance or 'difficulty' and we hope that every teacher will find that they are collecting ideas from across the whole range to meet their learners' needs.

HOW?

The How? section includes further guides for teachers and leaders regarding the implementation of WalkThrus as a tool for teacher development. This includes a repeat of the A|D|A|P|T strategy and more guidance for using WalkThrus in various professional learning scenarios.

The WalkThrus might be self explanatory on first reading, but the way ideas translate into improved practice is complex so it is essential that teachers and leaders think hard about how to engineer professional learning processes that are effective and sustained.

CLUSTERS

One of the tools we have developed is the idea of clusters. We found, through our experience in various training scenarios, that WalkThrus strategies are often strongly interconnected. It is powerful and efficient to combine linked strategies into a cluster so that teachers learn to use them in combination. We find that the 'If, Then, So that' structure helps with thinking through the choice of WalkThrus for a specific purpose. Readers can find a free downloadable cluster-builder toolkit to help them link WalkThrus from across all books and series to support them in their planning.

CONTENTS

WALKTHRUs 2

WHY?

REASONS FOR THE WALKTHRUs

It is important that everyone involved in sharing ideas about teaching understands the underlying rationale and evidence base, where one exists. This applies to all of the ideas we explore in each book, including the use of WalkThrus themselves. It also applies to the nature of successful professional learning. The Why? section explores the evidence around successful teacher development alongside a selection of the key ideas from influential educational thinkers and researchers, with several guest authors making contributions.

THE LEARNING MODEL

In our training, we always find it is very helpful to engage teachers with a simplified model of the learning process using the concepts of Working Memory and Long-Term Memory.

The diagram opposite draws on ideas from Cognitive Load Theory and the work of Dan Willingham. In this simple, un-annotated form, it provides a useful stimulus for discussion. The questions we ask are:

What does this diagram tell us about the learning process?

What are the implications for teachers?

Further questions to consider might include:

- How do we ensure students are thinking?
- How do we help them connect new learning to prior learning?
- Why do some students seem to forget things so easily?
- How do we become so fluent in some areas and find other things much more difficult?

On the next page spread is a more fully annotated version for reference. In a training situation, we recommend starting with the clear diagram to engage teachers' thinking and to explore their preconceptions before providing a more definitive labelled model. The model-building process is key to professional learning as identified in Practice with Purpose; all our WalkThrus are rooted in this model to some extent.

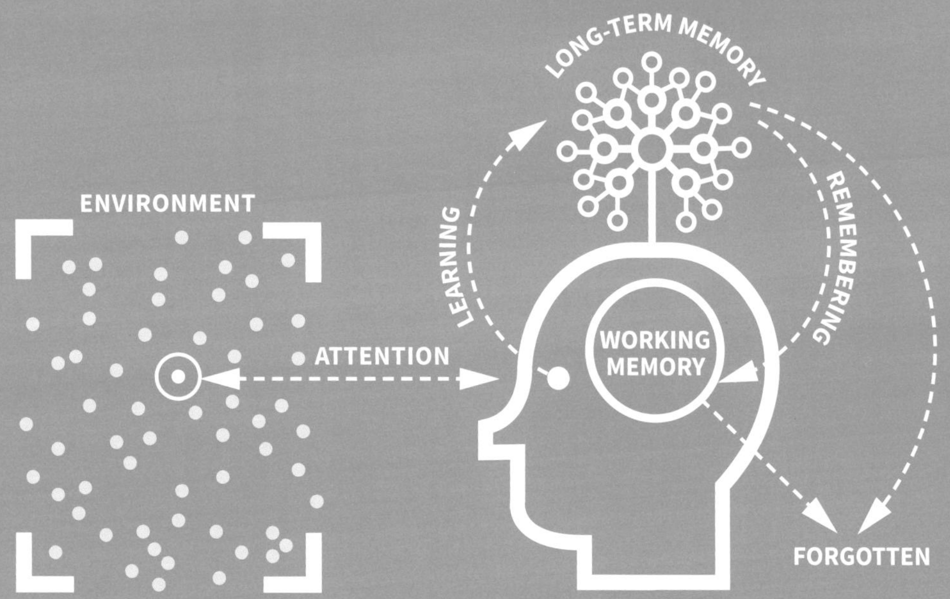
LONG-TERM MEMORY
ENVIRONMENT
LEARNING
REMEMBERING
ATTENTION
WORKING MEMORY
FORGOTTEN

KEY CONSIDERATIONS FROM THE LEARNING MODEL

ANNOTATED LEARNING MODEL

a BUILDING KNOWLEDGE AND EXPERIENCE
Each student has unique set influenced by: life and school experiences; home/social context; curriculum; reading. Other factors: motivation, sense of self, habits.

b SECURING ATTENTION
Design activities to foster focused thinking. Ensure clarity of communication. Develop study habits and routines to build concentration.

c PROCESSING IN WORKING MEMORY
Attend to the *bottleneck* problem of finite memory; present material in small steps. Use dual coding to increase capacity. Ensure students activate prior knowledge, linking retrieved information with new information.

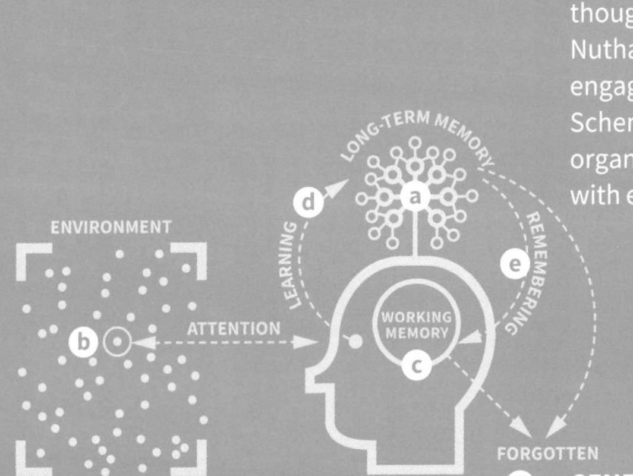

d STORING IN LONG-TERM MEMORY
Thinking is key: 'Memory is the residue of thought' (Willingham)
Nuthall's three-times rule suggests repeated engagement with key ideas.
Schemas develop as students select, organise and integrate new information with existing knowledge (Fiorella & Mayer).

'Understanding is remembering in disguise' (Willingham)

e GENERATIVE PROCESSES
Need variety, increasing depth, range and intensity of retrieval activities.
Include desirable difficulties: remove cue and recency; space and interleave practice.
Include big picture and detailed level recall.
Practise at higher frequency for fluency or automaticity.

WHOLE-CLASS TEACHING

Once we have an understanding of how learning works in terms of a simple memory model, the real challenge for teachers is to extend the implications for teaching an individual to teaching a whole class of students, each with their own schema-forming brains and their unique set of knowledge and experience. This issue is captured in Nuthall's *Hidden Lives of Learners*.

Many of our WalkThrus deal with the process of setting up classroom routines so that teachers are engaging all students in thinking, making connections, retrieval practice, developing fluency and identifying where individual students are struggling. Part of this requires developing a mindset where teachers move from thinking *has anyone understood?, does anyone know the answer?* to *does <u>everyone</u> understand?, does <u>everyone</u> know the answer?* This is the core challenge teachers face and it's all too easy to take the success of a few students to represent the rest. Our hope is that WalkThrus provide the framework for improving teachers' capacity for dealing with this challenge more and more successfully.

CHARACTERISTICS OF SUCCESSFUL PROFESSIONAL DEVELOPMENT

In this paper, Sam Sims and Harry Fletcher-Wood explore the evidence for six traits said to be essential for successful professional development. We have included five as the critiques are important to understand in terms of applying the WalkThrus. The sixth is *collaboration*. This is less vital than often thought. In the My Teaching Partner study, for example, it wasn't present and yet the programme was successful, with lasting impact two years later.

www.bit.ly/3bY7D6W

SAM SIMS

HARRY FLETCHER-WOOD

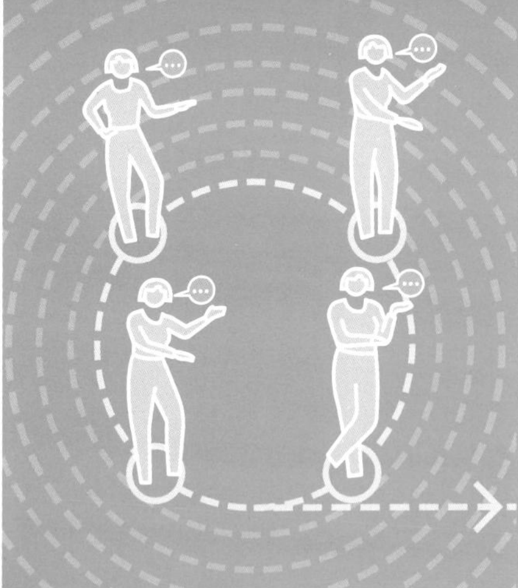

1

SUSTAINED | FREQUENCY IS CRITICAL, NOT TIME SPAN

Claim: Frequency, not time-span, is critical.

Critique: We can all agree that a one-day training day has limited impact in teachers' classrooms. The consensus view, consequently, is that PD is effective when it is sustained over time. Yet even if structured in terms of cycles, it still might lack impact – over a two-year period, teachers might face a fortnightly diet of entirely new material. For this reason, Sims and Fletcher-Wood say that what teachers need is repeated practice to change their ingrained habits. Frequency trumps the length of the time span.

2

PRACTICE-BASED | CREATE NEW HABITS

Claim: PD needs to contain an element of active learning or practice.

Critique: It's true that we find it hard to adopt new actions. This is important because we find it hard to adopt new actions if our habits remain unchanged. Even new goals seem to have little impact if old habits persist. However, practice during PD sessions isn't always meaningful; repeated practice of new techniques in the environment in which they will later be performed is the key to habit change. The associated review and feedback of coaching helps establish new robust cue-responses.

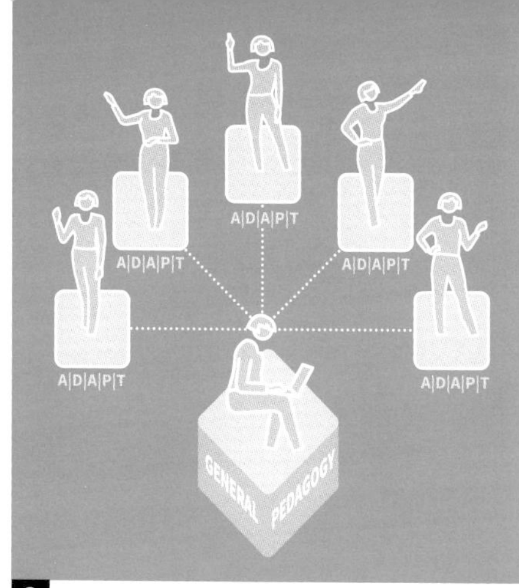

3

SUBJECT-SPECIFIC | GENERAL PEDAGOGY FITS ALL SUBJECTS

Claim: PD should be subject specific.

Critique: This isn't necessarily true. The Instructional Coaching approach of My Teaching Partner (MTP) was subject to a randomised-control study, revealing a positive statistically significant effect size on pupil attainment after two years. Significantly, the MTP programme contained no subject knowledge training, only general pedagogy. Yet, its success was seen across different subjects. It seems that the intense and frequent practice in classrooms, with specific subjects, was sufficient for teachers to adapt the techniques to various contexts.

4

EXTERNAL EXPERTISE | CHALLENGE THE FAMILIAR & REFRESH IDEAS

Claim: PD should include external challenge/expertise.

Critique: It's true that outside expertise can refresh and provide new strategies – however, it's not important who provides this level of challenge. It's the ideas that matter. Sims and Fletcher-Wood would like this view to be subject to further studies. From the WalkThrus point of view, the PD materials help teachers avoid the onerous task of collecting, curating and designing in-house publications – in each and every educational organisation.

5

TEACHER BUY-IN | PURPOSE & BENEFITS ECLIPSE VOLUNTEERING

Claim: Those who volunteer for PD succeed more than those obliged to participate.

Critique: Buy-in can be a product of the process rather than a prerequisite. Helen Timperley, in her 2011 book *Realizing the Power of Professional Learning*, points out that explaining the purpose and benefits of a PD programme has greater impact than requesting volunteers. This chimes with Viviane Robinson's work on the effectiveness of revealing the usually unarticulated theory of action behind the nature of the proposed strategy.

DOUG LEMOV'S PRACTICE PERFECT

Teach Like A Champion author Doug Lemov has written a book about how teachers learn. Its aim, as the full title reveals, is 'Getting Better at Getting Better'.

The book's 42 rules (OK, 'principles' if you prefer) help us move our focus from training days where we talk about techniques to classrooms where we practise them.

For that practice to be optimal, the techniques and activities need to be 'deliberately engineered and designed'. Here are five rules most pertinent to the deliberate use of the WalkThrus in PD programmes.

DOUG LEMOV

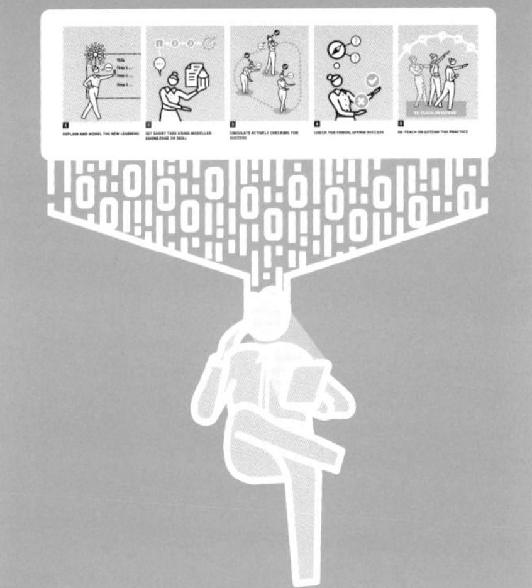

1

RULE 1 | ENCODE SUCCESS

A golden rule in teaching is not to let your students learn something incorrectly, as it takes great effort to override the error. For this reason, learners need to practise new methods correctly from the start. And for that to happen, the teaching techniques need to be explained so success invariably follows.

There is no value in romanticising errors. They dishearten and take valuable time to correct. Success, however, needn't be 100% perfection. But teachers need to know what 'getting it right' looks and feels like.

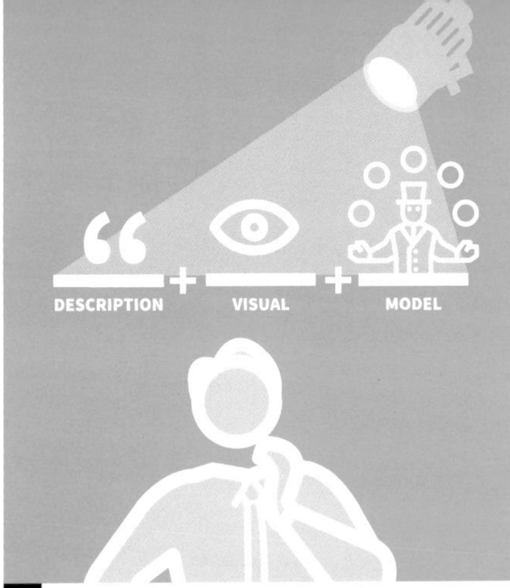

2

RULE 15 | MODEL & DESCRIBE

The ideal combination is the description, the visual and someone demonstrating what it looks like in action.

A description – however well written – leaves too much to the imagination. A visual on its own lacks an explanatory narrative. And a demonstration (see rule 16) doesn't necessarily reveal its key components to the untrained eye. But, as a trio, they help the learner 'triangulate' their perceptions as they move from one to the other. This multi perspective helps build an understanding of a technique to accelerate fluency.

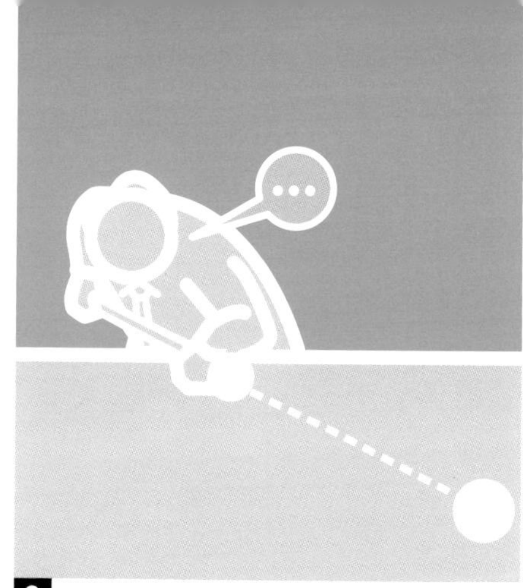

RULE 16 | CALL YOUR SHOTS

It takes an expert, writes John Bransford, to dissect what they see in classrooms and not be diverted by superficial detail. For non-experts, there is a danger of noticing and learning the wrong things.

Such errors of observation are avoidable. To 'call your shots' is to announce what your actions will be before executing them – as in some versions of the game of billiards where you have to notify which ball you intend to pot. Explaining a WalkThru to an observer focuses their attention, in much the same way, on the key actions involved.

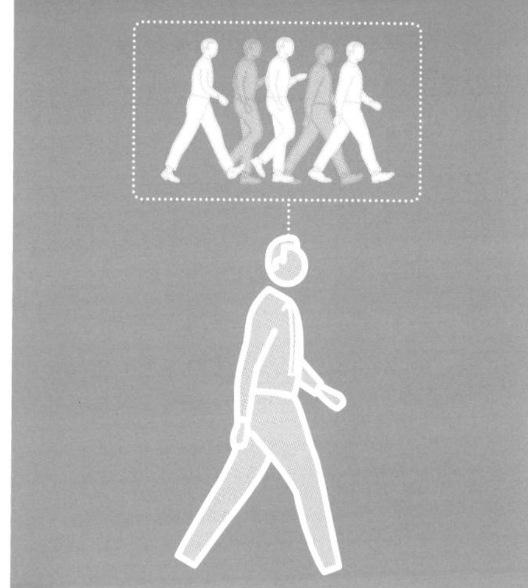

4

RULE 19 | INSIST THEY *WALK THIS WAY*

Much like discovery learning for pupils has been critiqued for being an inefficient way to learn, so it is with professional development. Leaving teachers to interpret vague verbal descriptions of methods is inefficient. Yet many teachers feel they ought to 'put their own spin on it', as Lemov explains.

Better – and completely legitimate – is to replicate the model presented. Imitation often needs to come first before more advanced variations are attempted. Rather than curbing creativity, it creates stability upon which to later forge adaptations.

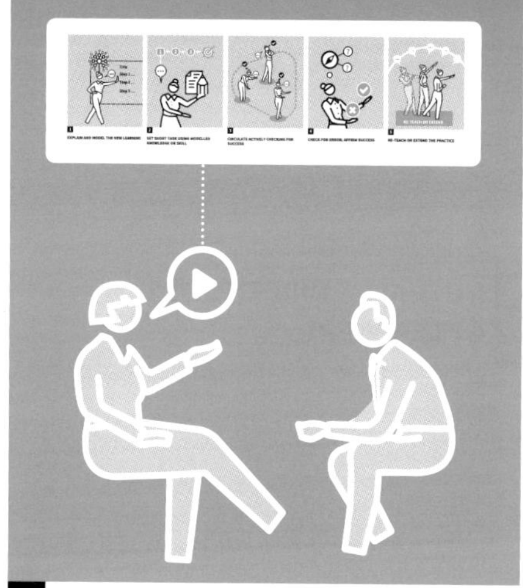

5

RULE 29 | DESCRIBE THE SOLUTION (NOT THE PROBLEM)

To draw another parallel with teaching students, we know how the use of the negative – 'don't' – is less likely to be as successful as pointing to what is wanted. Similarly with feedback for teachers. Lemov writes that 'Good feedback describes the solution – in concrete, actionable terms – rather than the problem.'

The WalkThrus are designed with this specific purpose in mind. And, alongside the Three Point Communication dynamic, they help establish exactly what the solution looks like, step by step.

NUTHALL'S HIDDEN LIVES OF LEARNERS

***Hidden Lives* is the culmination of 40 years of research. It is not a book about how to teach. As Nuthall says, it is 'primarily about the learning process as it occurs in ordinary classrooms'. Nuthall and his team explored the complexities of learning by setting up cameras and audio equipment, recording everything over several months, transcribing and collating the data. Their meticulous research revealed classrooms through students' eyes, offering insights into how learning happens within the complex world of the classroom.**

See *Nuthall's Hidden Lives of Learners in Action*

GUEST AUTHOR

CLAIRE STONEMAN

1

EFFECTIVE TEACHING: WE SIMPLY CANNOT TELL BY LOOKING

Nuthall opens the book with a salutary reminder: we simply cannot tell by looking whether teaching is effective. He explains that the evaluation of observable teacher performance is heavily influenced by current fashions in teaching. Further, the teaching that produces most learning varies from class to class and day to day. His message is that what we see in the classroom is just the background of teaching. The implication is to focus more on understanding student learning and the challenges students face.

2

LEARNING IS HIGHLY INDIVIDUAL

Nuthall highlights the complexity of the classroom. His team found that students already know about 40–50% of what the teacher is about to teach them. But this is not evenly distributed, and different students will know different things. Nuthall tells us that students learn from their experiences. The implication is to design curricula and learning activities that help students to encounter key concepts frequently. Activities should be linked to and build on students' prior knowledge so that they can make sense of them.

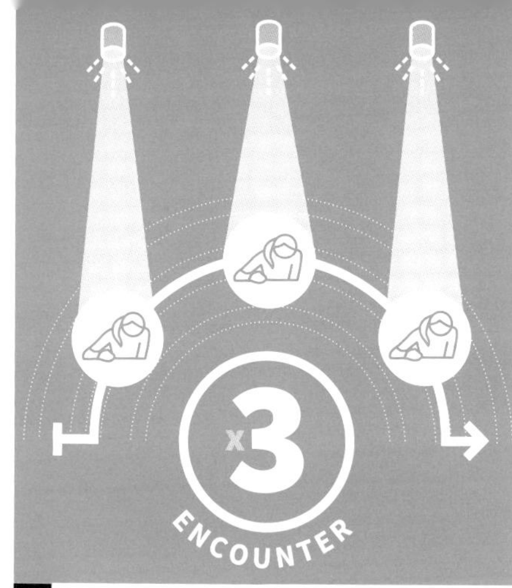

3

THREE IS THE MAGIC NUMBER

Nuthall's research shows us that learning happens over time. For a student to learn a concept and for it to be integrated into long-term memory, the student has to encounter a complete set of information about the concept on at least three different occasions. The implication is to design curricula and classroom activities so students encounter and revisit concepts a number of times in a variety of ways. The concepts are therefore more likely to be learned and remembered.

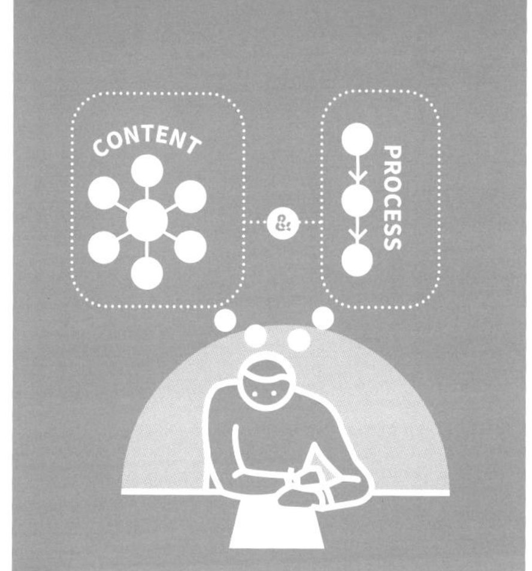

4

CURRICULUM CONTENT AND LEARNING ACTIVITIES ARE INEXTRICABLY LINKED

Nuthall explains that students learn what they do. Students learn not just the content of the curriculum but also the ways in which they encountered the content through different learning activities. The implication is to teach curriculum content and effective activities for learning the curriculum content, like self-quizzing. Progressively, students will learn these effective activities and apply them independently.

5

PEER CULTURE AFFECTS LEARNING

Nuthall's research highlights that peers are a major influence on student learning, even in individual activities. The classroom is full of complex interactions that teachers might not notice, including struggles for status, the shaping of self-concepts, and levels of engagement. The implication is to explicitly teach processes which create a supportive, collaborative, and respectful culture within a group. This is also an important consideration for school leaders when consciously crafting a school culture.

THE LEARNING SCIENTISTS' SIX STRATEGIES

Cognitive scientists Yana Weinstein and Megan Sumeracki, working for learningscientists.org, produced a superb series of guides for students, in collaboration with Oliver. The six strategies are designed for students to use themselves to enhance their learning, ideally modelled in the first instance by their teachers. Dual Coding is one of the six and is covered elsewhere in WalkThrus. The other five are summarised here. There is more information on their excellent website.

YANA WEINSTEIN

MEGAN SUMERACKI

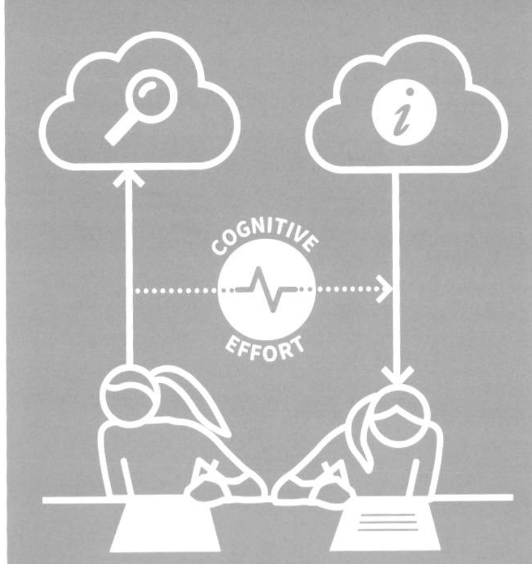

1

RETRIEVAL PRACTICE

We have a whole section in WalkThrus dedicated to the idea of Retrieval Practice. There are many ways to engage in this all-important process. The key emphasis from the Learning Scientists is to move away from simply re-reading notes – a common mistake that students make. Instead, they should *practise bringing information to mind* – engaging in generative processes and testing what they can remember without support before checking for accuracy.

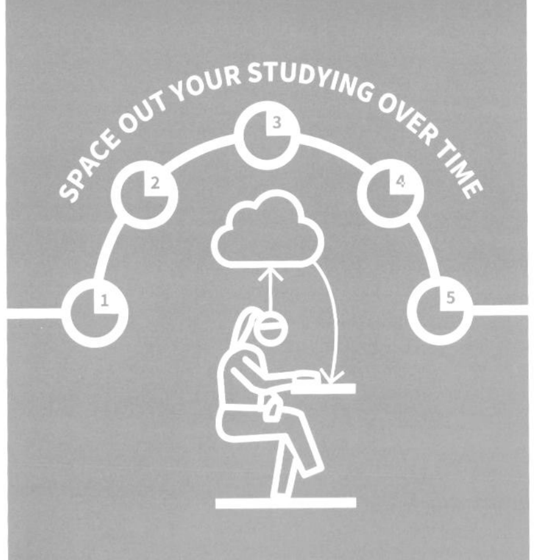

2

SPACED PRACTICE

Another common error students make is to cram their study on one topic in a long session. However, the research reported by Weinstein and Sumeracki shows that it is much more effective if students engage in shorter study sessions at intervals. Their message is *space out your studying over time*. This allows students to strengthen their retrieval, building a degree of fluency over time, even if it feels more immediately satisfying to do it all in one go, e.g. half an hour studying a topic per day for a week is more effective than 2½ hours all in one go.

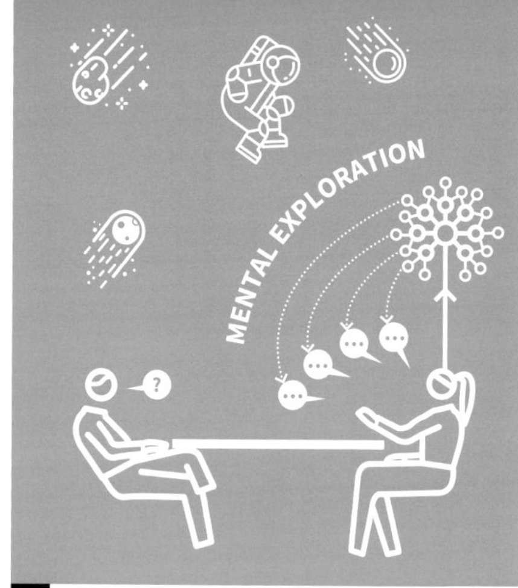

3

ELABORATION

This process is described in detail in our Volume 1 WalkThru **Elaborative Interrogation**. Weinstein and Sumeracki capture this neatly as *Explain and describe ideas with many details*. Students can improve their test performance significantly if they engage in mental exploration of their schemas using Why and How questions, alongside and beyond simply recalling specific factual information. They can also do this in pairs as part of **Peer-Supported Retrieval**.

4

CONCRETE EXAMPLES

This strategy is summarised as *Use specific examples to understand abstract ideas*. We have explored this further in the WalkThru **Abstract Models with Concrete Examples**. All too often, students try to study at a superficial level, learning definitions by heart, for example. However, it's only useful knowledge when they can give specific examples – such as an actual metal + acid reaction to illustrate the general pattern or an actual example of a *negative externality* in economics.

5

INTERLEAVING

An example of the Bjorks' idea of *desirable difficulties*, interleaving is not a strategy students use spontaneously because the experience of studying in this way can seem harder in the short term. However, longer-term recall can be strengthened significantly if students follow the suggestion to *switch between ideas while you study*. This means mixing up sub-topics within a subject during any given study session rather than studying them one at a time. The additional thinking involved strengthens learning.

LOVELL'S A|B|C|D|E OF COGNITIVE LOAD THEORY

Cognitive Load Theory is a collection of instructional recommendations based upon an understanding of how humans perceive, think, and learn. Originating from the work of John Sweller, each of the instructional recommendations has been validated through rigorous randomised controlled trials. CLT research is relentlessly practical. In the words of Sweller, 'The ultimate aim of cognitive load theory is to provide instructional effects leading to instructional recommendations.'

See *Sweller's Cognitive Load Theory in Action*

OLLIE LOVELL

GUEST AUTHOR

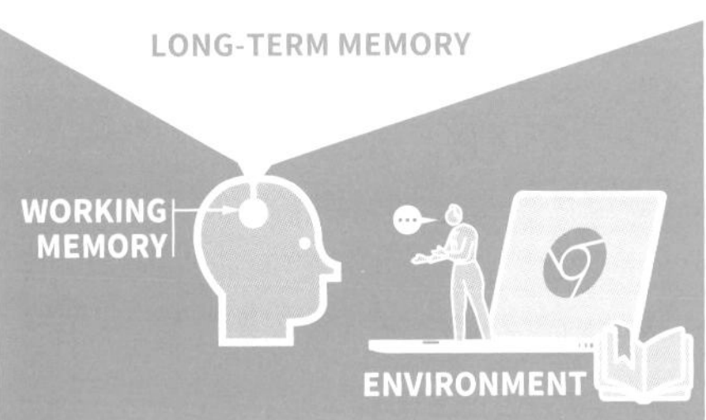

1

ARCHITECTURE OF HUMAN MEMORY

Humans utilise three key resources during learning: the **environment**, an unlimited external store of information; **working memory**, the site of our consciousness, a limited internal store that allows us to process only a few thoughts at a time; and **long-term memory** (LTM), an effectively unlimited internal repository of what has been learnt and remembered. Working memory is the only limited component of this system, acting as the bottleneck of cognition. CLT's recommendations address this bottleneck.

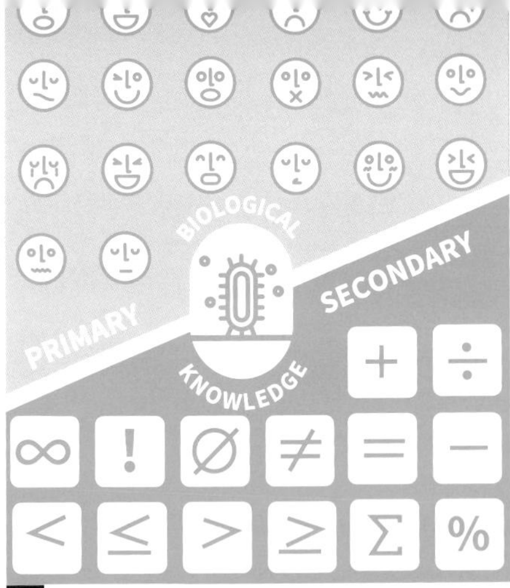

2

BIOLOGICALLY PRIMARY AND SECONDARY KNOWLEDGE

Biologically primary knowledge and skills are those that humans have evolved to acquire, e.g. the ability to recognise faces, solve problems, speak, listen. Biologically secondary knowledge and skills are only relevant because our culture deems them to be, e.g. reading and writing; academic domains such as science and mathematics. They have emerged relatively recently so we haven't evolved to learn them so easily. CLT focuses on instruction designed to help students acquire biologically secondary knowledge.

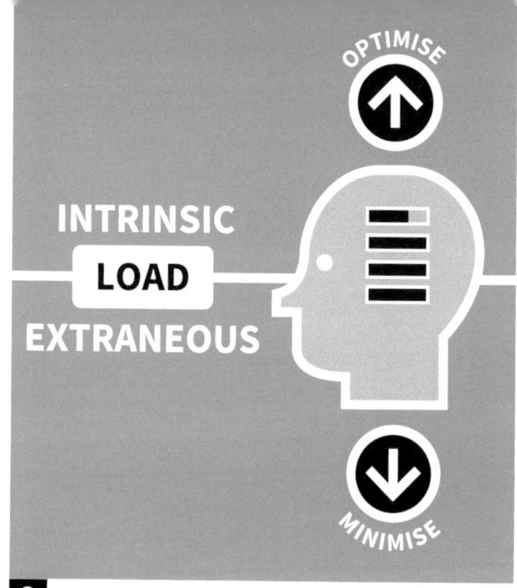

3

CATEGORISE COGNITIVE LOAD AS INTRINSIC OR EXTRANEOUS

Cognitive load is a term used to represent anything taking up space in working memory. Intrinsic cognitive load stems from ideas and concepts students must grasp to achieve the learning intentions at hand; it derives from instructional sequencing. Extraneous load results from students thinking about anything other than the core to-be-learnt material. CLT's fundamental recommendation is to *reduce extraneous load and optimise intrinsic load* and it describes ways to do this.

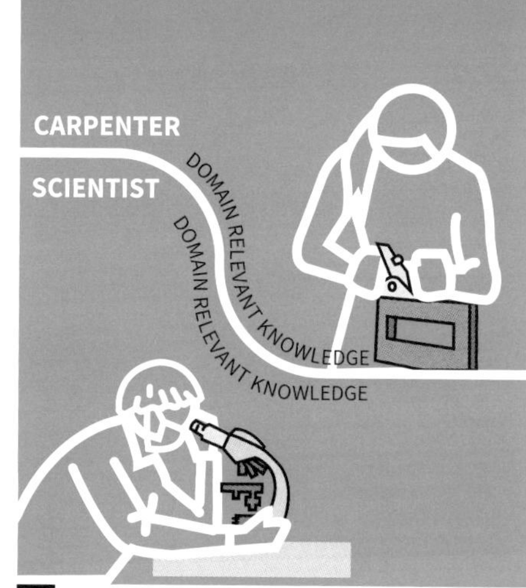

4

DOMAIN-GENERAL vs DOMAIN-SPECIFIC SKILLS

Domain-specific skills are tied to a domain, such as carpentry, chemistry or chess. There's a hypothesis that people can develop generic skills (e.g. problem solving) that work everywhere, but CLT suggests this is false; good problem solvers in chemistry won't necessarily be so in carpentry. CLT argues that only domain-specific expertise can be developed, by accruing relevant knowledge in LTM. Thus, a key role for teachers is to help students to acquire domain-specific knowledge.

5

ELEMENT INTERACTIVITY

Element interactivity is the source of all cognitive load. When students think about information elements (facts, figures, or ideas) or the interaction between them, it takes up working memory space. Novel information from the environment generates significant cognitive load, whereas mastered elements in LTM do not (supporting the importance of knowledge in LTM). Teachers can avoid cognitively overloading students by ensuring they don't encounter too many elements of novel information at one time.

LEARNING AS A GENERATIVE ACTIVITY

In *Learning as a Generative Activity*, Logan Fiorella and Richard Mayer explore how eight different strategies can be used by pupils to make meaning from any new information that is presented to them. These strategies are: summarising, mapping, drawing, imagining, self-testing, self-explaining, teaching and enacting. They involve pupils going through three key learning process: select information, organise it into a new form and then integrate it into their long-term memory.

See *Fiorella & Mayer's Generative Learning in Action*

MARK ENSER ZOE ENSER

GUEST AUTHORS

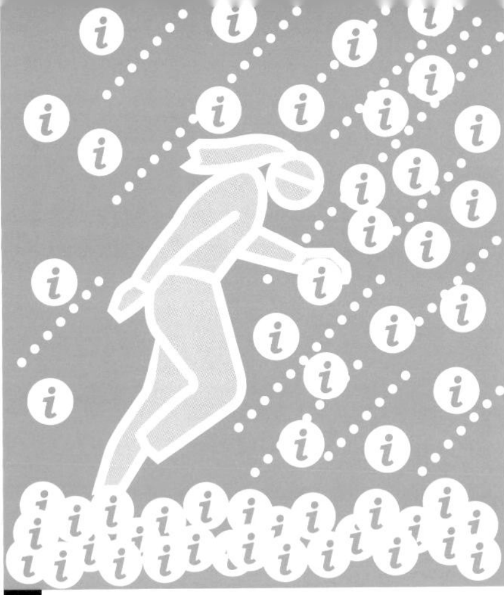

1

SELECT

We are bombarded by information all of the time. The first step in learning is to select what we will pay attention to and what we will ignore. Too often, learning activities do not generate learning because the learner is not selective: they transfer everything from one place to another or are only given the information they are expected to use.

An example of selection would be ***summarising***: the learner must decide the salient points in a passage; or in ***teaching***, where the learner must decide what information is the most important to pass on.

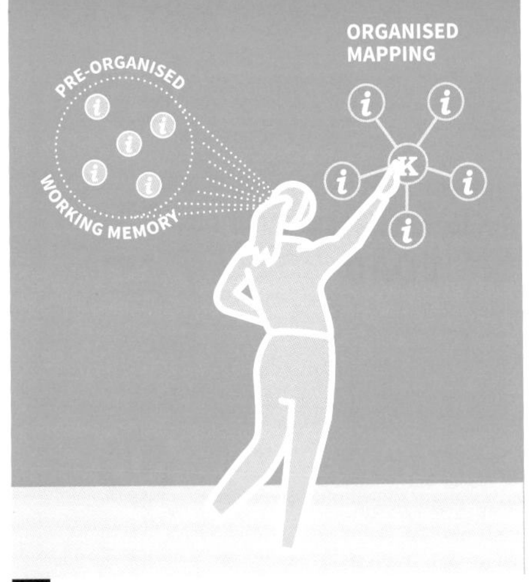

2

ORGANISE

We hold selected information in working memory and organise this here from fragments into something that has a meaning. If we want people to remember this information in the future, we want them to think hard about it. Learning may not be generative if the information is simply presented back in the same form. For example, ***drawing***: the learner must think hard about a written description or process to decide how to show it in an image. Or ***mapping***: a passage of text is organised under different headings with connections between the information shown.

INTEGRATE

Working memory is extremely limited; long-term memory is essentially limitless. For something to be learned, it needs to be integrated into our long-term memory and available for retrieval at a later date; we can then think about new things in light of what we already know, building understanding. An example of integration is ***imagining***: learners think about new information based on what they already know e.g. reading about development in Mali and imagining the impact that climate change will have. They are integrating new information with something they already know about.

4

METACOGNITION & MOTIVATION

Fiorella and Mayer write about metacognition and motivation being the *Mighty Ms* and they are central to the ideas within their work. By giving pupils these different strategies, they are able to think about their own learning and eventually decide when to deploy these different ways of learning, such as when revising.

The strategies also help to make the learning visible, and pupils can see the progress they are making. This tangible achievement is motivating.

5

BOUNDARY CONDITIONS

It is important that different generative learning strategies are used in the right place and at the right time. Some, such as ***enacting***, work best with very young children who struggle with abstract thought. Others, such as ***summarising***, don't work where the information is already given in a summarised form, e.g. in tables and diagrams in science.

We need to ensure the strategy doesn't become a barrier to learning – for example, in ***drawing***, if the learner spends too long thinking about the presentation of the image; or in ***imagining***, if they lack the prerequisite knowledge.

COGNITIVE APPRENTICESHIP: MAKING THINKING VISIBLE

Allan Collins, John Seely Brown and Ann Holum's 1991 paper posited the notion that we could transform the techniques of traditional apprenticeship to make explicit to our students the thinking processes required to apply subject knowledge to solving problems. Their Principles for Designing Cognitive Apprenticeship Environments are expressed within a 'framework consisting of four dimensions that constitute any learning environment: content, method, sequence, and sociology'.

See *Collins et al.'s Cognitive Apprenticeship in Action*

GUEST AUTHOR

JOHN TOMSETT

1

WHY MAKE THINKING VISIBLE?

Traditional apprenticeship taught the techniques which were observable. In an academic setting, the cognitive processes required are largely invisible and need to be surfaced. Then, to make the tasks meaningful to students, the aim in Cognitive Apprenticeship is to site the tasks in meaningful contexts which the students can understand readily. Lastly, unlike traditional apprenticeship, cognitive apprenticeship teaches thinking processes and skills which are transferable from one challenging task to the next.

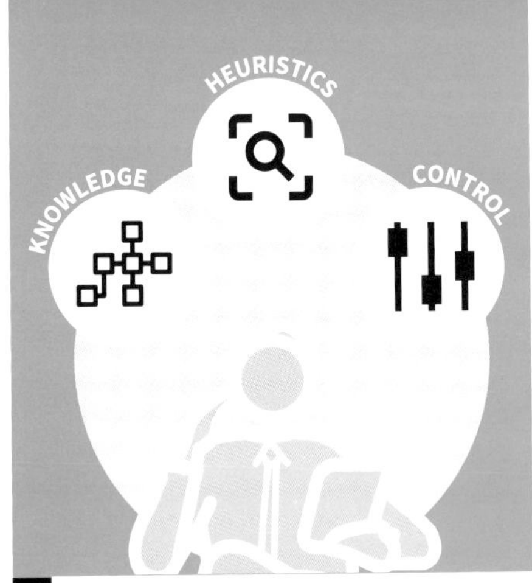

2

CONTENT | TYPES OF KNOWLEDGE REQUIRED FOR EXPERTISE

Domain knowledge is crucially important. Without it, there is no learning, but on its own it is not enough. You need heuristics, or techniques that usually work when attempting a problem. But when heuristics do not work, you require control strategies, or what we might call metacognitive skills, which help you think through different approaches to a challenge beyond the limited effectiveness of heuristics. Finally, within this first dimension, you need to know different methods of learning any of these previous three types of knowledge.

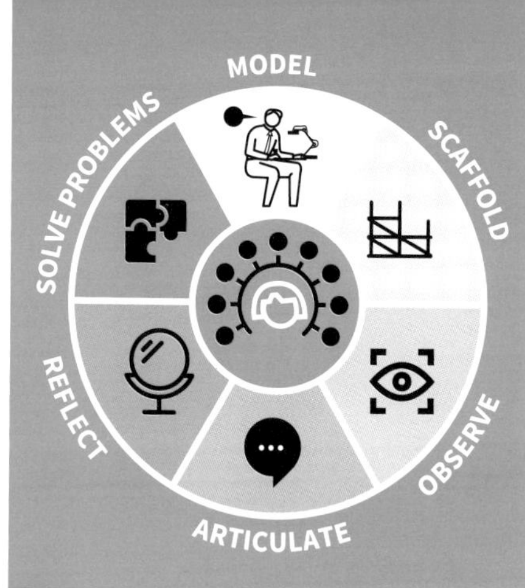

3

METHOD | WAYS TO PROMOTE THE DEVELOPMENT OF EXPERTISE

Collins et al. outline six elements:

- The teacher models a task or process; the students observe.
- Scaffolding support helps students complete a task.
- Teachers observe while coaching students to complete the task.
- Students articulate what they know and how they think when completing a task.
- On completion, teachers show students how to reflect upon their performance.
- The final stage is to ask students to identify and then solve their own problems.

4

SEQUENCING | KEYS TO ORDERING LEARNING

Collins et al. insist that you begin globally before looking at local skills. This gives the learner a 'conceptual map … before attending to the details of the terrain'. Tasks must be sequenced to ensure an increase in complexity and then teachers must diversify tasks to help students explore the breadth and depth of the subject domain. These tenets are sited within the subject domain, but also emphasise the transferability of the metacognitive skills as students tackle more diverse, complex challenges.

5

SOCIOLOGY | SOCIAL CHARACTERISTICS OF LEARNING ENVIRONMENTS

We have to ensure the learning is *situated* in contexts students find meaningful, encouraging them to use their knowledge actively with purpose rather than just passively receive it. Collins et al. encourage developing communities of practice where students find an intrinsic motivation for their learning which goes beyond pleasing teachers or gaining examination grades; where students exploit cooperation between each other to enhance the community's learning as a whole.

TRIVIUM 21C

Published in 2013, *Trivium 21c* by Martin Robinson has been a major influence on our thinking about curriculum. Subtitled 'Preparing Young People for the Future with Lessons from the Past', *Trivium 21c* explores the development of educational thinking through history, leading to a set of clear principles for contemporary curriculum design.

In this WalkThru, Martin Robinson has provided us with his own summary of the key ideas in the book. Trivium 21c in Practice on page 54 explores the implementation.

MARTIN ROBINSON

GUEST AUTHOR

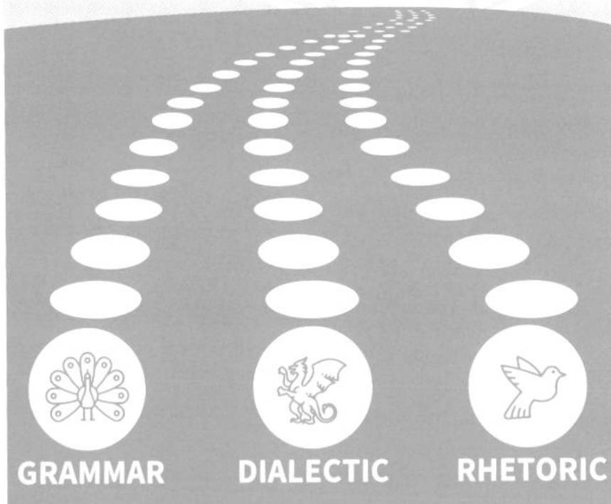

1

WHAT IS THE TRIVIUM?

Trivium is Latin for the place where three ways meet. This crossroads is the basis of the medieval idea of a liberal arts education in which the aim is to help pupils on the way towards wisdom and freedom. The trivium is the basis of teaching in many of the most prestigious education institutions in the world. For teachers, the trivium involves them in thinking about curriculum and pedagogy at the same time, charting a course through grammar, dialectic and rhetoric, which are the three ways, or arts, and are the core of all school subjects.

2

GRAMMAR

This is the 'foundational knowledge of all things'. For the teacher it involves the question 'What do my pupils need to know?' The facts, rules, precepts, concepts, practices, and skills – the essential building blocks that help ensure the child has the prerequisite information and how it connects to other knowledge. The pupil can begin to navigate this way by asking 'What do I know? What do I need to know?' In the first instance, the teacher will answer these questions.

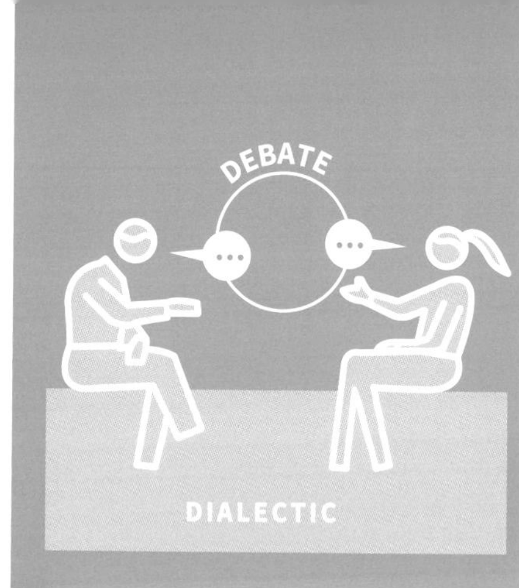

3

DIALECTIC

This involves investigating the quality of knowledge. Dialectic asks, 'Is it true?' It tests the learner and the knowledge through debate, argument, conversation. For the teacher it involves them in creating the conditions for investigation, practice and questioning of knowledge. Important parts of this art include Logic ('Does this make sense?'), Practice ('How best to do this well?'), Experiment ('What does this mean?') and Judgement (comparing and contrasting and understanding different perspectives). The teacher guides the pupil towards working in these ways.

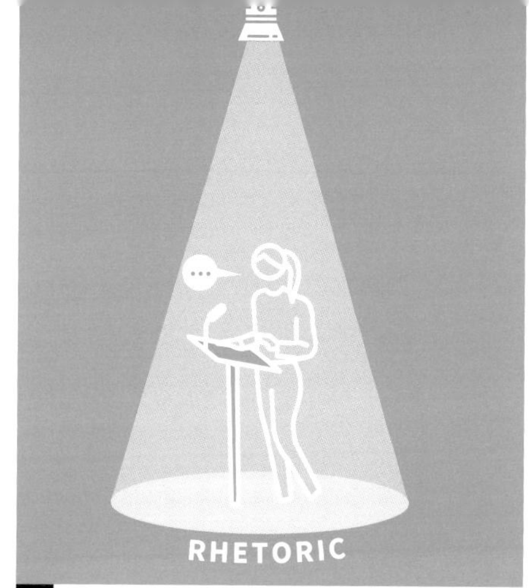

4

RHETORIC

This art is about expressing the knowledge gained through grammar and dialectic; the pupils' free expression of what they have learned. Classically it is associated with the spoken word in which the student expresses their thoughts beautifully, eloquently and persuasively; in academia, it includes the essay and the exam. This translates to all subjects: performance on the sports field or school stage, solving a maths problem or communicating results of an experiment or in an academic essay or exam. Rhetoric is where the pupil, in the words of Zeno, 'reaches out to the world with an open hand'.

5

WISDOM

The overall outcome of an education through the trivium is that each pupil will be a knowledgeable, thoughtful and eloquent human being equipped to tackle the natural, cultural and social worlds they find themselves in with a keen mind, unafraid of uncertainty and able to make the right choices. Able to be independent of their teachers when they leave school, these free thinking individuals are 'philosopher-kids' – not fully formed, but able to navigate the ways of the trivium confidently, asking, 'What do I need to know?', 'Is this right?' and 'How best to communicate this?' – knowing, thinking, communicating.

WHAT?

THE WALKTHRU SERIES

In this second volume, we have selected another 50+ ideas presented by Jenny and Joe as WalkThrus. The strategies are organised into the same six sections as in Volume 1, covering the range of activities that teachers need to explore with any class. It is our intention that, put together, the books should be regarded as forming one coherent curated set as a whole. There is no hierarchy between the books in terms of importance or difficulty and we hope that every teacher will find that they are collecting ideas from across the whole range to meet their learners' needs.

WALKTHRU SERIES

BEHAVIOUR & RELATIONSHIPS

01

It's essential that teachers create an environment in which all students feel they belong and feel safe; an environment that allows all students to thrive as individuals and as learners. This requires establishing appropriate learning-focused relationships where expectations are set high and where everyone knows the routines and the boundaries. This collection of WalkThrus covers some basic ideas and techniques to support teachers in achieving this. The ADAPT concept will be important as circumstances will vary significantly from one setting to another.

ASSERTIVENESS

Bill Rogers makes the distinction between the Indecisive Teacher – hoping for compliance and respect without insisting on it – and, at the other extreme, the Autocratic Teacher – relying on power dynamics to demand compliance. However, the Assertive Teacher uses positive, warm but insistent, decisive interactions to secure compliance and build respect. An assertive demeanour and mindset is the ideal for all concerned. It's a personal confidence that comes across through what we say in combination with physical presence, facial expressions and tone of voice.

WALKTHRUs IN THIS SERIES

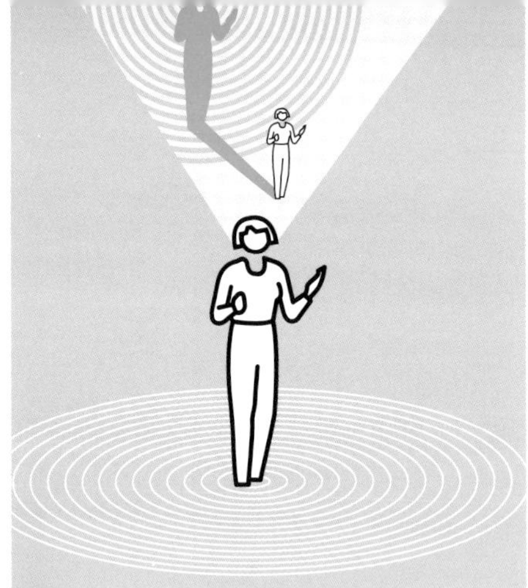

1

PROJECT NON-VERBAL CONFIDENCE

Our body posture and facial expressions convey a great deal about our emotions and intentions. An assertive teacher will project a sense of confidence through the way they stand – alert and positive rather than timid – and the way they walk around owning every corner of the space. They manage their non-verbal responses to communicate warmth and calm authority rather than anxiety or aggression.

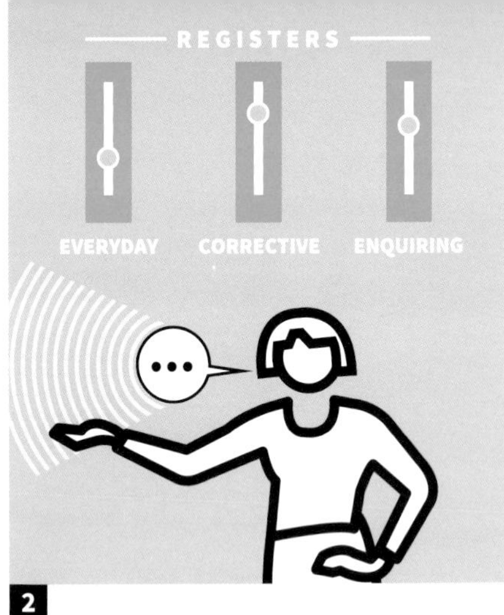

2

PROJECT YOUR VOICE CALMLY, FIRMLY

Voice control is a key teacher skill. It's not necessary to have a loud voice but it must reach into the furthest corners of the teaching space. Project to the very back, checking frequently that students can hear and that they are listening. It is useful to have at least two voice registers: one for normal everyday exchanges and another more corrective tone that communicates a level of additional firmness.

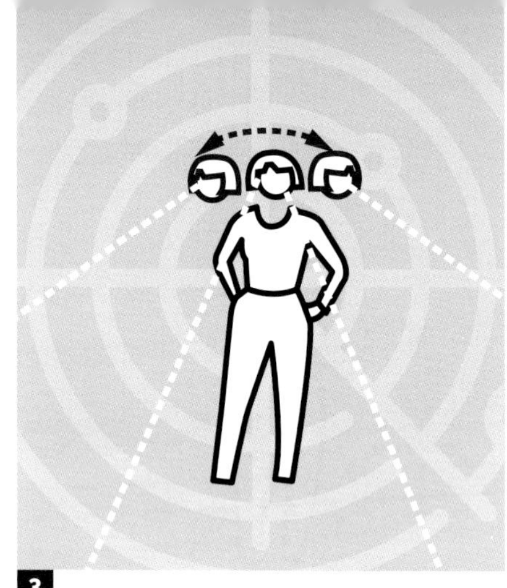

3

MAINTAIN EYE CONTACT

An unassertive teacher will often avoid eye contact. It conveys an awkwardness that students pick up on. This can be an unconscious response to genuine feelings but needs to be overcome. To model an assertive presence, it's vital to make eye contact with students in order to engage them in discussions and reinforce expectations. Scan the class continually, looking front and back and into the corners to ensure all students know you are including them, keen to hold their attention.

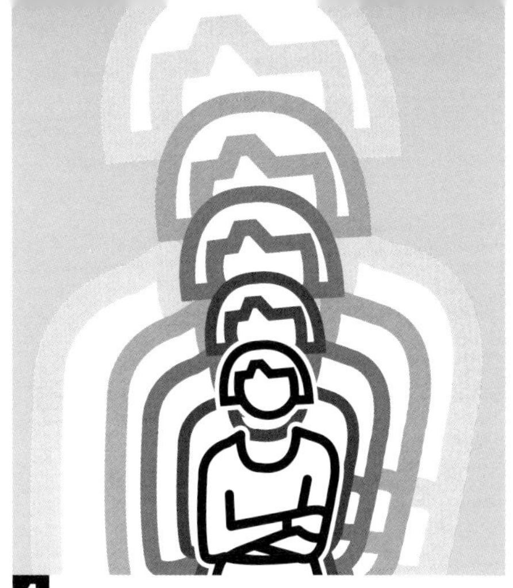

4

BE INSISTENT

In the majority of behaviour management scenarios, high expectations are maintained by continual reinforcement in a low key but firm and insistent manner. This means being clear that you mean what you say as far as possible. If you want students to put their pens down to listen, you insist that they do. If you want them to draw the graph in pencil, you insist that they do. You establish what you establish. (See Volume 1)

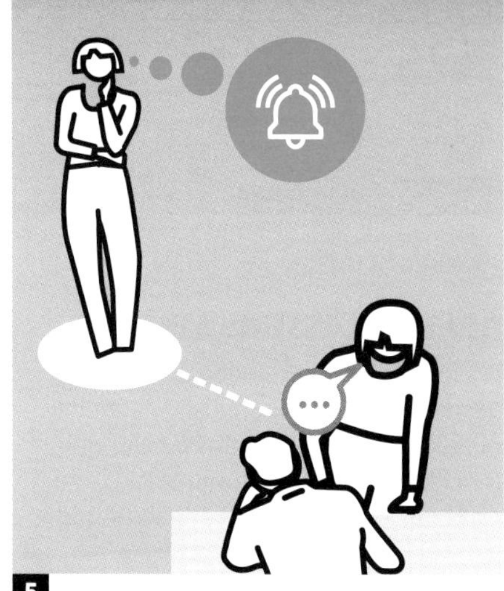

5

CHALLENGE AND AFFIRM

An assertive teacher will evaluate the standards of behaviour in their lessons continually. If things are not up to standard, they will take low level action every time, not allowing things to build up, requiring a much stronger intervention. If you are not happy with students' behaviour, address it right away. At the same time, it is important to use **Positive Framing** and to give affirmation to students when they meet the standards. *'Thank you, that's great. Everyone is listening and ready to go. Well done.'*

GETTING LESSONS STARTED

When a teacher and students are fully up to speed with their shared understanding of expectations and routines, it can be remarkable how quickly and efficiently a class can arrive, enter a room, settle and get stuck into some new learning within minutes. This requires all the elements in the process to be established, reinforced and made routine. Crucially, this process links behaviour management directly with learning. Making a great start to a lesson sets the tone for all that follows.

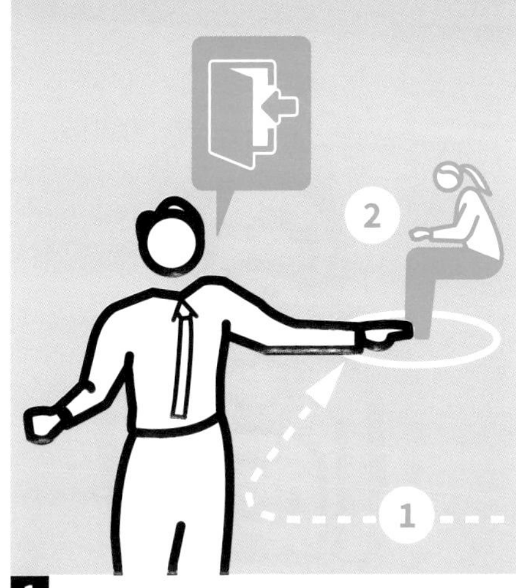

1

ESTABLISH ARRIVAL AND ENTRY ROUTINES

Entry and arrival should be high on your list of routines to work on when you **Establish Your Expectations** and **Rehearse Routines**. Decide exactly what you want students to do. This might include lining up outside your door or coming straight in; standing silently behind their chairs or sitting down immediately and getting their books out. Whatever you decide, build all the elements into a clear routine and rehearse it.

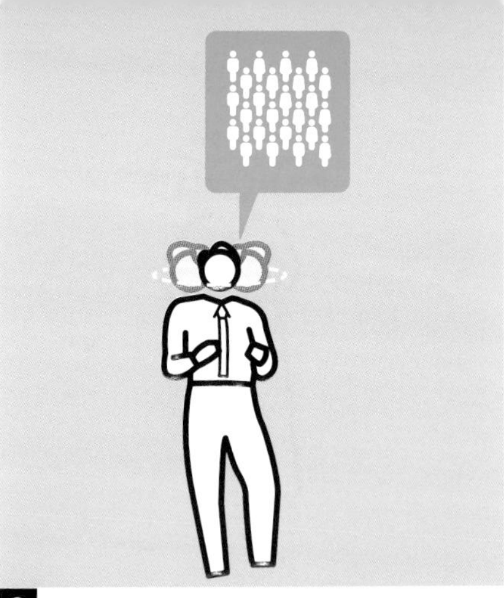

2

ADDRESS THE CLASS; TAKE THE REGISTER

Take time early in every lesson to establish and reinforce expectations, positive learning-focused relationships and the all-important sense of belonging. We feel this is best achieved by creating a calm moment when the teacher addresses the class directly with plenty of eye contact, free from other distractions. This can be when the register is taken or a moment when you offer a welcome and review learning goals.

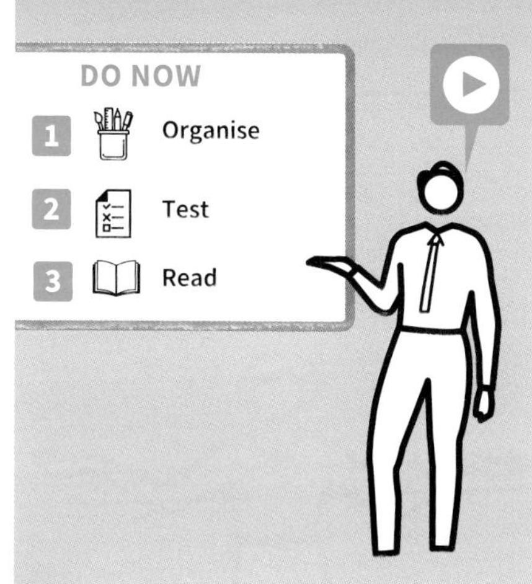

3

DO NOW: ESTABLISH A REPERTOIRE OF ENTRY TASKS

Devise a small repertoire of short practice tasks that students are familiar with that can be initiated by simple cues from a board message or verbal instruction. These are commonly called Do Nows after Lemov's *Teach Like A Champion*. Establish routines so students know to begin these tasks unprompted or to wait for a cue to start. The goal is to get them thinking as quickly as possible.

4

SET THE CONTEXT FOR THE LESSON WITHIN A SEQUENCE

Once the class is settled, after a Do Now task, gain their full attention (**Signal, Pause, Insist**) and explore how this lesson fits with the previous lesson and the wider learning sequence or topic. This framing is important in supporting students' self-regulation and schema-building. Ideally every student should know the wider purpose of any particular lesson.

5

DISCUSS SPECIFIC LEARNING GOALS

Wiliam and Leahy's Five Strategies include clarifying learning intentions as a vital element in formative assessment. *If we don't know where we're going, we'll never arrive!* Students do not need to write learning objectives into their books robotically. Rather, learning objectives should be explained, modelled and discussed. **Check for Understanding** from a sample of students to establish whether they have a good sense of what they are about to learn and why.

GATHER AROUND: DEMONSTRATIONS & STORIES

There are numerous scenarios when a teacher will want students to gather around, bringing them all closer together and/or closer to them so that they can see or hear something that requires closer attention than can be sustained from their usual seats. This is common for storytelling, especially with picture books; it is common for practical demonstrations in art, technology or science. Switching from one arrangement to another requires some thought to make it a smooth, calm process.

1

ESTABLISH A COMFORTABLE *GATHER AROUND* ARRANGEMENT

Consider how your students can sit or stand in an arrangement around the focus area so that everyone can see and hear what is happening in a relaxed state for a reasonable period of time. Rehearse this explicitly, especially if it is something you need to do quite frequently. Make the details of your expectations explicit and clear. Take time to establish them. A *stand so you can see* rule is a simple, useful expectation giving responsibility to students for organising themselves.

2

ESTABLISH A SIGNAL AND MOVEMENT ROUTINE

Once students know what the *gather around* configuration looks like, you can rehearse moving from the *at seats* position to the *gather around* position. This might be an organic movement of everyone at once, or something more structured – e.g. row by row – depending on the context. Establish a signal that students know is their cue to move.

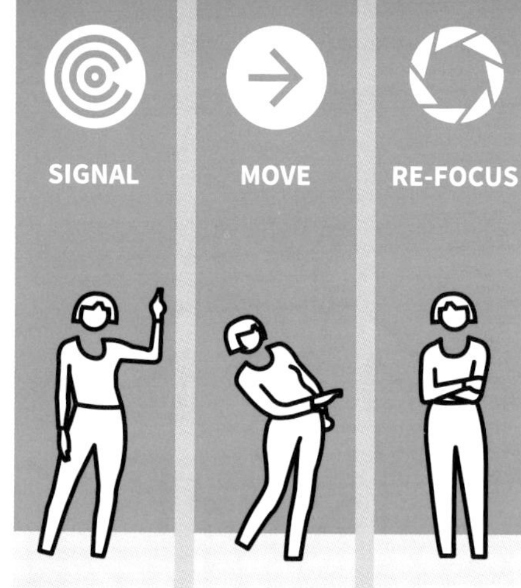

3

SIGNAL, MOVE, RE-FOCUS

The goal is for students to move from one set-up to another with minimum fuss. You can make this whole process as formal or informal as needed, assuming your expectations are always met.

Signal: Give the agreed signal to gather around.

Move: Monitor students as they go through the moving routine into the *gather around* position.

Re-focus: Once in position, scan the class, making eye contact and making sure everyone is now re-focused, relaxed and ready.

4

MONITOR FOR SUSTAINED ATTENTION

A gather around scenario can require a different type of monitoring, especially if students are standing up and are bunched together. Be sure to look up from your demonstration or book to scan and check for student engagement. Make students feel they are still seen by you; use **Cold Call** questioning to ensure they are all thinking about the material in hand. Pause when needed to recapture any individual student's focus. Take time to insist everyone is with you, part of the learning process, before continuing.

5

CHECK FOR UNDERSTANDING

The great value in these moments is in students seeing things with their own eyes and/or getting them closely involved in the narrative (of a story or non-fictional series of events or processes). Check that this is happening by periodically sampling students using **Check for Understanding** technique.

What do you think is happening at this point in the story? John?
What effect does this type of brush stroke have on the painting? Izzy?

KEEPING ON TASK

A common behaviour management challenge is to keep a group of students focused on a task with the required effort, intensity and independence, for a sustained period. This is easier to do when the task is a form of guided or independent practice and harder when students continually struggle. It is also easier when students have good habits built around a familiarity with the experience of working hard for an extended time, supported by high expectations that are reinforced so that their stamina for sustained effort has developed.

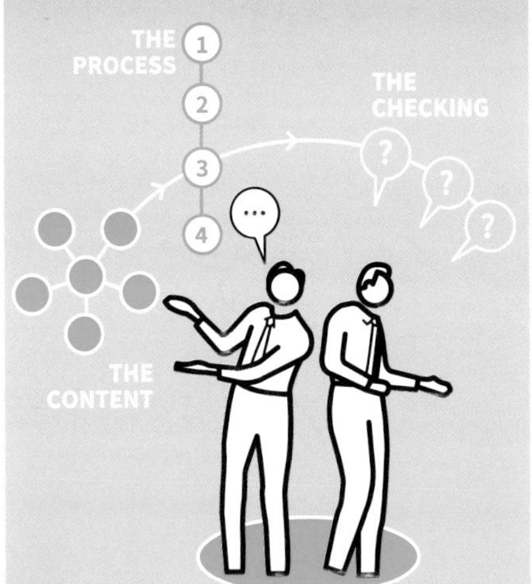

1

EXPLAIN THE TASK AND CHECK FOR UNDERSTANDING

If students are to sustain effort and attention, they need to know what they are supposed to be doing. After explaining the task, use the **Check for Understanding** process, sampling a few students, to ensure that students know what is expected from them, elaborating further as needed. It can be counterproductive to bypass this process, with teachers often needing to stop the class to re-explain later. It saves time to check in advance.

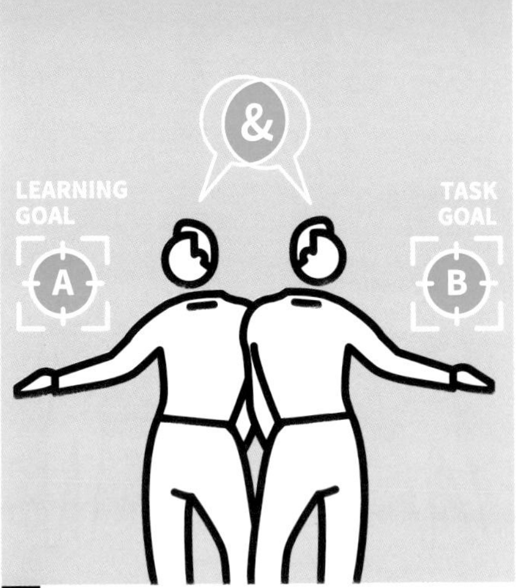

2

SET LEARNING GOALS AS WELL AS TASK GOALS

Learning goals: the knowledge, skills and understanding students should gain by completing the task, e.g. *You should be able to describe all the changes of state in the water cycle.*

Task goals: the products students should produce. e.g. *You should have finished labelling the diagram and written an explanation for each step.*

It's important for students to check their progress against both types of goal.

3

ISSUE TIME CUES & GOAL REMINDERS

Time cues: A key element in sustaining focus is to break down the time available into stretches that students can manage. This is a form of scaffolding. Discuss the expected time limit for completing the whole task and some stages within it so that students can monitor their progress.

Goal reminders: Task completion alone can be an illusion of learning unless the learning goals are reached. Be sure to issue learning goal reminders as well as task completion reminders. Not only *Have you finished?* but also *Have you learned it?*

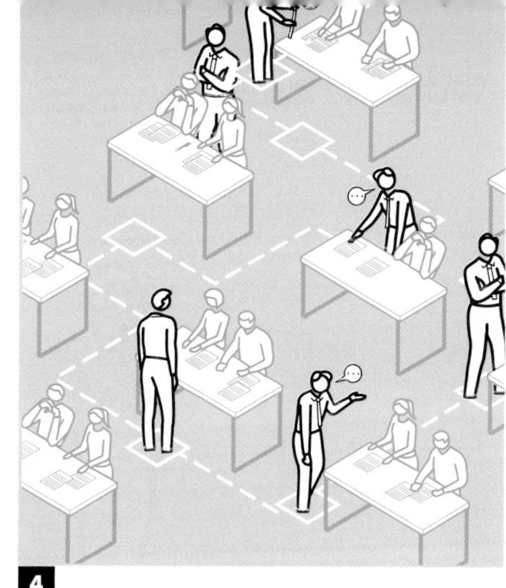

4

SUPERVISE ACTIVELY

Students are more likely to drift off-task if they do not feel their teacher's presence while engaged in the task. As discussed with **Guided Practice**, active circulation is a vital element in keeping students on task. The spirit of this is to communicate a sense that you are interested in what they are doing – not merely checking up on them. You can pick up on any difficulties at the same time as reinforcing learning goals, task goals and time cues with individuals.

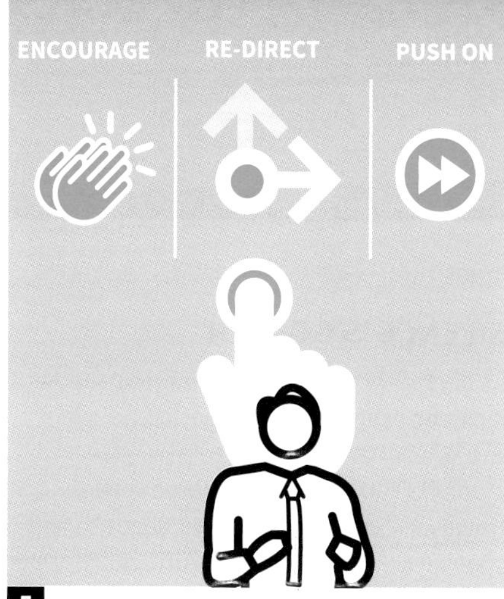

5

ENCOURAGE, RE-DIRECT OR PUSH ON

At a simple level, basic supportive encouragement is highly motivational for everyone. It also helps to anticipate a range of responses to any given task:

Some students will fly – they may drift unless the task is continually challenging. Be ready to push them on to the next stage in the learning.

Some students might struggle – they start giving up unless they get support and encouragement. Be ready to re-balance the provision of scaffolding with the need to foster independence.

SILENCE IS GOLDEN

As part of the repertoire of learning modes, it can be useful to initiate periods of silent working. In conditions of total silence, students can be incredibly productive. However the silence required needs to feel special; a kind of golden, luxurious silence that allows full concentration without distraction. It cannot be a harsh intense silence imposed in a disciplinary style. It needs to be a silence that students relish.

WALKTHRUs IN THIS SERIES

BEHAVIOUR & RELATIONSHIPS

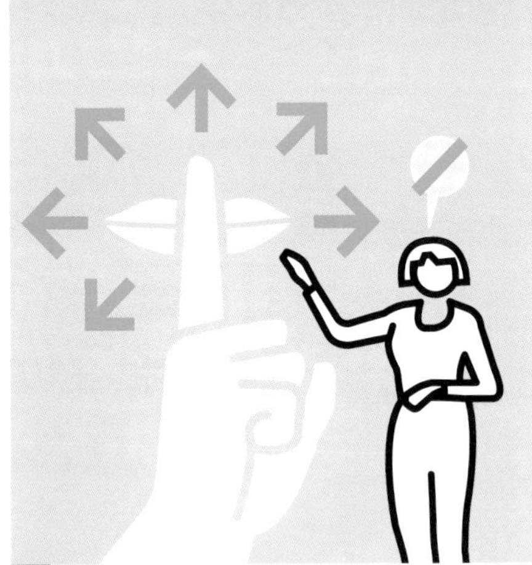

1

ESTABLISH THE PRINCIPLE: SILENCE IS ABSOLUTE

The first step is to establish that silence means silence. Nobody talks at all; it's a pin-drop silence where no one makes a sound. This includes the teacher and any support staff. It's very different to *keeping the noise down* or even *working quietly*. Teachers' silence is important for modelling purposes but also because, in obvious practical terms, any noise that breaks the silence ruins it and teachers' voices are no exception.

2

SET A SILENT WORK TASK WITH A CLEAR TIME LIMIT

Students relax into a silence if they know how long it will last. Indefinite silences can feel oppressive so, in initiating the silence, be clear that it will last for, say, 10 minutes. If that feels like too long, then start with shorter silences at first and build up students' stamina for silent working. Make sure that the task or reading activity is clear enough so that you do not need to give further instructions during the silent period.

3

MAINTAIN YOUR OWN SILENCE AND MODEL THE JOY OF IT

During the golden silence, avoid causing distractions yourself. Use the silent time to model focused attention on a task while monitoring students in a low-level manner. Where necessary, use non-verbal cues such as a finger to your lips to reinforce expectations. It's hard to expect students to maintain the silence if you cannot maintain it yourself.

4

REINFORCE THE FEELING THAT SILENCE IS GOLDEN; TO BE TREASURED

In order for silence to be embraced positively as a learning mode, it's important that you only ask for silence for the positive purpose of stimulating productive periods of concentration. It's not a time to kick back and relax or ever used as a form of discipline – a punishment for poor class behaviour. Try to model the joy of silence and celebrate the positive feelings of calm focus that it can generate.

5

END THE SILENCE GENTLY AND REVIEW THE WORK

Honour your time limits as precisely as possible so that students learn to trust and respect them when they are set. As the time limit approaches, avoid a rush of noise by talking softly, using **Cold Call** to select some students to share their ideas or the work they've produced. Alternatively, switch to **Think, Pair, Share** so that every student has an opportunity to air their ideas simultaneously.

TRANSITIONS BETWEEN ACTIVITIES

In numerous settings, the nature of activities and teacher-student interactions needs to change during the course of a lesson so that ideas and experiences are explored in the most appropriate manner to maximise learning. If transitions are seen as time-wasting or disruptive, it can be inhibiting and confining. However, once transition routines are established, it allows flexible, responsive teaching to flourish as teachers can switch between activities with confidence, adding variety, changing the tempo and increasing depth and challenge as required.

WALKTHRUs IN THIS SERIES

BEHAVIOUR & RELATIONSHIPS

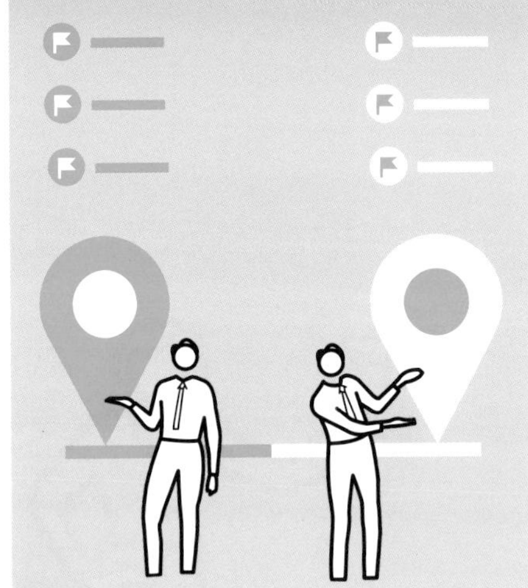

1

ESTABLISH EXPECTATIONS FOR EVERY ACTIVITY TYPE

As new types of activity are added to the class repertoire, run through the process of establishing expectations and rehearsing routines explicitly. Ideally, the number of different types of learning is manageable where teachers use them frequently enough for the routines to become embedded. If students are unsure what to do or what is expected, then transitions are much more likely to waste time and feel disruptive.

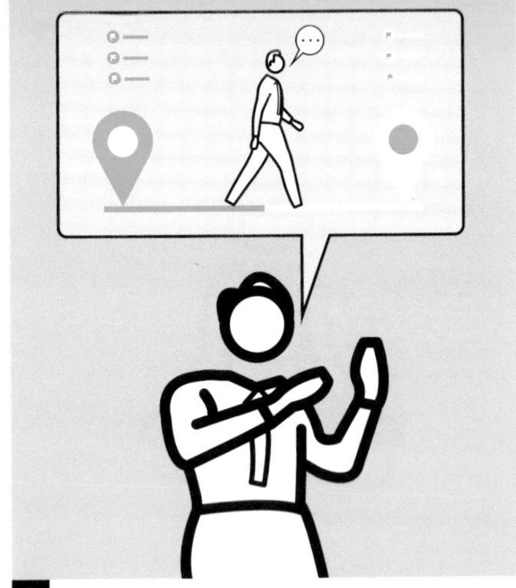

2

VERBALLY WALK THROUGH THE TRANSITION

Before initiating a transition, walk through it verbally using a familiar set of instructions: *When I give the signal, I'd like everyone to move into your practical groups in your normal positions. As always, you only need your pencil, ruler and exercise book; everything else should be tidied neatly on your desk. Walk slowly to your normal stations and show me you are ready.*

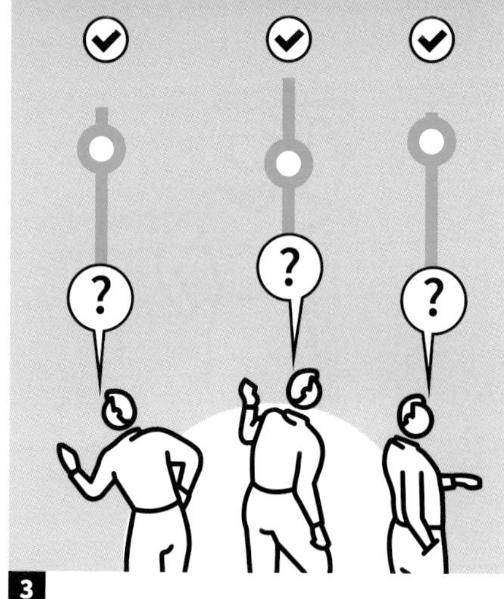

3

CHECK FOR UNDERSTANDING

This is classic territory for using this strategy as a matter of routine. Instead of asking rhetorical, ineffective questions like *Does everyone understand what to do?*, select one, two or three students to run through their understanding of what is expected:

Kingsley, remind us what you all need to do when I give the signal.
Amy, do you agree with Kingsley? Did he leave anything out?

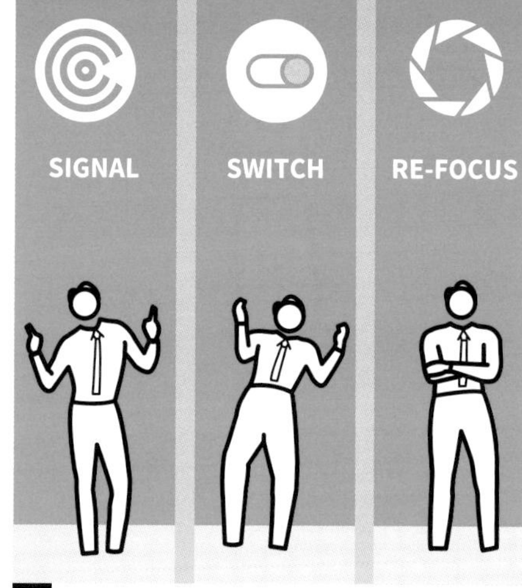

4

SIGNAL, SWITCH, RE-FOCUS

Signal: Give the agreed signal to start the transition.
Switch: Monitor students as they go through the routine, switching from one activity to the next.
Re-focus: Once they have switched, scan the class, making eye contact, making sure everyone is now re-focused, relaxed and ready. You may want them to get straight on with the next activity, in which case make this part of the transition routine explicitly.

5

REVIEW, REFINE AND REHEARSE TO IMPROVE EACH ROUTINE

The more fluid and fluent the transition routines are, the more likely you are to use them. Don't give up on them early on – time spent getting them right is time well spent. You will be able to remove some cues, pauses and checks as the transitions become more automatic. If something isn't working, change it and then rehearse and embed the adapted routines.

LESSON DISRUPTION

Disruption happens when one or more students' behaviour exceeds agreed respect and safety boundaries, interrupts the teaching and learning process or prevents it from proceeding. At one end of the scale it can be mild – easily and swiftly resolved; at the other end, it can be severe, requiring students to be removed from the class. The frequency and severity of these scenarios will vary significantly between contexts. It's important to know how school systems support teachers in each circumstance.

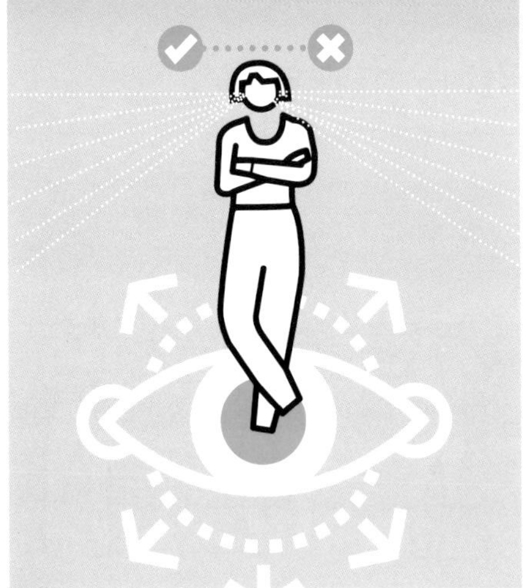

1

EVALUATE THE SITUATION

A central teacher function is to monitor and maintain standards of behaviour so students are safe, secure and unhindered in their learning. Maintain a pattern of continual background monitoring, referencing a set of expectations and boundaries so that behaviours that constitute disruption are easily and consistently identified. Evaluate every situation, keeping in mind the need for fairness and consistency, balancing the needs of individuals and the whole class.

2

TACKLE IT; DON'T TOLERATE IT

As discussed in **Establish Your Expectations**, it's useful to remember that you establish what you establish. If a student's behaviour is problematic, falling outside the boundaries, you must tackle it, choosing the most appropriate response. If you tolerate it, you effectively condone it, which can lead to bad habits forming. Intervene with low level issues early on before they escalate, leaving you with a bigger issue to tackle. Remember it is possible to be warm, kind and friendly as well as having very high expectations, strictly reinforced.

3

TAKE THE LEAST INTRUSIVE APPROACH FIRST

You have a range of options including:

- non-verbal reinforcement or private word with individuals or small groups
- public reinforcement using **Positive Framing**; using controlled severity (sounding cross) to communicate a more strict challenge or reprimand
- sanctions including detentions or short-term removal following the agreed protocols

Choose the least severe/intrusive approach possible but, for sure, do whatever is needed to address the situation.

4

ENACT AND NARRATE CHOICES AND CONSEQUENCES

Follow the steps in the **Choices and Consequences** WalkThru. Intervene to prevent the unwanted behaviours from continuing, then run through the options for the student(s) to follow. If their behaviour can be redeemed immediately, make that option clear. If they have already triggered a sanction, be clear to narrate the reasons:

You continued shouting out after the warning, preventing others from answering, so, as you know, that means you now have a lunchtime detention with Ms Shaw.

5

RE-FOCUS THE LEARNING

As quickly as you can, support the class to move beyond a disruptive incident by re-focusing the learning, perhaps with a recap of what had been covered so far in the lesson. It's important to model a calm *back to normal* adult response, not amplifying the drama or any incident, reinforcing that this is how students should also respond. This will be more important the more significant the disruption was to begin with.

PERSPECTIVE: THE DOT IN THE EMPTY SQUARE

This technique is helpful for keeping behaviour that falls below expectations in perspective. It's possible to fall into a habit of taking excellent behaviour for granted, letting it pass without comment, while always addressing poor behaviour and low standards. This risks creating an excessively negative atmosphere, where discipline feels heavy and the teacher seems continually critical. Bill Rogers, the Australian behaviour expert, suggests the dot in a square technique as an antidote to this habit.

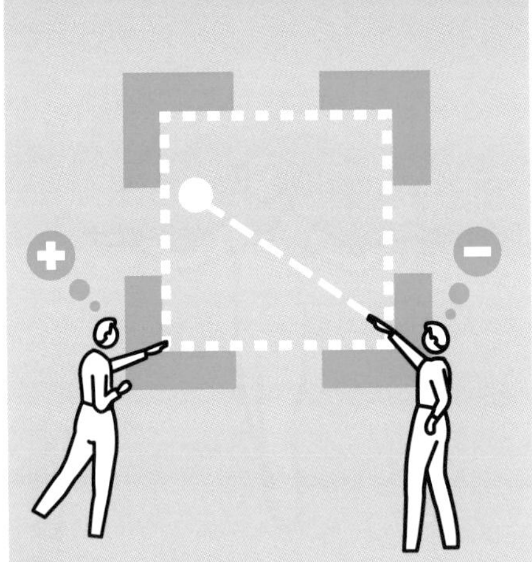

1

FOCUS ON THE EMPTY SQUARE, NOT THE DOT

In the analogy, the dot stands out but most of the space is empty. The dot represents negative behaviour in the context where the dominant behaviour is positive. In managing behaviour, remember not to lose sight of the empty square: the positive, on-task, kind, respectful, hard-working, cooperative behaviours that most students exhibit, even when one or several students are not meeting those standards.

2

AFFIRM THE ACTIONS OF THOSE RESPONDING POSITIVELY

Before addressing any negative, off-task behaviours, routinely reaffirm the positive behaviours:

Wow – we've got some superb homework here. Well done.

Excellent – great to see you all on time and ready to go!

Thank you to everyone listening and paying full attention; that's wonderful.

WALKTHRUs IN THIS SERIES

BEHAVIOUR & RELATIONSHIPS

3

RE-AFFIRM GENERAL EXPECTATIONS TO ALL

Use the fact that most students are able to maintain high expectations to reinforce the idea that this is what you expect from everyone and that you believe everyone is capable of meeting the standards.

Thank you – that's the level of concentration I know you're all capable of. Well done.

I'm sure we can get everyone producing work of this standard.

Great to see how well people are including the new words in their writing because they took time to learn them.

4

USE POSITIVE FRAMING TO ADDRESS THE *DOTS*

Of course you have to also address the negative behaviours – the dots – but this is easier to do in a climate dominated by affirmation and encouragement.

OK – now I need everyone eyes front and listening like the others.

Nearly everyone is arriving nicely on time; you two can do it too!

Thanks for all the great homework – now, Toni, James and Suzanne, yours will be great too so let's get that organised.

5

NARRATE CHOICES AND CONSEQUENCES FOR FUTURE ACTIONS

Where the dots represent more challenging or persistent poor behaviour, after the affirmation for the empty space majority, you still need to run through the **Choices and Consequences** routines.

Thanks to everyone who listened so well during the Cold Call questions. Nick and Nicole – I need you doing the same. You can either respond in the way I expect or there will be a detention and a phone call home.

CURRICULUM PLANNING

There is an important interplay between curriculum and pedagogy: what we teach and how we teach it. This set of WalkThrus builds on the ideas in Volume 1, exploring a range of concepts and strategies, helping teachers to design and deliver a curriculum that is challenging, rich in knowledge and experiences of different kinds and where attention is given to diverse perspectives and to students with special needs. Some WalkThrus relate to planning structures and making connections between subjects, and we're delighted to include Bennie Kara's section 'Diversity: Ways into Curriculum Building'.

TRIVIUM IN PRACTICE

Martin Robinson's *Trivium 21c* guides us through the principles and concepts of the three arts of grammar, dialectic and rhetoric. As well as providing a superb philosophical framework for considering the types of knowledge and experience that constitute an excellent education, it has practical application as a structure for curriculum review. This works at the level of a whole-school curriculum but also at the level of unit design within a particular subject.

MARTIN ROBINSON

WALKTHRUs IN THIS SERIES

CURRICULUM PLANNING

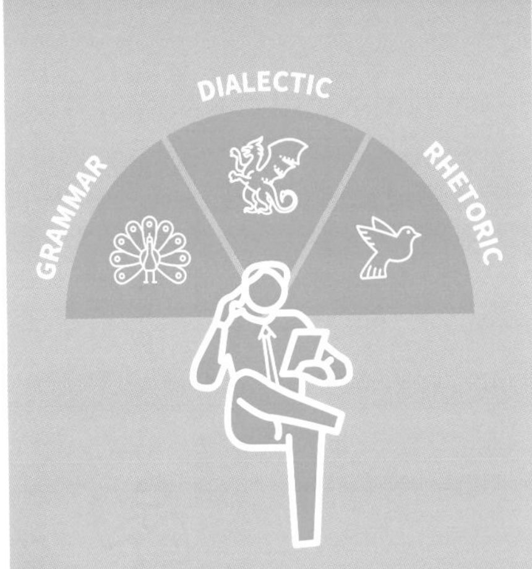

1

PLAN EXPLICITLY USING THE TRIVIUM AS A FRAMEWORK

When considering what to teach, it can be extremely powerful to plan your curriculum using trivium concepts explicitly. Put simply, this could be expressed as:

Grammar: What do you want students to know?

Dialectic: How do you want students to explore that knowledge?

Rhetoric: How do you want students to communicate or express this knowledge?

2

ESTABLISH THE GRAMMAR

Every subject has its grammar: the key elements of knowledge that every student should know. This will largely be determined by the traditions of the subject as established by the subject community within and beyond the school. However, your selection will also be shaped by school values and teacher preferences.

Use **Coherent Planning** and **Core and Hinterland** to ensure everyone has a clear sense of the knowledge content in each subject and how this adds up to a coherent overall curriculum.

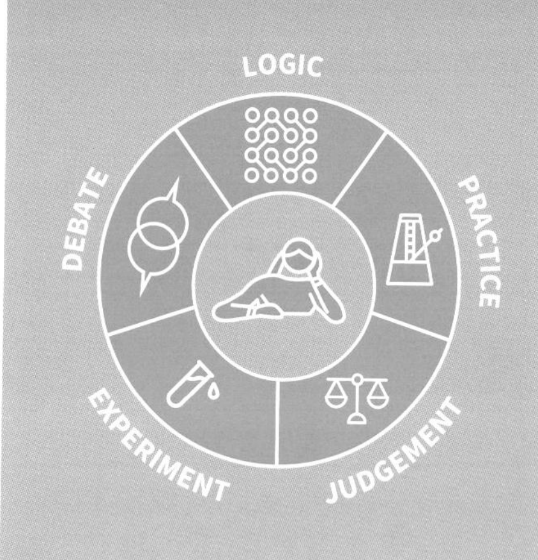

ENABLE THE DIALECTIC

Plan concrete learning experiences that will enable students to explore the grammar of the trivium; to investigate the quality of the knowledge. This will include:

Debate: questioning the truth; examining evidence.

Logic: reasoning; asking 'Does this make sense?'; explaining what we observe; making deductions.

Practice: 'How best to do this well?'

Experiment: testing ideas; gaining first-hand experience.

Judgement: exploring different perspectives to compare and contrast.

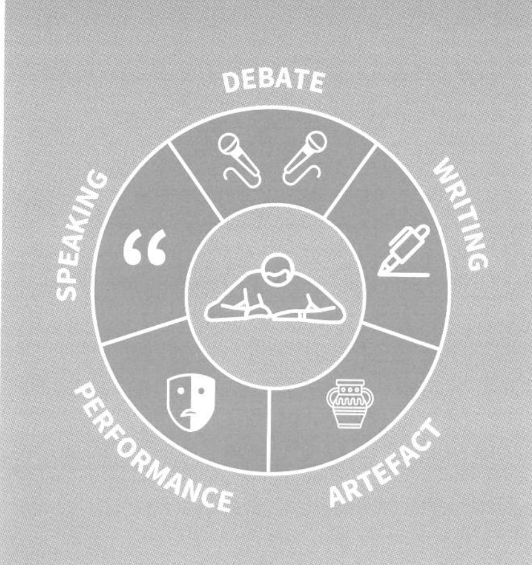

DEVELOP THE RHETORIC

Consider the specific forms in which students will express their ideas, communicating what they've learned, sharing their perspectives. This could include:

Formal speaking: for example, oracy.

Debate: giving a presentation to an audience.

Writing-based products: writing an essay; a report on an investigation with graphs and tables; a written project showcasing students' research and understanding.

A performance: in music, sport or drama.

An artefact: a piece of artwork, coding, woodwork, electronics.

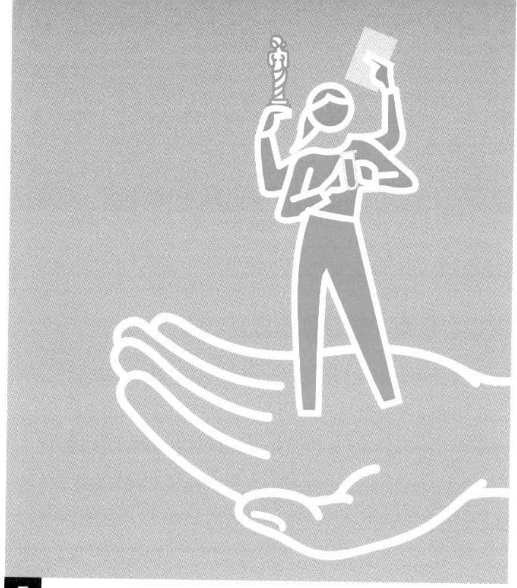

FOSTER WISDOM

In the spirit of the trivium, where the whole is greater than the sum of the parts, review your curriculum at a big-picture level and at a unit level to check that all three of the arts are given due weight. Make adjustments as needed. Are you explicit enough about the grammar? Are the elements of dialectic planned explicitly or too ad hoc? Is there variety and richness to the forms of rhetoric? Overall, are students being led to a place where they are engaging in the three arts independently, like Robinson's philosopher-kids?

MODE A : MODE B

In *The Learning Rainforest*, Tom defines the loose concept of Mode A and Mode B teaching to explore the most appropriate blend of strongly instructional teaching (Mode A) with other, often more student-led, teaching and learning modes (Mode B). We have devoted a series of WalkThrus to Mode B teaching ideas. Here, we will explore Mode A : Mode B as a curriculum planning concept. It's not about doing one or the other; it's about getting the right blend for your context.

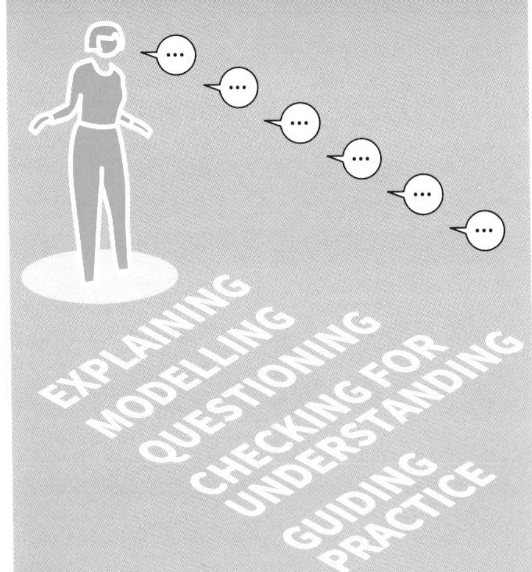

1

PLAN THE MODE A CORE

Every teacher needs to be able to deliver high-quality instructional teaching. This is Mode A:

- **Explaining**
- **Modelling**
- **Questioning**
- **Checking for Understanding**
- **Guiding Practice**

In curriculum terms, it is useful to identify all the key knowledge areas that will require explicit instruction. It could be nearly all of them or just a portion, depending on the subject context.

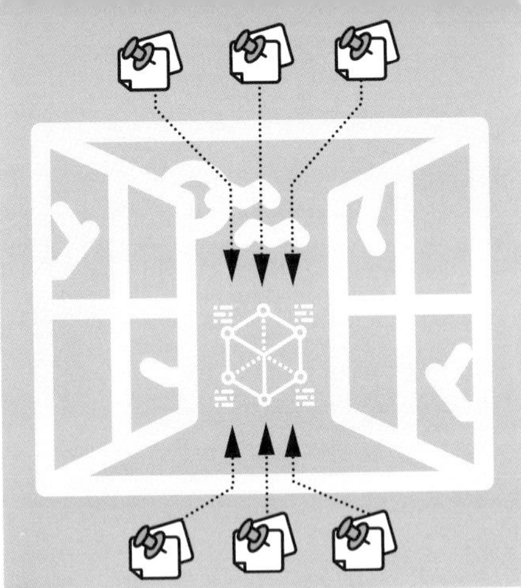

2

PLAN MODE B ELEMENTS FOR SCHEMA-BUILDING

Mode B teaching usually involves set-piece activities that require explicit planning. Plan opportunities for students to deepen their knowledge and understanding beyond teacher instruction:

- **Enquiry Projects**
- **Independent Learning: Pre-reading**
- **Museum/Gallery visits**
- **Open Response Tasks**
- **Oracy: Debating**
- **Oracy: Instructional Inputs**
- **Making/Designing**

3

PLAN MODE B ELEMENTS FOR PERSONAL DEVELOPMENT

Plan Mode B elements that have value for their potential in developing students' personal confidence, independence and capacity for collaborative working, in addition to supporting their understanding of the specific knowledge at hand:

- **Collaborative Learning**
- **Oracy: Public Speaking**
- **Oracy: Recitation and Performance**
- **Self-Directed Learning**

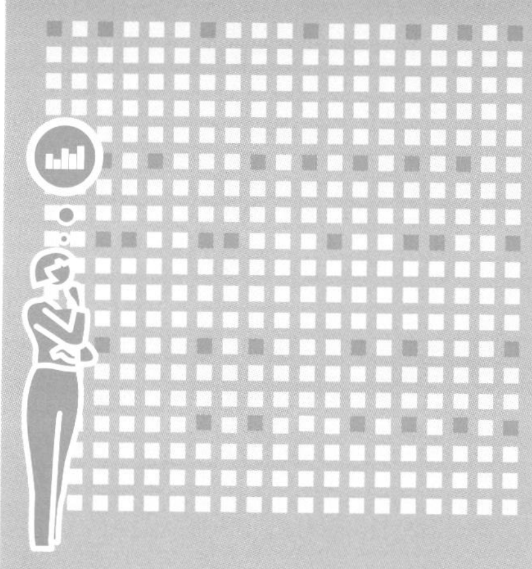

4

GET THE FREQUENCY RIGHT

Unlike Mode A teaching, which will be a daily default for most teachers, Mode B elements can be woven into the curriculum at varying frequencies. Some elements might be daily, some weekly or monthly; some might happen once per unit of work or even just once a year. Used judiciously to optimise their impact, Mode B elements offer a depth and richness that supplements the staple diet of Mode A.

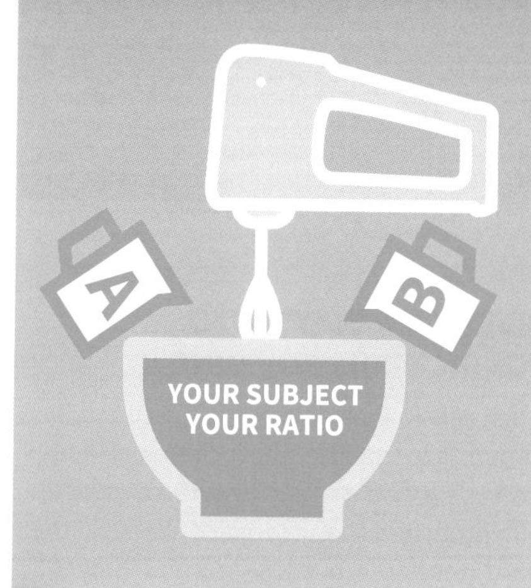

5

BLEND MODE A & MODE B OVER TIME

The optimum blend of Mode A and Mode B is highly context specific. Tom suggested in *The Learning Rainforest* that, as a science teacher, his A:B split was roughly 80:20. But that is a subjective approximation. There are no hard and fast rules and whole lessons could easily be devoted entirely to one mode or the other. The point is to integrate the elements into the curriculum as a whole to maximise its depth and richness.

DIVERSITY: WAYS INTO CURRICULUM BUILDING

When considering diversity in the curriculum, the aim is to usualise* the inclusion of ideas, stories, experiences and histories of people with protected characteristics. We avoid the word 'normalise' because 'normal' implies a right way of being. We usualise to show that all experiences are part of the fabric of society. Diversity in the curriculum is essential to create global citizens who have an awareness of where they fit into the world.

*Reference *Usualising*: term coined by Sue Sanders, founder of Schools Out, a charity supporting schools to become safe spaces for LGBT+ students and teachers.

BENNIE KARA | GUEST AUTHOR

WALKTHRUs IN THIS SERIES

CURRICULUM PLANNING

1

EXPAND THE UNIVERSE

Our established canon of knowledge is centred on post-enlightenment, Western European thinking. Recognising that ideas are the product of global cultures requires us to expand boundaries. Does your curriculum reference positive content originating from outside Western Europe? This expansion of boundaries is not merely geographical; it can also be applied to chronology. Teaching pre-enlightenment thinking means that the foundation of subject knowledge is secure and broad.

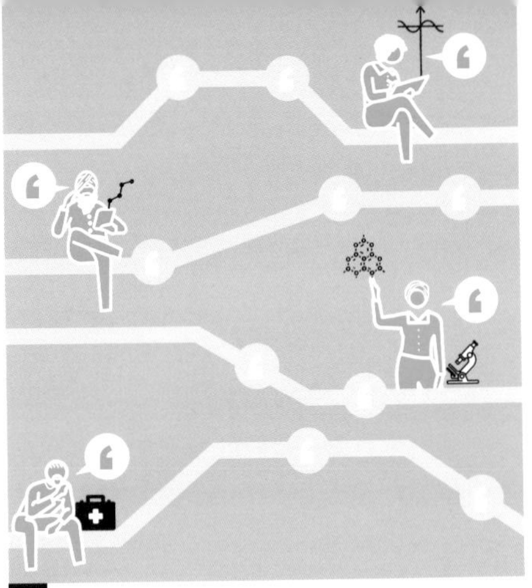

2

HIGHLIGHT PARALLEL STORIES

Decentring the curriculum so one perspective is not privileged over another, try telling parallel stories. This works particularly well in subjects where a range of perspectives on the topic can be taught. Voices that have been hidden or ignored can be brought to the fore and celebrated, especially using non-fiction sources. Students are allowed to commit to their schemas a balanced viewpoint on the topic. It's a powerful tool for building empathy and understanding, countering the idea that there is a single story to be learned.

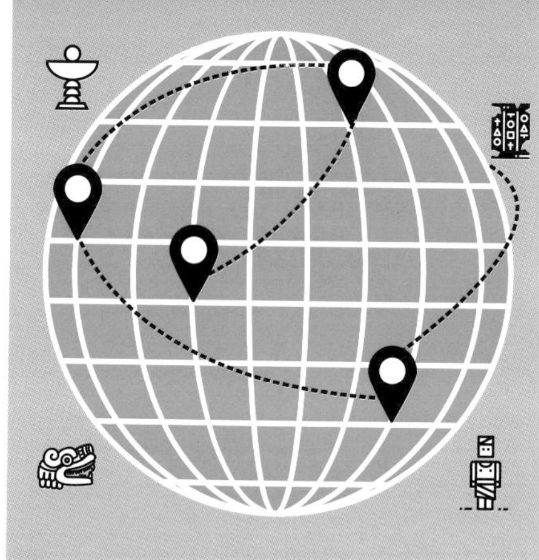

3

MAP MIGRATIONS

Migration is a central tenet of diverse schema building; knowledge itself has *moved* across time and cultures, e.g. linguistic migration – the language of your subject originated somewhere. In addition to Latin and Greek, explore the etymology of words from languages such as Sanskrit and Persian and the usage of loan words. Apply migration to knowledge itself – e.g. in medicine, art, design, religion and music. Explore the migration of global cultural ideas towards modern Britain.

4

DIVERSIFY FACES

Finding role models – the *faces* of your subject – seems simple. But all too often, we default to obvious, well known, Western European models. A simple check of your own subject knowledge will help you to discover a broader range of people to whom you can attribute the development of your subject. Are there people outside of white, Western Europe who were important in the formation of your subject? Are there representations of diverse bodies in your subject area? Who are the *hidden figures* or your subject?

5

COUNTER DOMINANT NARRATIVES

Instead of a curriculum where race, gender and disability are mainly rooted in victim narratives, include positive representation. Go beyond teaching slavery and the Holocaust or gender narratives of victimhood, illegality and medical controversy. Go beyond external perceptions of disability or neurodiversity. Actively use examples and narratives countering this dominance. What is the received *truth* children are led to believe? Actively provide a more balanced perspective.

AUTHENTIC CONNECTIONS

In numerous curriculum contexts, there are opportunities to make powerful links between the knowledge and experiences gained in different traditional subject areas. Sometimes this is referred to as interdisciplinarity or, more simply, cross-curricular links. Subjects do not exist within a rigid silo, as if there are no overlaps with other areas, but it is important to make any connections authentic, driven by the benefit to understanding each of the contributing areas in more depth. There is no value in linking subjects artificially for the sake of it.

1

ESTABLISH A COHERENT VERTICAL CURRICULUM FOR EACH SUBJECT

Follow the processes of curriculum planning for subjects on their own to begin with. These Volume 1 WalkThrus will help:

- **Designing a Knowledge-Rich Curriculum**
- **Sequence Concepts in Small Steps**
- **Coherent Mapping**
- **Blend Knowledge and Experience**

Doing this first will ensure that each subject retains its internal coherence while also flushing out ideas for possible connections.

2

LOOK FOR CONNECTIONS BETWEEN SUBJECTS

Working collaboratively across subject teams, look for areas where students would benefit from interdisciplinary connections being planned explicitly. This might include:

- Key concepts, common to each subject but explored in different ways.
- Different aspects of a text, a period in history or geographical location.
- Different learning opportunities from common experiences such as field trips and visits.

3

INTEGRATE OVERLAPPING KNOWLEDGE

Where the same concepts are encountered in different subject disciplines, it pays to make strong connections explicitly, integrating examples from the contributing subjects and even teaching them as one topic where possible, especially at primary level.

Climate change and weather are good examples. These include aspects of geography and science. Concepts, terminology and case studies can be planned as an integrated whole.

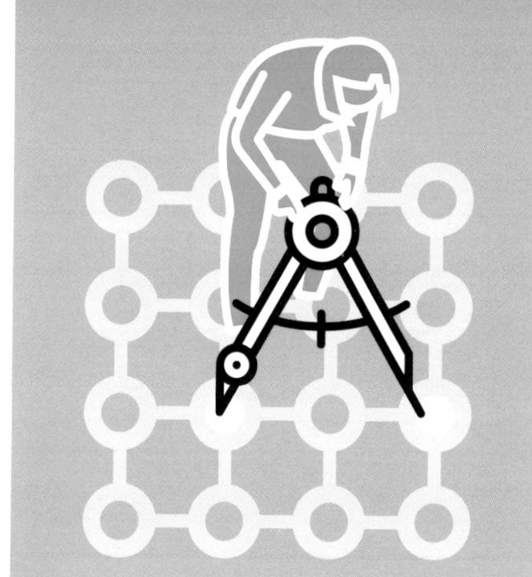

4

COORDINATE PARALLEL CONNECTIONS

Where linked ideas are encountered in multiple subjects running concurrently, coordinate approaches so that they reinforce each other, deepening understanding by seeing ideas in different contexts, rather than it being ad hoc, creating confusion:

- Measurement and graphs in maths, science, geography, technology: *units, formulae and measurement methods can be coordinated.*
- Multiple links between literature and history: *BAME history/literature; Dickens/ Victorians; war poetry.*

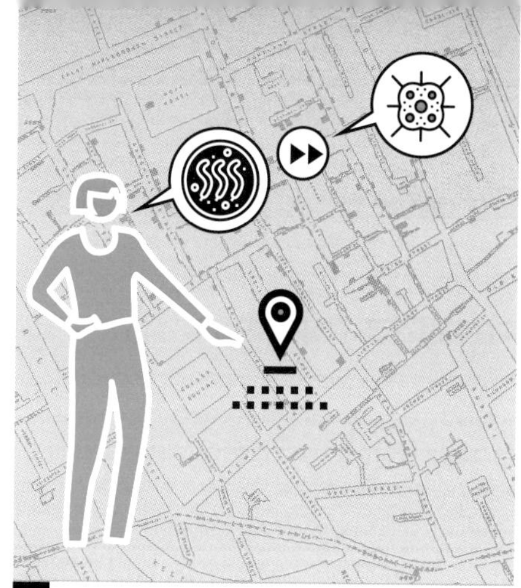

5

PLAN ASYNCHRONOUS CONNECTIONS

There is no need for all curriculum connections to be delivered at the same time. If you know where connections can be made to prior learning or to future learning in other subject areas, it is helpful to make the links explicit:

- John Snow's discovery of cholera in London in 1854 in history forms a background for discussing microbes and disease in science some time later.
- A geography sustainability unit picks up ideas about renewable fuels taught in science earlier.

THEMES & TOPICS

It's a common practice in primary schools (to a much lesser extent in secondary schools) for subjects to be combined via overarching topics or themes.

Primary schools sometimes teach nearly everything except maths and English through topics of this kind. This can work well, with potential benefits in terms of coherent schema-building and efficient time planning, provided that the integrity of the contributing subjects is maintained, not corrupted by the imposition of the theme.

Sometimes local events and contexts provide material for strong topics, allowing students to see how, for example, history, technology, geography and religion interconnect in their local area and community.

WALKTHRUs IN THIS SERIES

CURRICULUM PLANNING

1

CHOOSE THEMES OFFERING AUTHENTIC DEEP LEARNING GAINS

Ideas to build excellent themes around:

Places: West Africa, Beijing, The Himalayas

Periods of History: The Middle Ages, 1920s, 1960s, The Iron Age

Environments: Deserts, Oceans, The Local Area

Events: The Olympics, WWII

People: Nelson Mandela; Emmeline Pankhurst

Concepts: Freedom, Rights, Journeys, Rites of Passage

Technology: Transport or communication over time and around the world

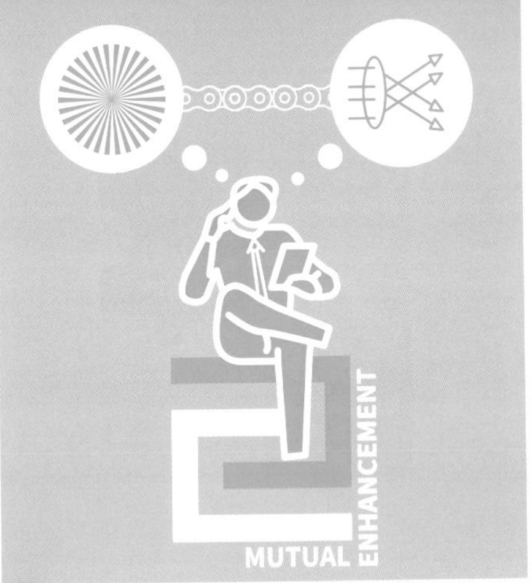

2

APPLY THE TEST OF MUTUAL ENHANCEMENT

In a unit on colour, students can explore both art and science, examining the properties of light, the eye and the application of colour in painting.

They work together.

Only link a subject to a theme if, by doing so, you positively contribute to students' understanding and experience. If connections are tenuous or contrived, don't include them. Look for **Authentic Connections**. Including The Black Death or Snow White in the colour-themed unit is obviously very superficial.

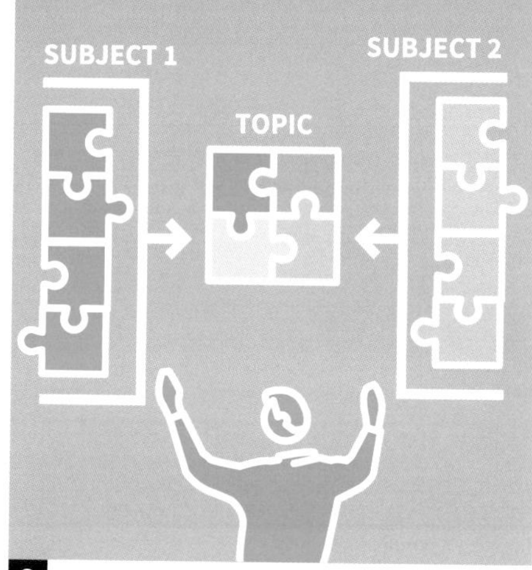

3

MAINTAIN SUBJECT COHERENCE

Across a series of themes or topics that span the curriculum, ensure that the concepts within each subject build logically over time. For example, geographical understanding often starts with our local area, then key national and wider global reference points: cities, continents, oceans. Randomly studying Peru in Year 3, because of Paddington Bear, may not help their deeper conceptual understanding of geography. Make choices that maintain that coherence as far as possible.

4

SET KNOWLEDGE GOALS – OF ALL KINDS

Refer to **Blend Knowledge & Experience** in Volume 1. It is important to specify the knowledge and experiences all students should acquire from a themed topic, to ensure details are not lost. This is especially true where enquiry projects are woven into the learning process. However, it can be useful to frame the topic with a big question:

- Could humans live on Mars?
- What was everyday life like in the 1850s?
- Why do people hold festivals?

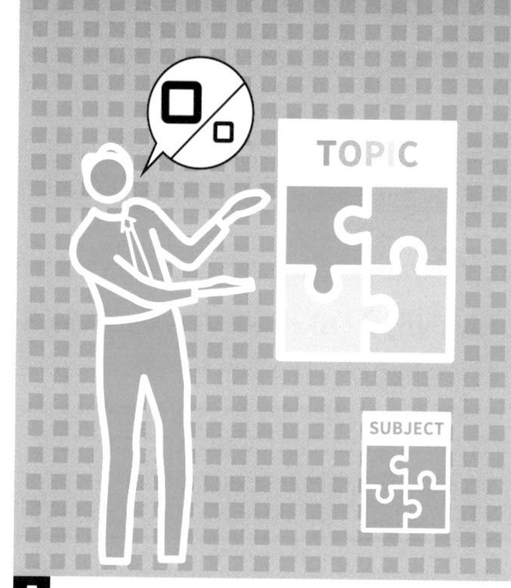

5

BLEND TOPICS WITH SINGLE SUBJECT TEACHING

Rather than shoehorning every element of the curriculum into a topic or themed unit, it can help to blend topic work with other single subject elements across the curriculum. In a particular six-week sequence, you might teach science and geography through a themed unit while teaching history and art as separate subjects. This is better than forcing the art curriculum into the theme unless it fits naturally.

LEARNING OBJECTIVES vs TASKS

Graham Nuthall's research clearly illustrated that there is an ever-present risk of confusing task completion with learning. It is possible to perform all manner of tasks and take part in activities, following instructions or joining in with the class, without actually connecting ideas to prior knowledge, building secure links and consolidating new learning.

Teachers need to be aware of this and focus on setting explicit learning objectives rather than focusing on task completion. Of course good tasks will support learning but it's important to be clear about our priorities.

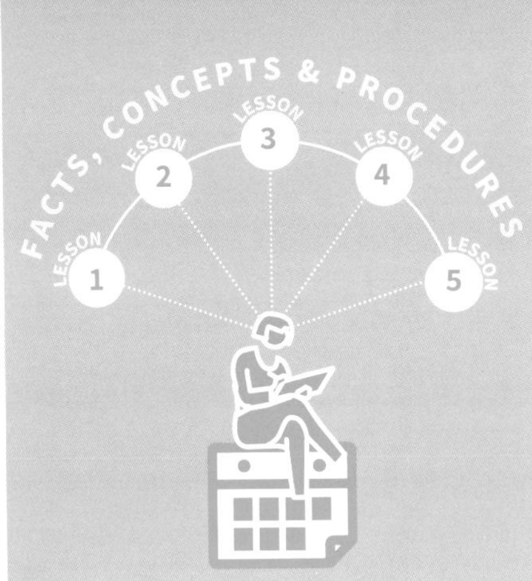

1 PLAN LEARNING OBJECTIVES SPANNING A SERIES OF LESSONS

Take account of your overall curriculum plan and students' prior knowledge to decide what the learning objectives should be for a series of lessons, not just one lesson at a time. Good learning objectives will include:

- The specific facts, concepts or procedures students should know and understand, building on the knowledge they already have.
- The skills students should be able to perform independently or with increased fluency, developing their existing skills.

2 MAKE SHORT- AND LONG-TERM LEARNING OBJECTIVES EXPLICIT

A real example might be:

- Long term: know the structure and function of each of the organs in the digestive system.
- Short term: know how enzymes in the stomach and intestines work to digest and absorb different food types.

The teacher can't be totally sure how far students will progress in any one lesson but, with the overall objectives in mind, they and their students can check how far they've got and how much further they still have to go in explaining all the functions of all the organs.

WALKTHRUs IN THIS SERIES

CURRICULUM PLANNING

3

DISCUSS, CLARIFY, CHECK FOR UNDERSTANDING

It's important for students themselves to understand the learning objectives. This helps them to make sense of ideas that they encounter and to monitor their own progress. Remind students of the big picture for the topic in hand and use questioning methods to ensure they understand what the learning goals are. It is not important whether students write down learning objectives for each lesson; avoid making this an unthinking routine that students might do without understanding. Use **Check for Understanding** to sample the class.

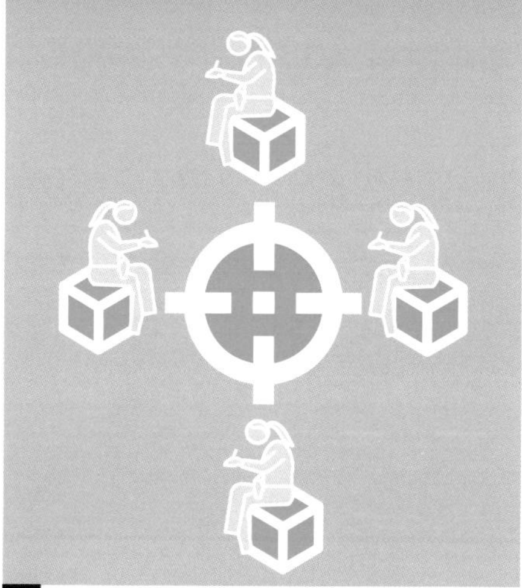

4

DESIGN TASKS THAT SUPPORT THE LEARNING OBJECTIVES

Once everyone is clear about what students should know and be able to do, explain the tasks. These should be designed to ensure students can gain the knowledge they need. As well as the teacher's **Explaining and Modelling** input, take account of Willingham's idea that *memory is the residue of thought* and ensure all students have to think, making sense of new ideas in terms of their prior knowledge. As far as possible, include generative learning activities so students have to select and organise information. (See **Make Everyone Think**.)

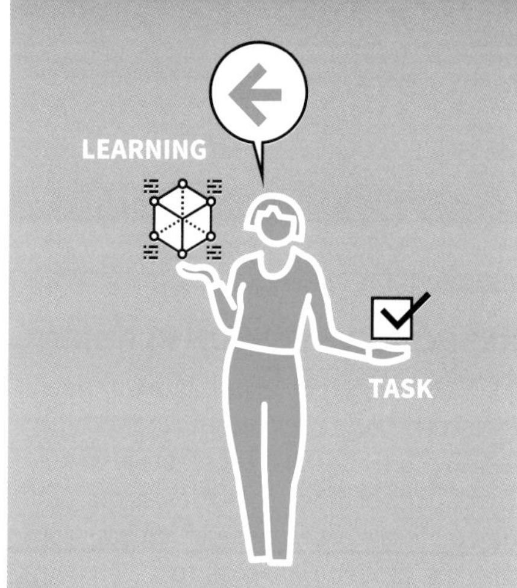

5

FOCUS ON ACHIEVING LEARNING GOALS OVER TASK COMPLETION

During lessons, make sure you reinforce the learning goals: *Have you learned it? Can you do it? Can you explain it?*

Be careful not to over-do the task completion messages – *Have you finished? Is the table complete? Have you produced enough writing yet?* These alone do not mean students achieve the learning goals. A focus on task completion risks masking the true extent of student learning. Training students to check their own learning with self-quizzing and self-review is part of the process.

RESPONSIVE LESSON PLANNING

A key challenge for teachers is to translate their curriculum planning into the specific learning activities that constitute lessons. These units of time, spread across the timetable, are a well-understood basis for thinking about how to construct effective learning sequences.

However, it is usually much more effective and time efficient if teachers plan learning that spans a longer sequence of curriculum content before focusing on each individual lesson. This allows them to focus on deeper learning goals and respond as students progress at varying rates.

WALKTHRUs IN THIS SERIES

CURRICULUM PLANNING

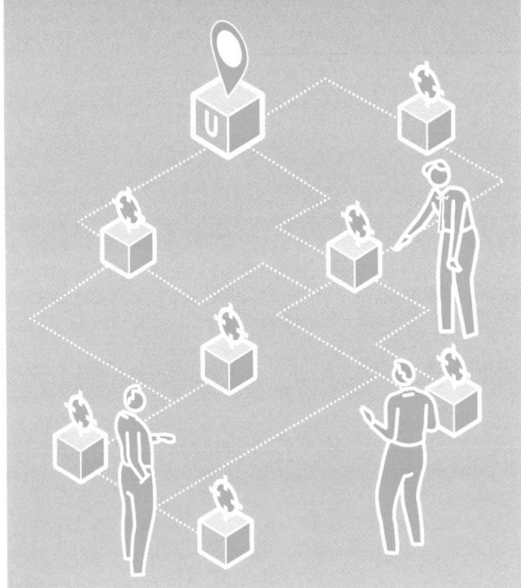

1

PLAN AND SEQUENCE UNIT-LEVEL LEARNING INTENTIONS

Before planning lessons, map out the learning for the unit as a whole. Volume 1 WalkThrus cover several aspects of this:

- **Designing a Knowledge-Rich Curriculum**
- **Coherent Mapping**
- **Blend Knowledge and Experience**

Establish a very clear set of precise learning intentions for all students such that, by the end of the whole unit or sequence of lessons, they should have learned X, Y, Z as in **Learning Objectives vs Tasks**.

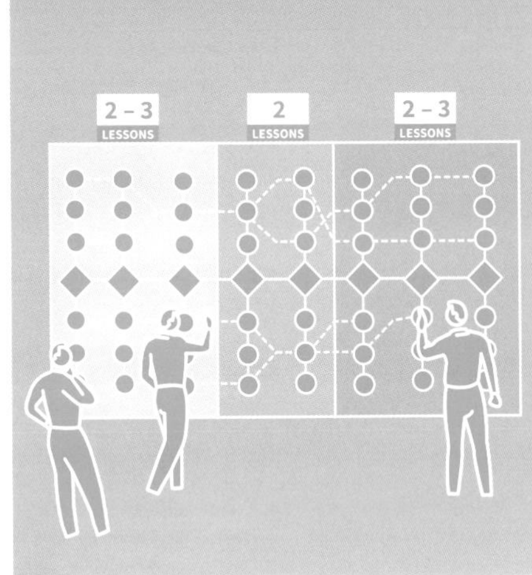

2

BREAK DOWN INTO MULTI-LESSON SERIES

Taking account of the time available, map out an approximate timeline for covering the curriculum content over a unit. This should be provisional, allowing scope for agile adjustments in overall pace at various points. A rough medium-term timeline allows you to gauge the depth and intensity of the learning you need to aim for.

In the short-term, designing series of around 4–8 lessons gives a tight enough focus for the learning intentions, each lesson forming one step in a longer learning arc.

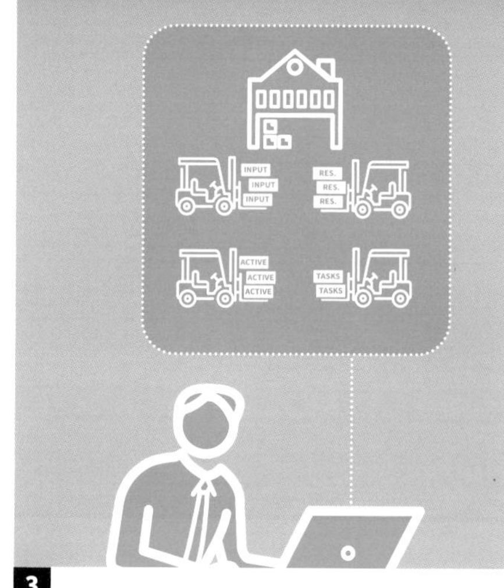

3

DESIGN ACTIVITIES AND ASSEMBLE RESOURCES

Using ideas from **Learning Objectives vs Tasks**, design teacher inputs, activities, practice tasks and resources needed to secure success for every student. Planning 4–8 lessons in one go allows scope for some lessons to focus on teacher exposition and modelling or perhaps guided and independent practice.

In planning activities, you do not need to decide in advance exactly when they will happen; instead you prepare them, ready to deploy at the moment you feel students are ready.

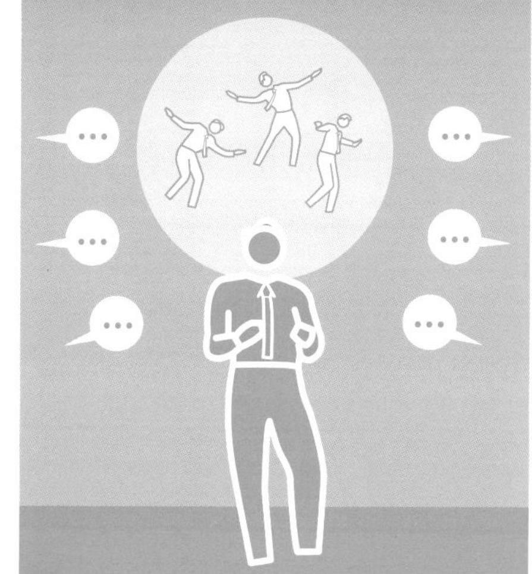

4

BE AGILE IN REAL TIME, ADAPTING TO STUDENTS' RESPONSES

If you are using a good range of formative assessment methods, questioning and checking for understanding, guiding practice closely, you will be able to gauge whether students are making progress towards the overarching learning intentions. Be agile in your thinking, ready at all times to move ahead faster or to go back and re-teach. There is no merit in sticking rigidly to a lesson plan if you determine that a different approach is needed. Act right away, for the whole class or specific individuals.

5

RE-SHAPE THE UNIT PLAN LESSON TO LESSON

After each lesson in a series, take stock of the progress students have made, as far as you can tell, and plan the detail of the next lesson, adjusting your overall plan as needed, depending on the time you have left. You may need to intensify some aspects of practice; re-teach or re-model some key elements; set different practice tasks in class or for home study. You may even need to remove some planned activities to accommodate more consolidation or jump ahead – a normal healthy feature of good responsive planning.

TEACH TO THE TOP

Every class is a mixed attaining class. The challenge for teachers is to pitch material so everyone is challenged and supported to make good progress. Rather than pitching to the middle or letting the least confident students' difficulties lower expectations for everyone, teaching to the top implies a default approach – a teacher mindset – where the highest attaining, most confident students drive the overall pitch and depth of learning. This is the best way to raise standards for all, providing supports to reach ambitious goals rather than pitching low and offering higher attainers occasional extra challenges.

WALKTHRUs IN THIS SERIES

CURRICULUM PLANNING

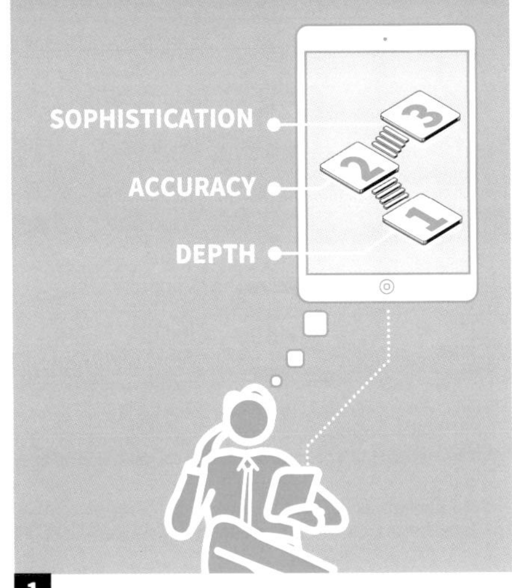

1

PLAN FOR DIFFICULTY & CHALLENGE

Follow the steps in the **Pitch It Up** WalkThru. Ensure that your curriculum is rich in challenge, including elements of difficulty that will stretch everyone in the cohort. You might need to adjust the level of challenge and difficulty responsively depending on the degree of success your students experience. But through good curriculum planning (see Volume 1), you should have a sense of the material that will represent genuinely ambitious knowledge goals in any subject for a particular class.

2

IDENTIFY THE HIGHEST ATTAINERS

Note we use *mixed attaining* class rather than *mixed ability*. *Ability* can be misunderstood, sometimes regarded (falsely) as a fixed characteristic. With that caveat, it is important to identify the set of specific students who are the most confident and knowledgeable based on objective assessments. Find out what they are capable of without presuming any limits. This might require setting very demanding tasks early on just to test where they begin to experience significant difficulty.

3

TEACH SO THE HIGHEST ATTAINERS ARE ALWAYS CHALLENGED

This is the heart of the concept. Plan and teach so that the conceptual depth and sophistication of the material or the degree of practical difficulty are always demanding for your highest attaining students. This should be supported by the questions, tasks and problems you set. Those students should never feel that they are being held back or that the work is too easy. This high challenge approach benefits everyone.

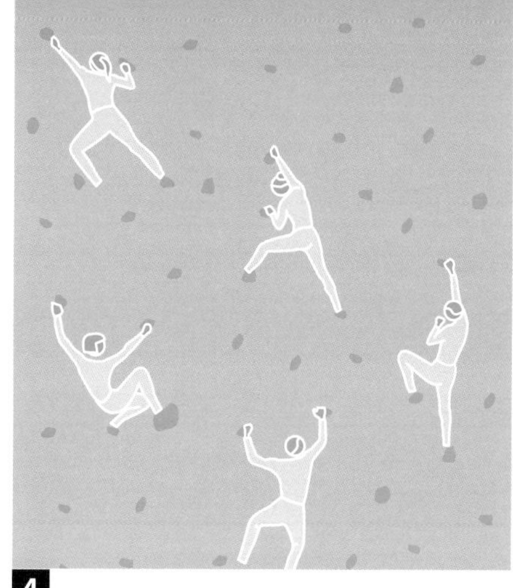

4

PROVIDE SCAFFOLDS AND SUPPORTS

Having planned the pathway for the top, plan appropriate forms of scaffolding to support the remaining students to reach the same standards, albeit with more help, guidance and time. This approach minimises the chance that a curriculum is *dumbed down* and switches thinking from *How can I make it easier for you?* to *How can I help you climb higher?*

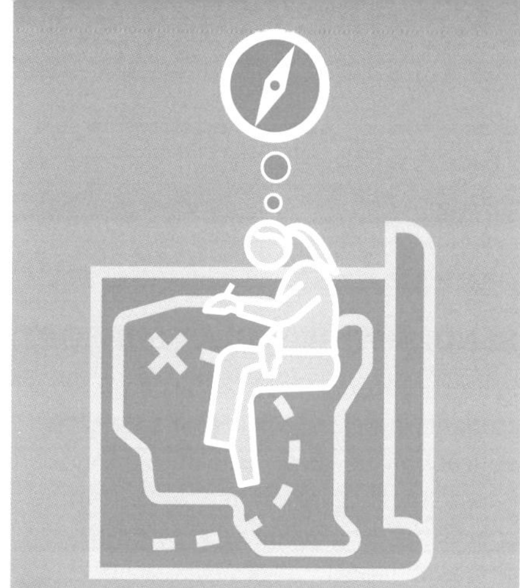

5

VARY MODES OF GUIDED AND INDEPENDENT PRACTICE

It's vital that high challenge is not viewed as constant struggle. Everyone needs practice, including high attainers. Less confident students will need more guided practice; more confident students can move rapidly to independent practice. Plan a range of practice tasks within your Teach to the Top approach, adjusting in response to students' level of performance and fluency at any point.

SEND: AIM HIGH, PLAN SUPPORT

In most contexts, there will be one or more students in a class with identified special educational needs or disabilities (SEND). Those students are entitled to expect their special needs to be fully addressed in an embedded way by all of their teachers. This is not simply a moral obligation; it is required by law. It's a core element of any teacher's practice to ensure all SEND students' needs are fully met. This means supporting individual students to meet high standards; it's essential not to lower expectations or project stereotypical assumptions about what they can and cannot do.

1

EXPLORE YOUR SEND STUDENTS' SPECIFIC LEARNING NEEDS

For every class, make sure you are fully aware of any documented SEND students and their specific needs. This will involve seeking out and reading any documentation – taking the initiative to do so, not waiting for it to be presented to you. Depending on the students' age and circumstances, you may need to discuss cases with SEND specialist staff, parents and the student themselves in order to plan appropriately, following any technical guidance as needed.

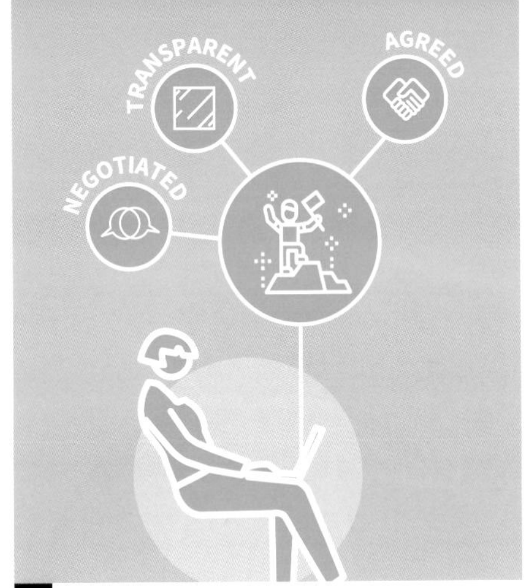

2

PLAN AMBITIOUS LEARNING GOALS

Armed with knowledge of your students' special needs, plan curriculum goals for them as individuals. Clearly this depends on the nature of the curriculum and their needs but the first principle should be that SEND students' goals should not deviate from everyone else's in terms of standards and depth, to the greatest extent possible. Engage in a process where any goal adjustments are transparent, negotiated and agreed.

3

PLAN TAILORED SCAFFOLDS AND SUPPORTS

Take heed of general and individualised technical guidance in order to make adjustments or additions to curriculum materials and lesson plans to support SEND students to succeed. Different areas of SEND will require very specific types of support. Even where external support is strong, an important principle is that it is you, the teacher, who carries responsibility for ensuring supports are available and deployed effectively.

4

TEACH INCLUSIVELY

With supports in place, teach the class including all SEND students as a whole. It's vital that SEND students receive direct instruction and engage in discussion and dialogue alongside everyone else; that any sense of being outside the main group is eliminated or minimised. Support SEND students to participate at every opportunity, keeping in mind that this is their entitlement, not some kind of bonus.

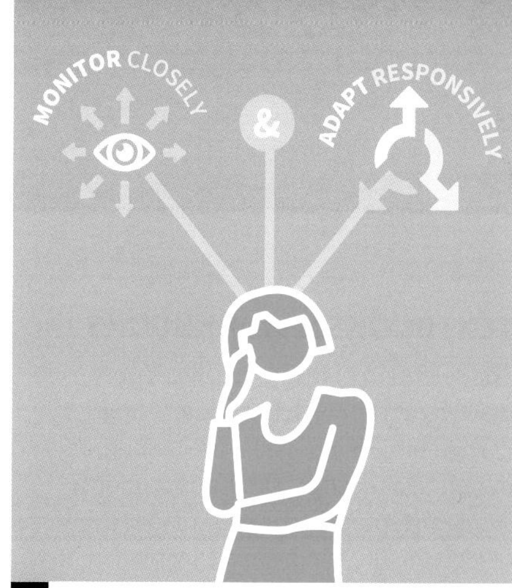

5

MONITOR CLOSELY; ADAPT RESPONSIVELY

It can take time to learn exactly what works to maximise a student's success and confidence. Monitor and adapt as responsively as possible, always keeping expectations high. Identify and separate issues around impaired physical access or cognitive processing from issues of effort and motivation and respond accordingly. Keep close contact with parents and specialists to resolve difficulties.

TEXTBOOKS & WORKBOOKS

The selection of resources to support delivery of the curriculum is a key part of curriculum design. There are numerous benefits to teacher teams and students where pre-prepared, ready-made resources of high quality can be used, instead of busy teachers creating their own materials in addition to everything else. Where a good textbook is available or where students can follow the tasks set out in a high quality workbook, teachers can focus more on their explanations, questioning, feedback and checking for understanding.

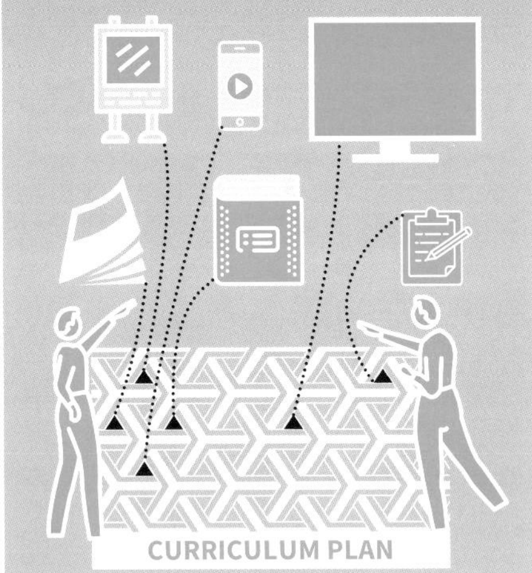

1

MAP THE RESOURCES TO THE CURRICULUM PLAN

Your curriculum should drive resource planning; not the other way around. Select resources aligning with your curriculum plan and map across, choosing elements you will use. There is no need to follow a published scheme in a particular order; your own sequence should guide you. Supplement published resources with your own, avoiding reinventing the wheel or feeling confined. In terms of quality, ask whether your homemade PowerPoint is really better than the spread in the textbook.

2

ENSURE ALL STUDENTS CAN ACCESS THE RESOURCES INDEPENDENTLY

A key benefit to using textbooks and workbooks is that students can access them independently, during lessons and in between lessons. In some contexts, it isn't sufficient to make them available – for example in a library or online. You need to give each student their own, checking they can and do access the material. Set an early task that requires students to refer to the material independently as a way to flush out any access issues.

3

MODEL THE USE OF RESOURCES IN LESSONS

Students will not necessarily know how to use a textbook or workbook. Every aspect can and should be modelled explicitly:

Reading: how to navigate the text; encountering unknown terms; where to find information; skimming and scanning.

Comprehension: making sense of arguments, diagrams, explanations.

Making notes: how to select and record information.

Questions and answers: how to use the resource for self-assessment.

4

ESTABLISH LEARNING ROUTINES

Most textbooks and workbooks are more useful if used routinely as part of the learning process. Frequent use allows students to develop effective study habits, focusing on the content, not the mechanics of using the resources. Good routines to establish might include:

- How to check for errors using the back of the book answers.
- How to set out notes in a certain style.
- What to do if you don't understand a word.

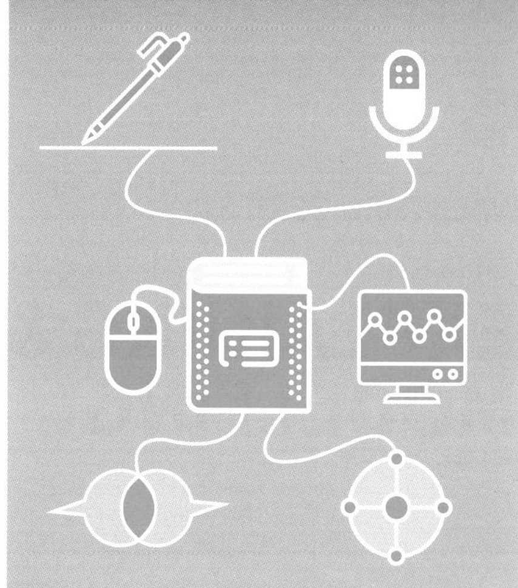

5

BLEND WITH OTHER LEARNING MODES

A common objection to using textbooks and workbooks arises when they are perceived to dominate the learning experience excessively. Taking account of the range of knowledge and experiences students need for effective schema-building, ensure you use these resources judiciously. Even if you find it beneficial to use them in most lessons, make sure other learning modes have their place to add variety and depth to the learning process.

WALKTHRU SERIES

EXPLAINING & MODELLING

03

A central feature of effective teaching is the process of enabling students to develop their knowledge and understanding of concepts and processes and the ability to apply their learning to a range of situations. Explaining and modelling are vital elements of any teacher's repertoire of techniques. Drawing on the evidence base described in the Why? sections in both Volumes 1 and 2, these WalkThrus cover several key aspects of effective teachers' practice, from using exemplars and analogies to giving practical demonstrations. We are also delighted to feature four WalkThrus written by Alex Quigley, focusing on reading strategies.

PRE-READING INSTRUCTIONS FOR COMPLEX TEXTS

Fundamentally, the school curriculum is mediated by our students' academic reading ability. As reading skill opens up access to the curriculum, it is vital to focus instruction on successfully mediating the reading of complex texts, from science textbooks to historical sources. We cannot, and should not, dumb down our text choices. Instead, we need to pitch it up. But if we are to teach challenging texts, we need to ensure pre-reading instructions can offer access points into the text for all students.

ALEX QUIGLEY | GUEST AUTHOR

WALKTHRUs IN THIS SERIES

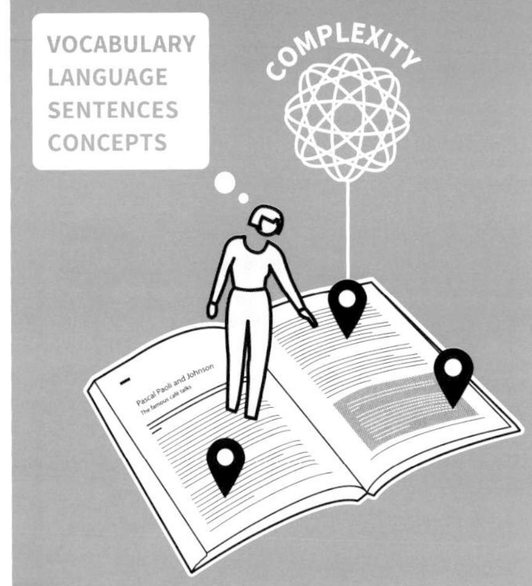

1

UNDERTAKE A *READY RECKONER*

All texts can prove complex in different ways. As such, a teacher can select a manageable portion of the text (e.g. the first 200 words, or a page from a chapter) and then evaluate the complexity of that portion. Some aspects that determine text complexity include:

- Rare, academic vocabulary
- Language features e.g. metaphors
- Sentence length
- Range of complex concepts or big ideas

Determining just how complex this sample passage proves will lead to decisions about pre-teaching.

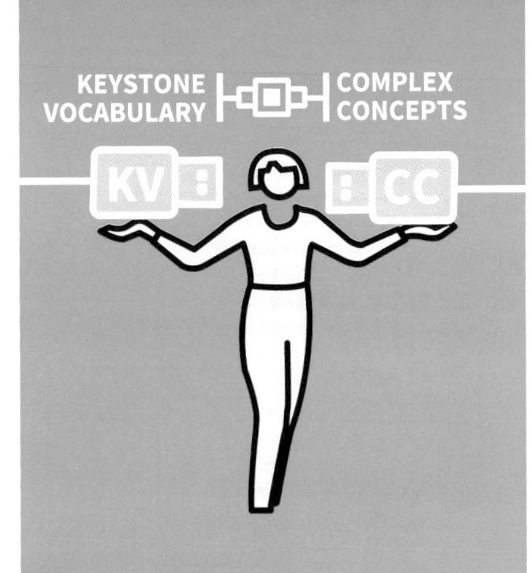

2

CONNECT COMPLEX CONCEPTS AND *KEYSTONE VOCABULARY*

For complex texts, it is important to identify and pre-teach sophisticated concepts, such as particles and energy in science, alongside explicitly identifying the related core vocabulary that is essential to communicating those concepts. A small number of keystone (fundamental to the schema of the text) vocabulary items can be explicitly pre-taught. These vocabulary items, such as *atoms, molecules* and *ions* for the scientific concept of particles, should be identified, taught and revisited as part of a coherently mapped reading curriculum.

3

ACTIVATE PRIOR KNOWLEDGE AND *RELATE*

A key aspect of pre-reading instruction, to ensure students can understand a difficult academic text, is to explicitly activate students' prior knowledge. For example, when reading a Shakespearean sonnet in English literature, it is important to relate it to other poetic genres and knowledge related to Shakespearean plays studied. Many novice students can miss seemingly obvious connections. Connecting keystone vocabulary items to words they know already allows for better developed schemas for the text.

4

PROBE & QUESTION

Before reading a text in class fully, a small number of **Probing Questions**, via **Cold Calling**, should be directed at individual pupils to ascertain a representative level of prior knowledge for complex concepts and *keystone vocabulary*. For example, in history, a probing question about students' knowledge of Tudor kings and queens can precede reading a source that evaluates the Wars of the Roses. Limited responses may lead to recalibrating how much pre-reading instruction is required to develop students' schemas before they go onto reading further texts.

5

PLAN FOR PAUSES

Complex academic texts can place a high demand on our students' working memory. Simply following each sentence can initiate a high demand for prior knowledge and vocabulary recognition. As such, it is helpful to identify specific pauses in the text, with a small number of targeted questions to **Check for Understanding** before initiating reading once more.

ALEX QUIGLEY

WHOLE-CLASS READING ROUTINES

Teachers read academic texts in the classroom to their students on a daily basis. This can total thousands of acts of academic reading. Subsequently, reading to a whole class can prove routine and habitual, which can in turn see it enacted without much reflection, resulting in variable success. Teachers can make more evidence-informed decisions about how to more precisely read to the whole class. There are a variety of options for whole-class reading, with different classroom approaches benefiting different reading outcomes.

WALKTHRUs IN THIS SERIES

EXPLAINING & MODELLING

1

EVALUATE YOUR WHOLE-CLASS READING OPTIONS

The most common approach to whole-class reading is teacher-led whole-class reading. This offers a reading role model who can read with a high degree of skill and fluency. It does not, however, have benefits of developing students themselves as fluent readers. The following approaches can support students' reading:

- Choral reading: students read along with the teacher in unison.
- Paired reading: small groups read collaboratively, aiding students' own reading skills (though it may lack the fluency of the teacher reading).

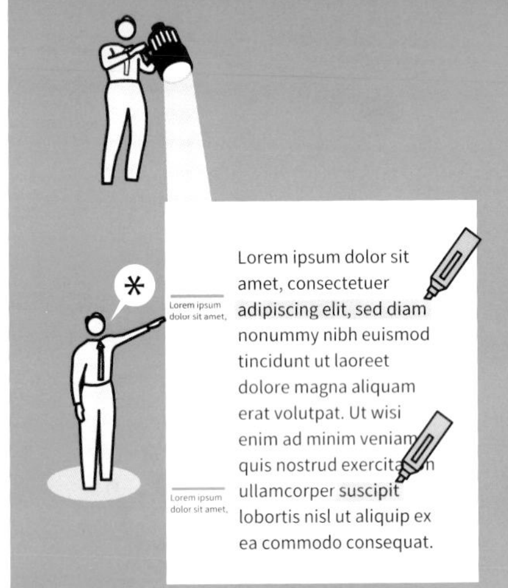

2

ANNOTATE & PRACTISE

Though teachers are busy, a productive use of lesson planning can include concise annotations for a complex academic text to be read in class. Brief annotations, such as underlining key words and phrases to stress and emphasise, can both support the performance of reading (which can aid student reading comprehension) and identify keystone vocabulary. For significant passages, a speedy practice of reading the passage aloud should aid fluent teacher reading.

3

EXPRESS & STRESS

An adept reading performance in class can aid the understanding of complex concepts. Teachers should read with a smooth pace, but also explicitly emphasise and stress the most important vocabulary items in a text. Of course, many academic texts include dense noun phrases which are unfamiliar for students. For example, in geography, noun phrases like *global atmospheric circulation* and *conservative plate margin* require careful, clear expression, whereas other words need to be stressed appropriately to convey their importance to students.

4

CHUNK & STOP

Given that academic texts can be so dense with complex vocabulary and concepts, how you chunk down a text into readable parts can determine how well students process their reading. Textbooks typically offer natural chunks and stopping points to check understanding, but these are not always evident, and often the teacher has to identify stopping points independently. In other types of texts, apt stopping points can be identified at the planning stage.

5

ESTABLISH THE GIST

Whole-class reading for a sustained period of time can place a high cognitive demand on both the teacher and students. It is therefore important to plan to consolidate understanding. For example, it can be helpful to give the concise gist of the text, or elicit this information from students, along with the targeted identification and re-reading of important sentences to ensure clarity and to reiterate the most important concepts of the text.

ALEX QUIGLEY

DEVELOPING READING FLUENCY

Reading fluency is an important prerequisite for students to read effectively and to comprehend the academic texts they read in class. Automatic and fluent reading is essential for students to concentrate their working memory resources on the complexity of the text. Researchers* have identified four dimensions of reading fluency:

- Expression and volume: varying expression and volume to match the content
- Phrasing: identifying clauses and emphasising words that are read together
- Smoothness: avoiding breaks or pauses
- Pace: an even, conversational rhythm

*Prof. Tim Rasinski's *Multi-dimensional Fluency Scale*

WALKTHRUs IN THIS SERIES

EXPLAINING & MODELLING

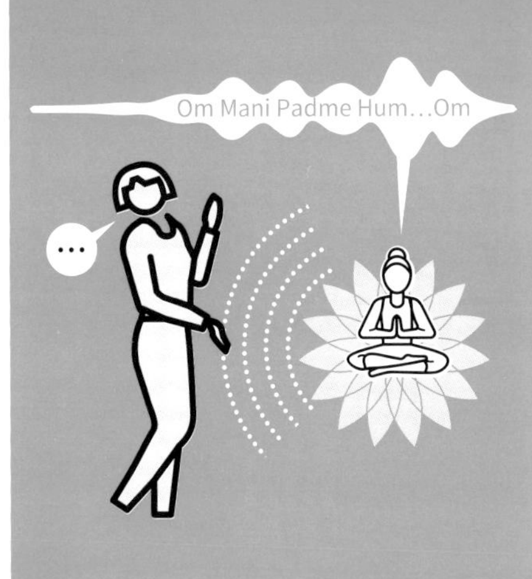

1

TEACHER MODELLING OF READING FLUENCY

It is helpful for students to hear models of fluent, skilled reading of academic texts. Modelling reading fluency can include the explicit review of the teacher's performance, using the language of fluency as described in the aforementioned fluency dimensions. Equally, the teacher can initiate an explanation of their own reading performance. For example, an RE teacher may discuss their phrasing of Buddhist chanting to ensure comprehension of the textbook chapter.

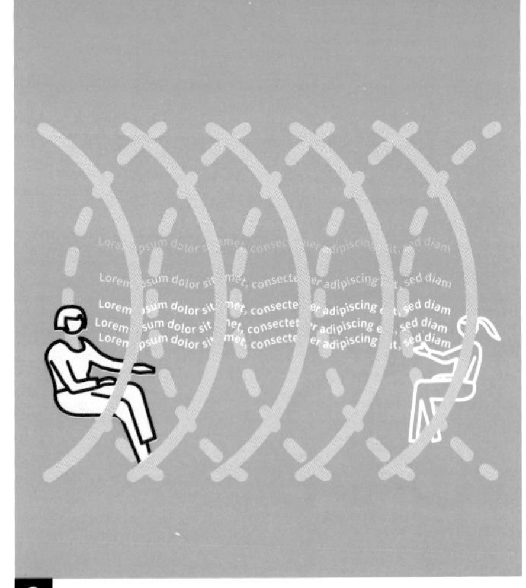

2

ECHO READING

Echo reading describes when a teacher models a passage, with the specific follow-up of pupils then reading the same passage. This is appropriate for an important passage to be read in class, such as a poem in English literature, or an important political speech in history. Having experienced the expert teacher version, some apt imitation can increase students' own reading fluency. Additionally, the repetition of this approach can foster a helpful consolidation of the reading content.

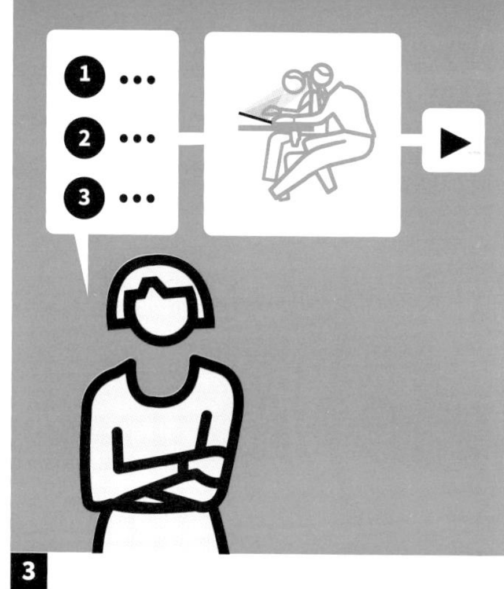

3

PAIRED READING

Students can be directed to read in pairs, such as reading alternate sentences of a given shared text, or repeating sentences after their partner has read them. This approach can support students to effectively assess the fluency of one another, offering a metacognitive support to further improve their own reading fluency. Whole-class talk about reading fluency is likely a prerequisite to maximise the gains from the collaborative approach. Clear, precise instructions are required for this collaborative strategy.

4

SEGMENTING SENTENCES

Many students struggle to notice the subtle cues offered by a textbook author or a poet. When they read, complex sentence structures trip them up and dense noun phrases, like 'organic, nutrient-rich materials' when describing soil erosion in geography, are not read with clarity or fluency. Identifying phrases (e.g. following the text with a visualiser) in meaningful chunks is often necessary to aid fluency, which in turn supports reading comprehension. For younger pupils, chunking such phrases with your fingers on the page can offer an additional support.

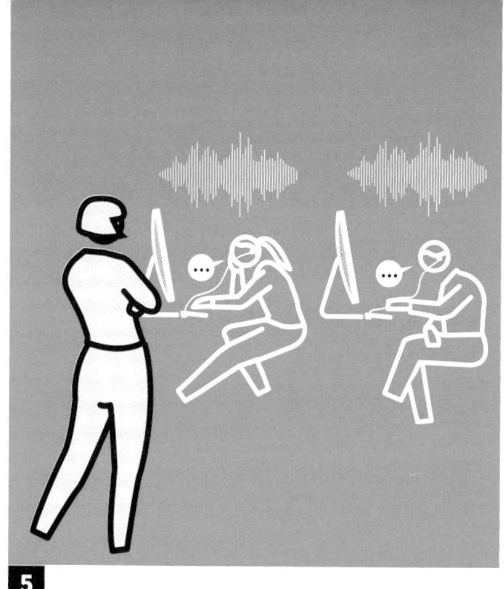

5

READ & RECORD

Digital technology offers manageable and meaningful opportunities to foster, and record, reading fluency. For example, students can record their own reading performances before then critiquing their own performance, or that of their peers. Equally, the teacher can play back their reading – both for repetition to consolidate understanding and to foreground aspects of reading fluency in performance.

ALEX QUIGLEY

SUMMARISING ACADEMIC READING

Reading may appear to be a natural act for so many students. Crucially, however, many students can read with a degree of fluency, but they lack the background and vocabulary knowledge to fully comprehend a tricky text. Many novice students fail to actively develop a rich schema for the text they are reading. They do not initiate the reading strategies of experts, who habitually make predictions, question and summarise the text. As such, explicitly teaching reading comprehension strategies, such as summarising, can prove a powerful tool to enhance reading comprehension.

WALKTHRUs IN THIS SERIES

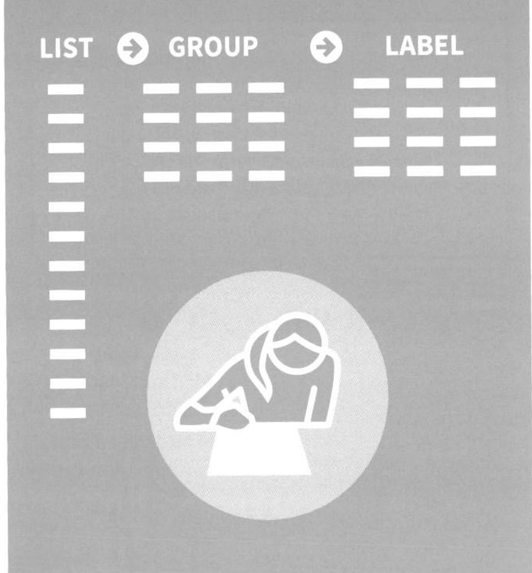

1

LIST, GROUP, LABEL

A well-established strategy to synthesise key information in the service of summarising an academic text is *list, group, label*. First, select a small number of key topics or ideas from the text. Then list as many vocabulary items and ideas related to the category or categories. Then work to more accurately cluster those words and ideas into sub-categories. This stepped approach to summarising meaningful details from the text helps students to explicitly make connections and to develop a rich schema for the text.

2

SHRINK & SUMMARISE

Many novice readers can struggle to identify and isolate the most salient features in a given academic text. Teachers should therefore explicitly model how to summarise in a concise and more purposeful manner. For example, *6-word summaries* can offer a quick and succinct approach to distilling the essential meaning of a text, no matter how lengthy. With repeated practice, students can begin to independently summarise in concise and precise ways. Students should be encouraged to reflect on the success of their single-sentence summaries.

PROMPT QUESTIONS

How do you know that...

What's your evidence for...

What questions do you have...

3

SUPPORT YOUR SUMMARY

Students should be encouraged to elaborate upon their summary by providing supporting evidence, either in written format, or via verbal explanations. This simple act of self-explanation can help students better connect their developing schemas for any given text. The teacher can offer simple question prompts to initiate accountable talk, whereat students explain and elaborate upon their short summaries, such as:

- How do you know that…?
- What is your evidence for…?
- What questions do you have…?

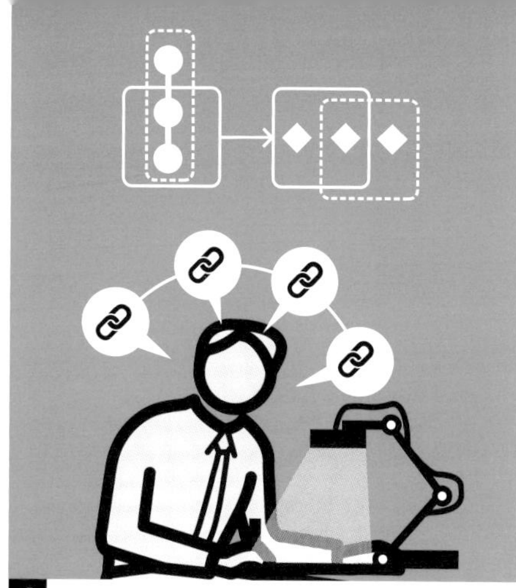

4

GO GLOBAL

Novice students commonly fail to enact the schema-building strategies of expert readers. They may read a textbook chapter on genetics and inheritance in science, but then fail to make connections to their prior reading and knowledge of living organisms and cells. Teachers can explicitly model *global inferences* – making connections between related concepts or topics – with strategies such as visually mapping related topics. Students can be encouraged to zoom in on individual words and sentences, before then zooming out to the big picture of the text.

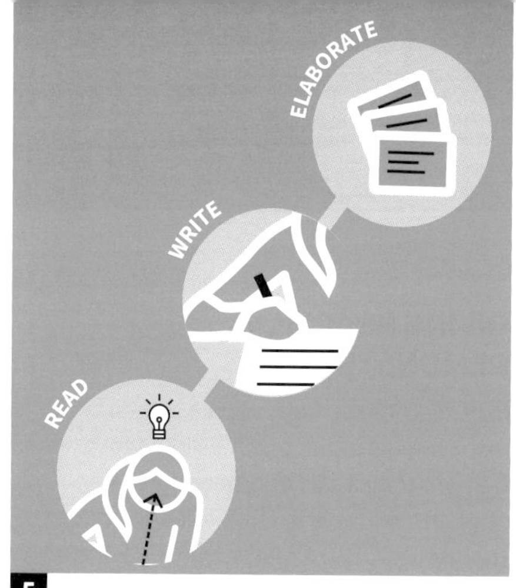

5

READ, WRITE, ELABORATE

It is well understood that writing about what you read provides a record of what has been read. Ample research even indicates that further elaborating on your reading can enhance its comprehension. Various study strategies, such as encouraging the design of summary flashcards, help students to explicitly transform the information from a given text and to summarise it in a concise record. Of course, such tools offer a resource for practising retrieval and for revisiting the academic text in an active, productive fashion.

GIVING PRACTICAL DEMONSTRATIONS

In numerous settings, as part of their instructional input, teachers need to demonstrate a skill or procedure that students will have to learn to perform themselves or an experiment to illustrate some natural phenomenon. The goal is to ensure that all students make sense of what they are seeing in order to develop their understanding at the level required. It pays to rehearse the practical elements, controlling the various materials and equipment alongside producing the narrative, so that the learning points are not masked by extraneous complications.

WALKTHRUs IN THIS SERIES

EXPLAINING & MODELLING

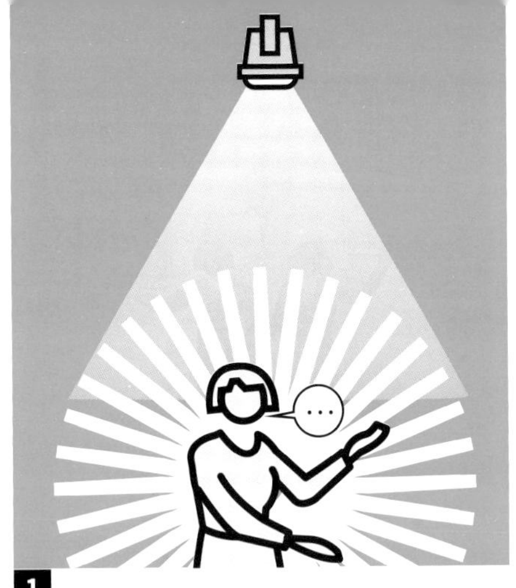

1

SECURE ATTENTION

If the demonstration needs students close up, use the routines in **Gather Around: Demonstrations and Stories**, initiating the procedure for students to move from their seats into their positions, giving full attention.

Alternatively, position your visualiser so that students can all see the demonstration on the screen as you run through it. This can be useful for effects that can't be seen clearly by a whole class when gathered around.

2

SET THE SCENE

Taking account of students' prior knowledge, explain the demonstration in the context of the wider curriculum. Teach students all the vocabulary they will need in order to explain what they see using **Deliberate Vocabulary Development**. Show diagrams alongside the real-world equipment so students can see how schematic simplifications relate to what they see. Cue up the demonstration, adjusting the equipment as needed so students can focus on the key effects you want them to observe.

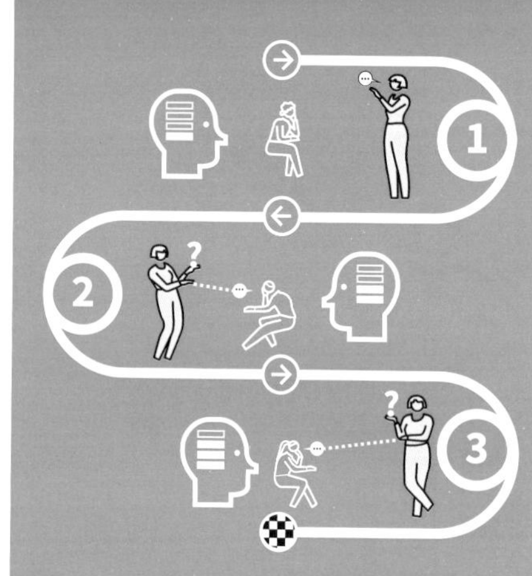

3

DEMONSTRATE IN SMALL STEPS

Taking account of the issue of cognitive load, run through the demonstration in small steps. Make students think about what is happening, not only any dramatic *attention grabbing*. At key points, use **Cold Calling** to ask students about what they are seeing, ensuring that they rehearse using any new terminology. They should be able to name all the tools, materials and apparatus. They should be able to rehearse sequences of steps mentally and verbally, in the correct order.

4

CHECK FOR UNDERSTANDING

Make it an explicit aim that all students can explain what they see. Connect what is seen to concepts and models. Ask probing questions that require students to:

- Explain what they are observing.
- Give reasons for steps in a procedure.
- Relate observation to theory.
- Predict and explain cause-and-effect relationships between inputs and outputs.
- Test their predictions and discuss the outcomes.

5

CONSOLIDATE THE LEARNING

There is always a risk that some students will have been watching without learning much. After the demonstration, set students a generative task that requires all of them to process the knowledge gained from watching and listening, making connections to prior knowledge and interrogating their understanding. Without this step, the episodic memory of having watched a demonstration can easily override the deeper conceptual understanding you may be hoping to develop.

DUAL CODING: DIAGRAMS

The core of Paivio's dual coding theory is based on matching a visual with a word for the retrieval of simple content. That's useful as far as it goes. But when the challenge is the understanding of more complex material, teachers need to use diagrams.

By converting abstract concepts or intricate processes into visual structures, key ideas are explained in a way that psychologists say is more *computationally efficient*. That's to say concepts become easier for students to understand by being visual, explicit and concrete.

However, for this strategy to be successful, the teacher must first teach how to read and create diagrams for different purposes.

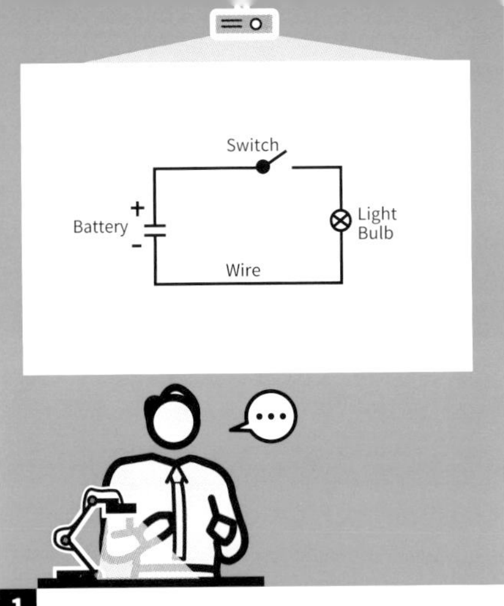

1

ESTABLISH A VISUAL OR SYMBOLIC LANGUAGE

Before diagrams can be used routinely, teach students the common symbols. Make a table or list to check students' recall and understanding over time.

Connect symbols to real-life objects and processes:

- How real electrical circuits and circuit diagrams relate
- How chemical symbols relate to particle diagrams and word equations
- How arrows represent forces and flows
- How timelines work

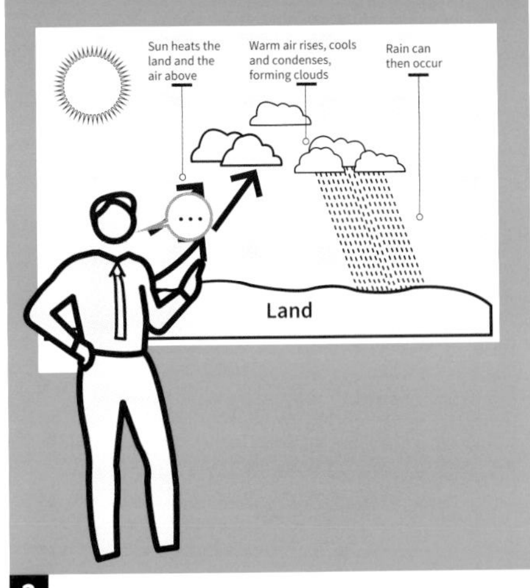

2

REPRESENT THE ESSENTIALS; LEAVE THE REST OUT

Strip out all the material that is not essential to explain the concepts you are trying to teach. Keep the symbols as simple as possible, while ensuring they remain identifiable. Use block shapes instead of detailed pictorial representations so that diagrams are easy to produce and manipulate. Remove the background or any objects not involved in the processes.

3

REPRESENT PROCESSES, MOVEMENT AND TIME

Teach students how you represent dynamic processes as well as static situations. For example, the use of arrows to show moving from the *before* to the *after* in any process. Establish a code for moving in certain directions or rotating.

Use flow diagram symbols to show procedures and decision points with different possible outcomes.

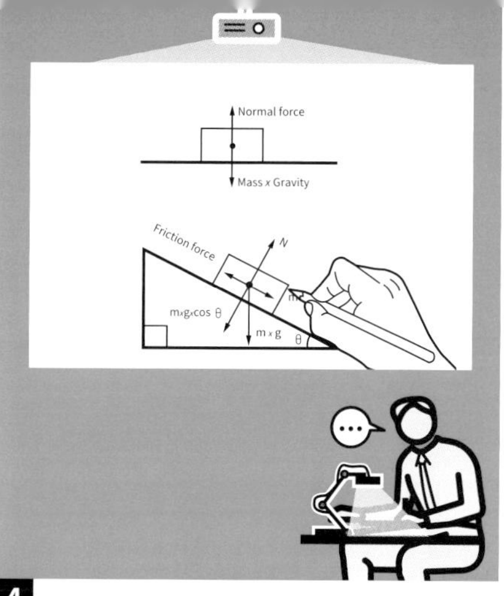

4

GENERATE IN REAL TIME, DUAL CODING VERBAL INFORMATION

Diagrams can work as static representations, but it can be powerful to create them in real time to support a verbal explanation. Using a visualiser or whiteboard, capture the steps of your explanation in symbolic form. This helps students to see processes develop, to visualise changes as they occur and to understand causal links, reinforcing the verbal narrative.

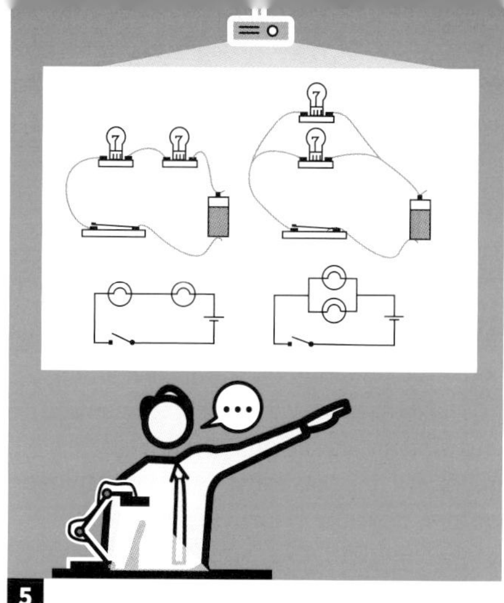

5

RE-CONNECT REPRESENTATION TO REALITY

Ensure students can translate diagrams back into real situations. This can include asking them to:

- Set up apparatus based on a diagram.
- Provide a narrative of an event or a change process, following the steps in a diagram.
- Solve a problem that is presented in the form of a diagram.
- Explain a phenomenon verbally using a diagram as the only reference.

ANALOGIES

In the schema-building model of learning – as described by Willingham, Shimamura and others – we can only really learn new material if it makes sense in terms of things we already know. Knowledge builds on knowledge. With this in mind, new abstract conceptual ideas can sometimes be best understood by constructing an analogy, referencing the behaviours of something familiar and more concrete. If we make the links clear, then, if we understand how a concrete example behaves, it helps make sense of the more abstract or less familiar idea.

1

CONSTRUCT ANALOGIES BASED ON FAMILIAR CONTEXTS

Well-established analogies used within specific subjects are normally successful because they connect to familiar contexts. For example:

- With electricity, a powerful analogy can be made with the properties of water flowing in a system of pipes.
- Aiming for the top of a mountain but taking small steps relates to numerous goal-setting scenarios.
- Sporting analogies can help to explain competitive attack/defence situations like battles.

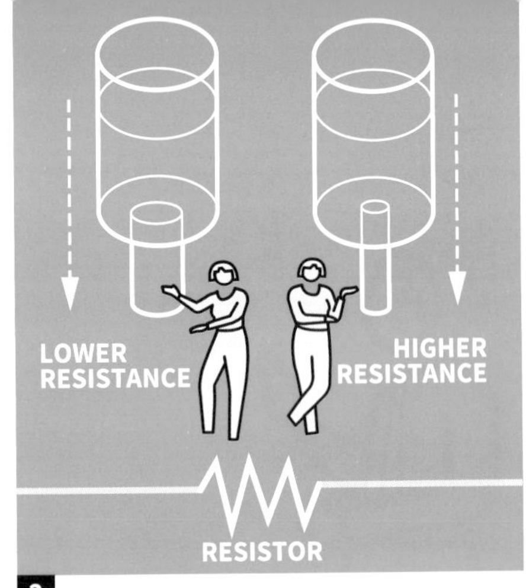

2

ESTABLISH THE PARALLELS EXPLICITLY

Take care to make very explicit links that explain the different features of the analogy. For example, with electricity, the rate of water flow is analogous to electrical current. Thinner pipes make it more difficult for the water to flow; this is analogous to higher electrical resistance. A bank overdraft is analogous to negative numbers on a number line. Borrowing more makes the total more negative.

Check for Understanding very carefully.

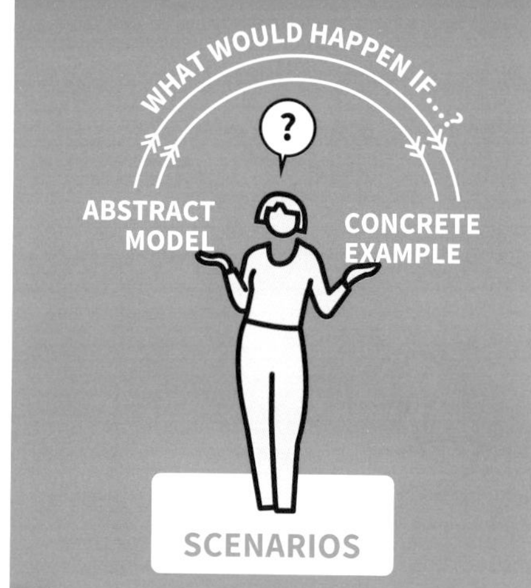

TEST THE ANALOGY IN DIFFERENT SCENARIOS

With the parallel elements established, explore how the more concrete example behaves:

What would happen to the rate of water flow if we made the pipes wider?

What happens to my bank balance if I pay back some debt?

Then link this to the way the analogous abstract example behaves:

The electrical current increases if we reduce the resistance.

I move in the positive direction if I take away a negative number.

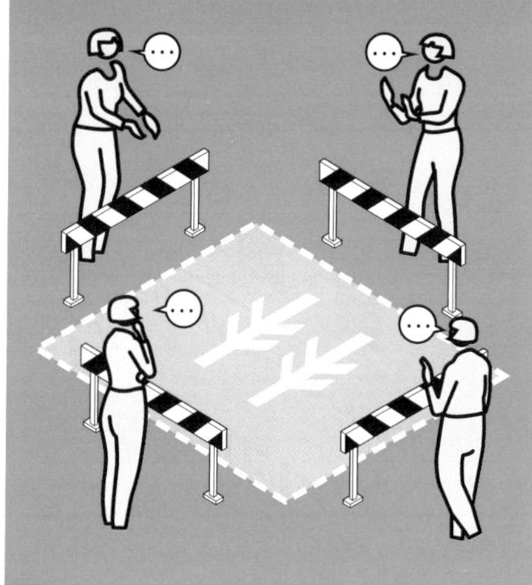

ESTABLISH THE LIMITS EXPLICITLY

Be careful not to stretch an analogy too far. If you are talking about *taking away cold* with a thermometer analogy for negative numbers, the physical reality of this starts becoming dubious. It might still help make sense of negative numbers but it can also add confusion. Opposing armies and football teams are only similar to a degree! Discuss the limits and ask questions. In the water flow analogy for electricity, can there be drops of electricity? What is analogous to voltage?

5

CHECK FOR UNDERSTANDING

Analogies are useful if they help to bridge from concrete prior knowledge to new abstract ideas. Make sure that this has happened through forms of questioning and formative assessment.

Check for Understanding to sample the class and establish whether the analogy is helping. Be prepared to add detail to the analogy or to try a different one until the abstract concepts start to make sense.

SEND: ADDRESSING COGNITIVE DIFFICULTIES

Drill down beyond broad special needs labels to establish and understand what any student's areas of need are. Whether these are moderate or severe cognitive impairments or communication difficulties or fall into the category of specific learning difficulties, teachers need to know what they are. Even where a known condition such as dyslexia, dyscalculia or dyspraxia is identified, each student will have their own needs within those umbrella definitions. Follow the steps in **SEND: Aim High; Plan Support**.

1

FIND AND BUILD ON SECURE GROUND

However difficult a student finds the learning in hand, they will have a baseline of things they can do successfully. It's important to find out what that baseline is and use it as a platform for building from. This will include aspects of literacy and language, communication skills, personal confidence, past knowledge and experience, physical skills, mental or spatial models. Getting to know your students in this way is very powerful.

2

IDENTIFY PRECISE BARRIERS

Through the course of the teaching process or through forms of assessment, try to find out exactly where students struggle. The more precise you are, the more likely you will be able to design appropriate scaffolds, practice tasks or interventions. It's important to balance this with maintaining high expectations. Sometimes students can tell you where they start to struggle so a good dialogue with them and their support teachers and parents is also very important.

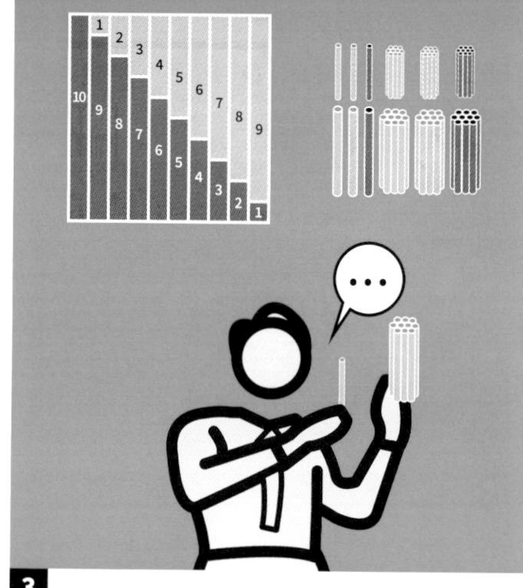

3

KEEP CONCEPTS AS CONCRETE AS POSSIBLE

Cognitive difficulties are often most in evidence when the learning moves from concrete to abstract. In maths, for example, it is important to build a solid foundation understanding of number and place value using concrete resources – rods, counters, shapes, patterns of objects – so number operations make sense in a concrete realm. Similarly, the meaning of new words and/or abstract models for scientific phenomena need to relate to the world students can understand.

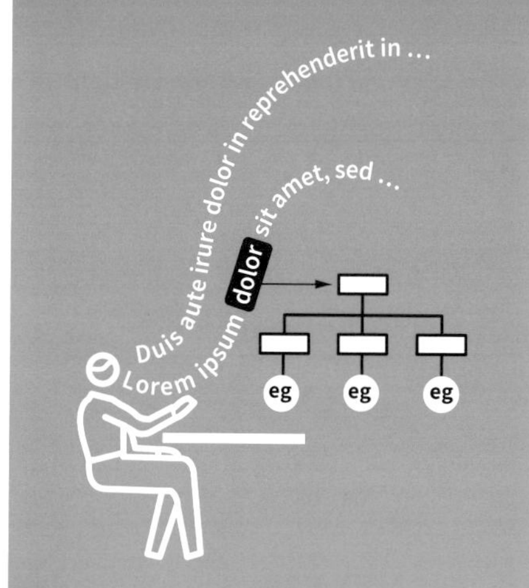

4

REINFORCE LANGUAGE ELEMENTS

Give students plenty of practice with key vocabulary both in terms of meaning and fluency. Connect words to objects and phenomena very explicitly; engage students in high frequency fluency-building activities so that they can use language with confidence in the appropriate contexts. Sometimes SEND students lack confidence and teachers are anxious about putting them under pressure – but this should not lead to them being engaged less or getting less practice than they need.

5

EMPHASISE GUIDED PRACTICE

Follow the ideas in **Guided Practice** extensively. Build confidence by supporting students to succeed in a task, prompting and scaffolding as much as is needed to secure a positive successful outcome.

Then, repeat this with less guidance and support.

Avoid the scenario of stress-inducing floundering but withdraw support steadily as students' confidence and fluency improves.

COMPARE, CONTRAST & CATEGORISE

One of the strategies described by Shimamura as part of his MARGE Model (Volume 1) is to frame concepts using the 3Cs: Compare, Contrast and Categorise. This helps students to learn in several ways:

Attend: to provide a focus for students' attention, linking new ideas to existing ideas.

Relate: to help organise information in order to store and retrieve more effectively and fluently. (This links to the ideas in **Big Picture, Small Picture**.)

Generate: to give a structure to retrieval practice activities.

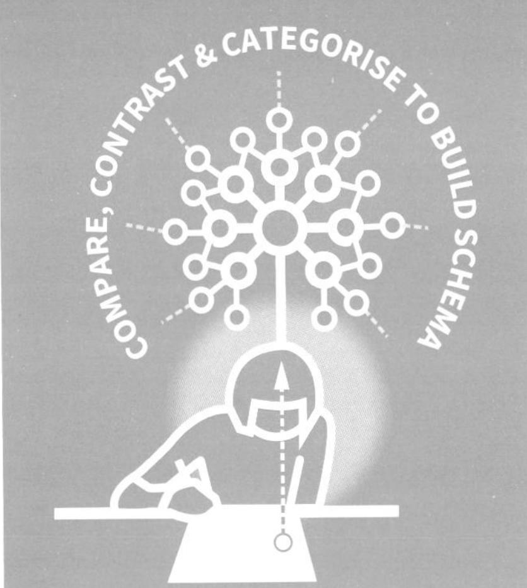

1

DELIBERATE SCHEMA-BUILDING

Students inevitably encounter ideas in complex, unpredictable ways, and then face the challenge of making sense of them.

Explaining ideas using the 3Cs helps students to make sense of concepts by front-loading this sorting process, presenting ideas in an organised fashion, deliberately and purposefully. They still need to make sense of the ideas for themselves but the modelling and scaffolding embedded in the 3Cs supports them in the process.

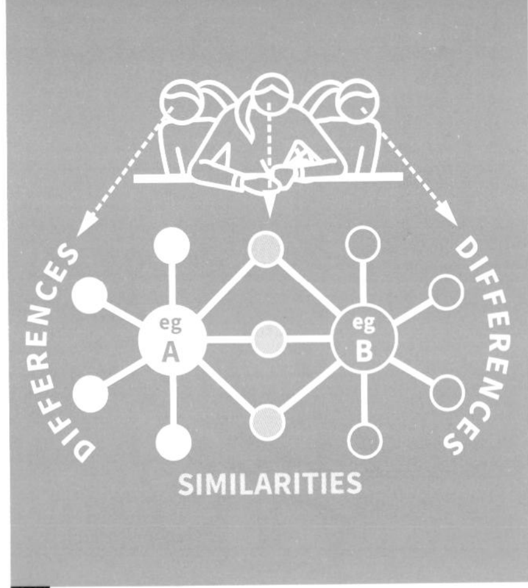

2

COMPARE: LOOK FOR SIMILARITIES AND DIFFERENCES

Features of different examples are often better understood by comparing them than by studying them in isolation:

- A range of perspectives and beliefs
- Examples of art, music, works of literature, design
- Exemplars of writing, in terms of quality or style
- Competing methods, strategies, explanations

In presenting ideas, set up two or more examples. Engage students in looking for and describing similarities and differences.

3

CONTRAST: EMPHASISE DIFFERENCES, ALTERNATIVES, CONFLICTS

Contrasting is a more specific aspect of comparison, emphasising differences in order to form a deeper understanding of each of the alternatives. Key questions to use include:

- Which example is more effective?
- Which idea explains what we see more successfully?
- How are these perspectives different? Can they both be right?

Where appropriate, ask students to rank examples in terms of accuracy, quality, effectiveness so that they have to explore their different features.

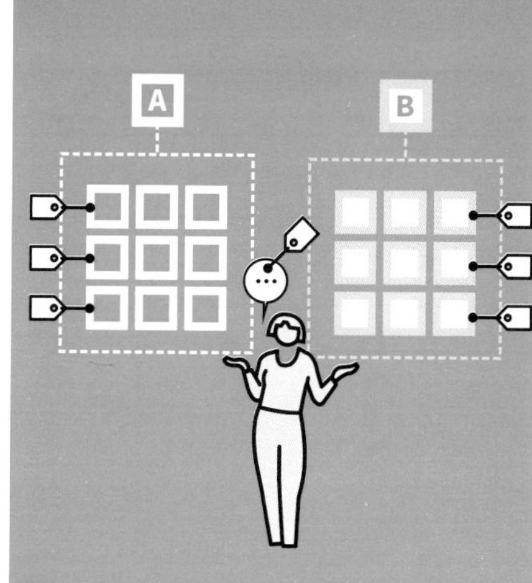

4

CATEGORISE: DEFINE, SELECT AND ORGANISE

Present ideas in ways that engage students in understanding the defining characteristics of different categories and then organising examples according to the definitions: different categories of *materials, living things, energy sources, literary and musical genres, art movements, grammar terms, tenses and cases in languages, historical periods, facts and beliefs, political movements.*

More generally, common categories are advantages and disadvantages or positive and negative effects.

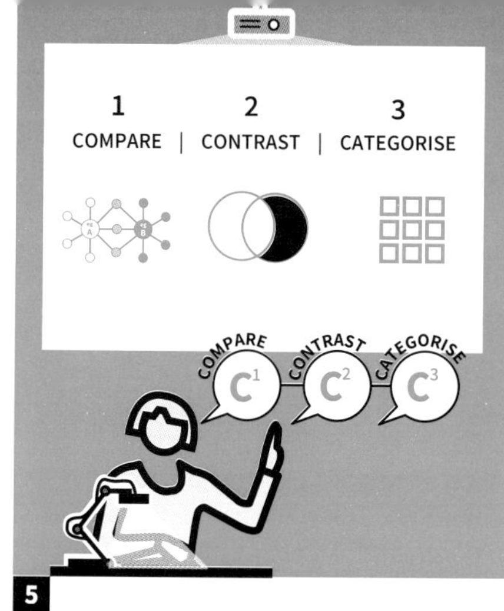

5

APPLY 3CS IN NEW CONTEXTS

Begin by teaching students to compare, contrast and categorise using familiar examples, modelling the process very deliberately and checking for understanding.

Then introduce new and unfamiliar examples so that students need to apply their knowledge of defined categories or features of high and low quality examples to evaluate and organise examples independently. Vary the level of guidance given according to students' success.

Finally, include 3Cs questions as part of **Weekly & Monthly Review**.

Attempt | Develop | Adapt | Practise | Test

EXEMPLARS

A central feature of learning in multiple subject areas is the process of engaging with examples of work similar to those that students are aiming to produce themselves. This could be creative products, performances, short or extended pieces of writing, reports, essays or projects. In preparing to model and explain the process for achieving success, referring to real exemplars of varying quality can help to communicate the requirements far more effectively than could be done using descriptors or criteria lists alone. Exemplars bring the ideas to life, making them tangible.

WALKTHRUs IN THIS SERIES

EXPLAINING & MODELLING

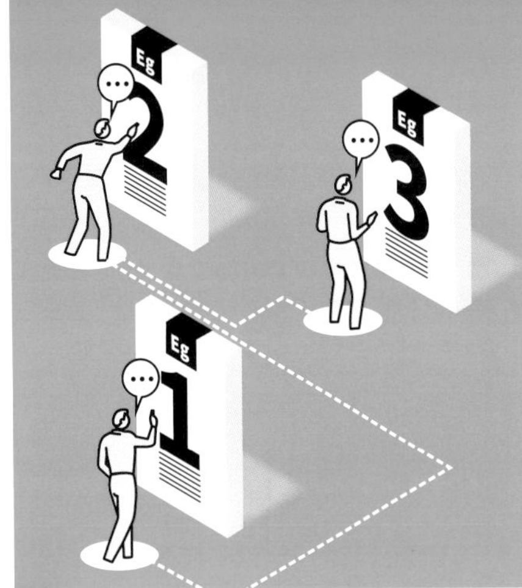

1

INTRODUCE AND EXPLORE EXEMPLARS ONE AT A TIME

Make sure that each example is explored fully. Consider the best way to do this in practice so that everyone can see it or read it.

- Does everyone need a copy?
- Can everyone see it clearly if presented on a whiteboard or presentation?
- Does it need to be viewed close at hand?
- Would a visualiser be the best way to share the exemplar?

For each exemplar, consider its features. Explain and discuss reasons why the exemplar is successful and how it could be better still.

2

COMPARE AND CONTRAST EXEMPLARS SIDE BY SIDE

Very often the features of one exemplar become more evident when compared to others. Apply the ideas in **Compare, Contrast and Categorise** to two or more exemplars relevant to the learning at hand:

- Writing sample A can be seen to be *more sophisticated* or *more succinct* than sample B. This makes more sense in comparison.
- Still life drawing A captures tone and perspective in a more naturalistic style than samples B and C, which are more stylised and abstract.

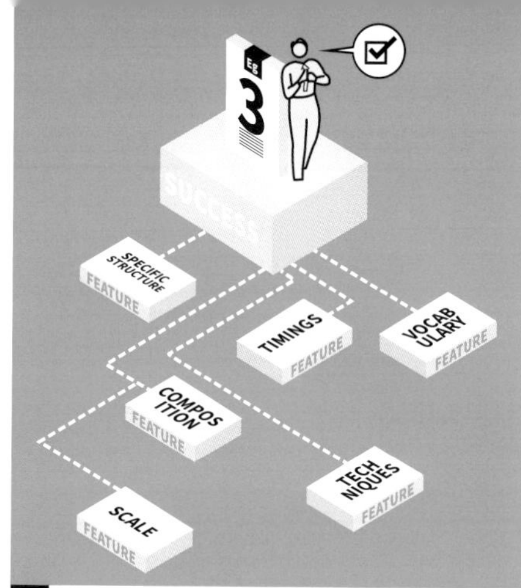

3

ESTABLISH PRECISE FEATURES OF SUCCESS

After exploring an exemplar as a whole, identify the specific features that might then constitute *success or excellence*. Focus on elements that students can later emulate in their own work. This might include specific structures and vocabulary in writing; compositional elements and techniques in art; any quantifiable elements such as word length, scale, timings.

Make a list that can later be used as **Success Criteria** for students' own efforts. This can be framed as a *mark scheme* in some contexts.

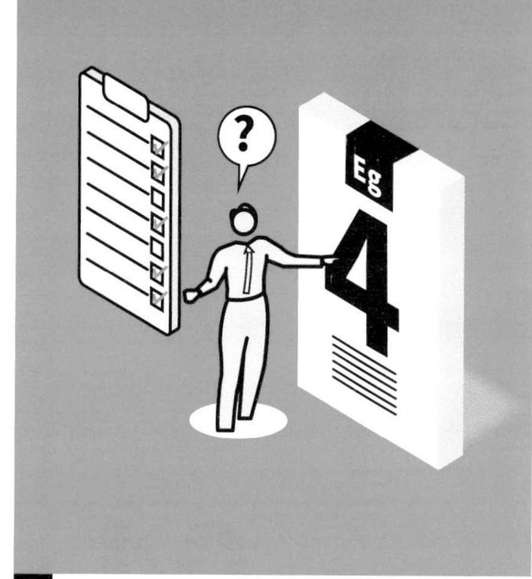

4

CRITIQUE FURTHER EXEMPLARS

Test out the validity of the success criteria on other examples. To begin with, this needs to be modelled. Show students how criteria are evidenced in a new example. **Check for Understanding**. The goal is for students to recognise the features of success in the exemplars and the key hinge points that move work from being mediocre to being excellent.

When ready, invite students to evaluate exemplars themselves, fading back the level of instructional guidance as needed.

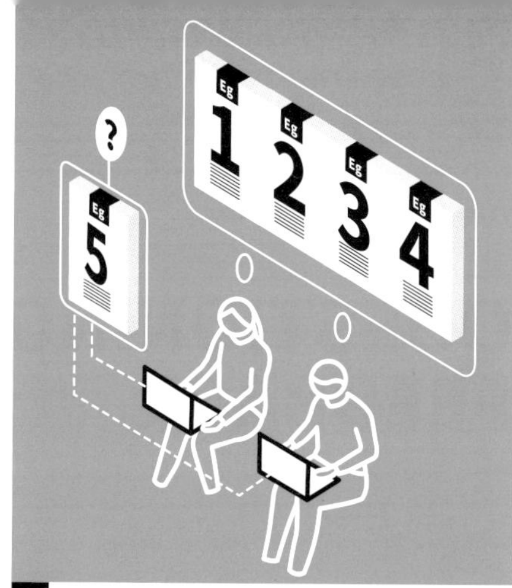

5

APPLY THE LEARNING WITH GUIDED AND INDEPENDENT PRACTICE

The end point of explaining and modelling with exemplars is not only for students to have seen them or to have made a copy for their notes; it is for them to be able to transfer the ideas, producing their own work at the required standard.

Ensure there is an opportunity for students to put their learning into practice on their own work, with **Guided Practice** and then **Independent Practice**.

QUESTIONING & FEEDBACK

All teachers ask questions and give feedback. However, there can be a significant range in the extent to which these practices have an impact on securing deeper learning with all students in a class. It is important for teachers to develop the capacity to be responsive, adjusting the explanatory inputs and tasks according to how well students are doing in making sense of the material. These WalkThrus set out a repertoire of effective questioning techniques that, together with the selection in Volume 1, form the default day-to-day practice in any classroom, enabling a teacher to gain a good sense of how well students are learning. There are also some key feedback techniques that help all students to move forward, deepening their understanding or gaining fluency.

NO OPT OUT
PAGE 98
Dealing with 'I don't know' responses

RANDOMISED QUESTIONING
PAGE 102
Choosing students randomly instead of cold calling

REDRAFTING
PAGE 106
Opportunities to repeat and improve

SPOT YOUR MISTAKES
PAGE 110
Helping students generate their own feedback

HANDS UP FOR ASKING OR IDEAS
PAGE 100
A routine for students to ask questions

NORMALISE ERROR & UNCERTAINTY
PAGE 104
Creating a climate for tackling students' difficulties

SELECTIVE MARKING
PAGE 108
A strategy for giving focused feedback

SUCCESS CRITERIA
PAGE 112
Identifying the key elements of success

NO OPT OUT

No Opt Out is a strategy originally defined by Doug Lemov in *Teach Like a Champion*. It's a very powerful routine to establish for the situation when students don't know an answer or offer '*I don't know*' as a kind of defence, protecting themselves from having to think too hard or expose their uncertainty. If done in the right spirit, it supports students to build their confidence, increasing their knowledge and overriding unhelpful defence mechanisms. It conveys to students a belief that '*I know you can do this*' as well as reinforcing high expectations of engagement and thinking.

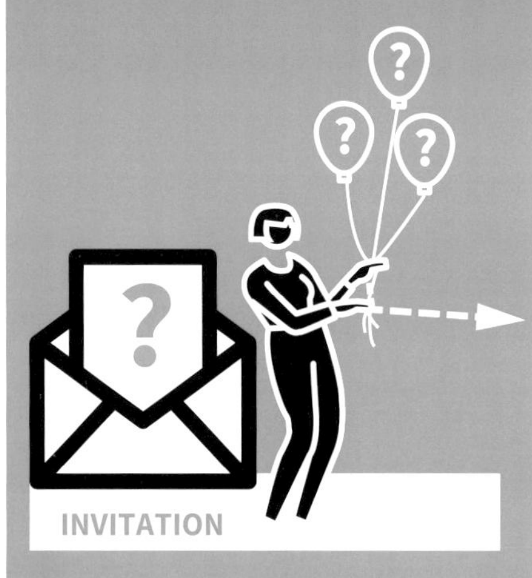

1

ASK A QUESTION AND COLD CALL

During a questioning exchange, follow the first **Cold Call** steps, beginning by asking a question that is addressed to the whole class.

Don't accept hands up or calling out.

Give some thinking time.

Select a student to respond, making it feel like a warm invitation to participate – not a *gotcha*, trying to catch them out.

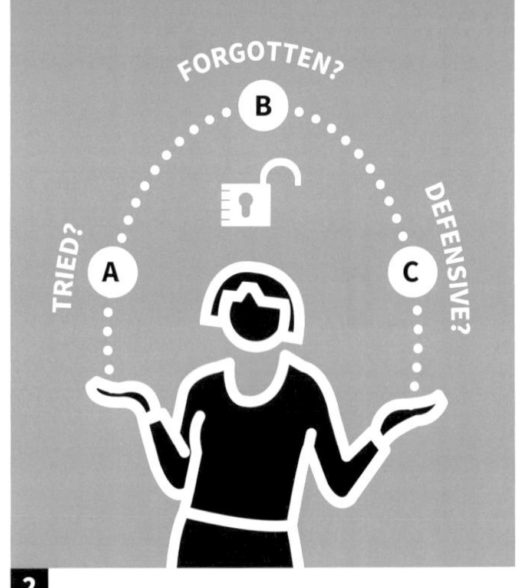

2

EXPLORE '*DON'T KNOW*' RESPONSES

When a student says '*I don't know*', explore the reason by asking follow-up questions and giving prompts.

Try to establish whether they don't know, having tried to work it out; whether they have forgotten; or whether they are simply putting up a defence.

WALKTHRUs IN THIS SERIES

QUESTIONING & FEEDBACK

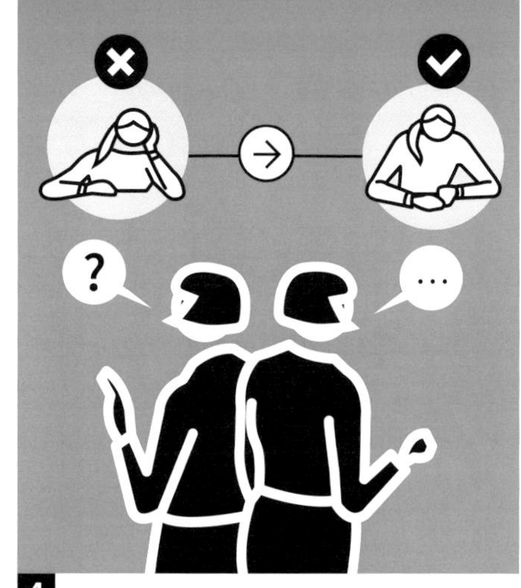

3

PROVIDE THE CORRECT ANSWER

Either:

Ask other students to provide an answer or to share their ideas.

If you get a good answer, move to step 4.

If, after asking 3–4 students, nobody you asked knows the answer, ask for a volunteer: does anyone know?

Or:

Simply give the answer yourself. Tell the class directly.

4

GO BACK AND CHECK FOR UNDERSTANDING

This is the key to **No Opt Out**. Having obtained or given a good answer, check that all the students who answered with '*I don't know*' now do know and understand. This might include asking them to:

- Repeat the definition or meaning of a word.
- Re-explain the concept or procedure.
- Repeat the instructions.

This allows them to rehearse their thinking and practise using vocabulary; a preliminary step in supporting long-term learning.

5

BREAK THE '*DON'T KNOW*' DEFENSIVE HABIT

Once a routine is established, students learn that a '*don't know*' response is never the end of the process; they will be expected to engage with what follows:

What's 19 × 9? Michael? *Don't know.*

OK...John? *I have 10 × 19 is 190; take away 19, gives me 171.*

Thanks. So, Michael...what is 19 × 9?

Michael responds. He isn't allowed to opt out. He's kept in the fold of '*knowers*'.

HANDS UP FOR ASKING OR IDEAS

In combination with **Cold Calling**, where the teacher selects who responds, it is important for students to have a means of asking questions, offering ideas or making spontaneous observations. Where **Cold Calling** is the norm for teacher questioning, 'hands up' becomes available as a signal for when a student wants to make a contribution of this kind. It's a helpful distinction to make, preventing classroom exchanges becoming stifled with students feeling they can't be spontaneous or offer ideas and observations. It also allows students to ask for help when they're struggling.

1

ESTABLISH THE EXPECTATIONS

Establish the process explicitly with a two-way meaning:

- If you have a question, an idea or want some help, raise your hand.
- If you raise your hand, I will assume that you have a question, an idea or want some help.

This is different to when we **Cold Call** questions. *When I ask a question, I will choose who I want to respond.*

2

WELCOME THE INPUT AND REINFORCE THE EXPECTATION

During the flow of a lesson, if a student raises a hand, welcome their input while reinforcing the expectations around it:

Jason raises a hand:
'Thank you Jason, what's your question – or do you need some help?'

If this happens while you are **Cold Calling**, reinforce the opposite: '*Thanks Jason, but we're giving everyone time to think; I'll select someone to answer in a minute.*'

3

ANSWER THE QUESTION

If the question feeds into the material at hand, either answer it directly:

'Great question Jason. The reason is…'

Or use **Probing Questioning** to see if the student can answer their own question:

'Can you see the connection here? Why was this step needed?'

If the question is potentially distracting:

'Great question Jason. I'll come back to that in just a while.'

Then make sure you do.

4

OR ENGAGE WITH IDEAS

In order to support deeper learning, it is helpful to explore ideas, beyond simply airing them.

'Daisy – a great idea. Why do you think that?'
'Sam – that's really interesting. What effect would that have?'
'Chris – nice idea. Do you think that would work in practice?'

While remaining open to divergent thinking, even a basic dialogue raises expectations in terms of depth of thinking and the process of linking ideas to the concepts under discussion.

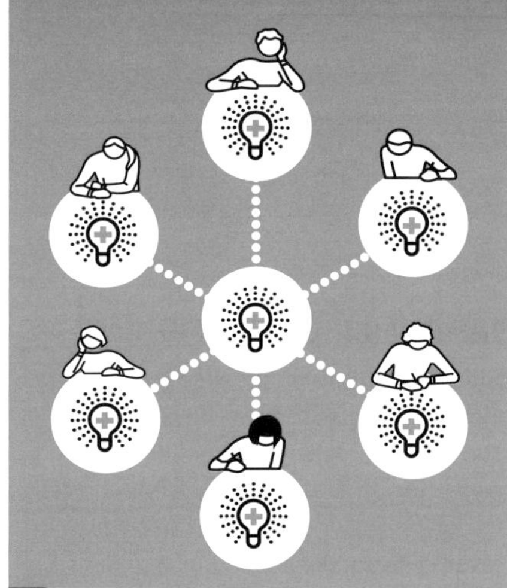

5

ENGAGE OTHERS AND CHECK FOR UNDERSTANDING

Ideally, students' questions and ideas should benefit everyone in the class. To ensure everyone is involved, use **Check for Understanding** techniques, sampling the room to check that others have heard and understood.

'Clara – what do you think of Daisy's idea? Would you agree with that?'

Reinforce the expectation that students' contributions flow from having listened to what other students have already said.

RANDOMISED QUESTIONING

One of the pitfalls of questioning is our unconscious bias to focus on certain students in a room, while avoiding or neglecting others. Even if well intentioned, it's not always possible to be sure that this isn't happening. It could be that certain students appear overly shy so we protect them; it could be that enthusiastic respondents are given priority. Randomising the questioning takes the choice of who to ask out of your hands and, used judiciously, can be a useful supplement to **Cold Calling**.

1

SET-UP A RANDOMISING SYSTEM; ESTABLISH THE ROUTINE

Examples include:

- Lollipop sticks: each student's name on a stick, chosen from a pot, then replaced.
- A number generator: each student has a number which could be chosen randomly.
- Name selection software: students' names entered into an electronic selection tool.

Each tool needs to be introduced with some explicit rehearsal so the process is time efficient.

2

ASK THE CLASS THE QUESTION AND GIVE THINKING TIME

Once the random method has been established, students know that they could be asked to answer. Ask a question so that everyone can see or hear. This includes everyone in the thinking process. It should be explicit that anyone might be asked.

Give an appropriate amount of thinking time for the difficulty of the question before the random selection.

3

INITIATE THE RANDOM SELECTION

When ready, start the random selection.

Pick out the lollipop stick.
Generate the number.
Run the name selector.

Remember the purpose: to select a student in an unbiased manner. It's not to create a huge drama out of the anticipation.

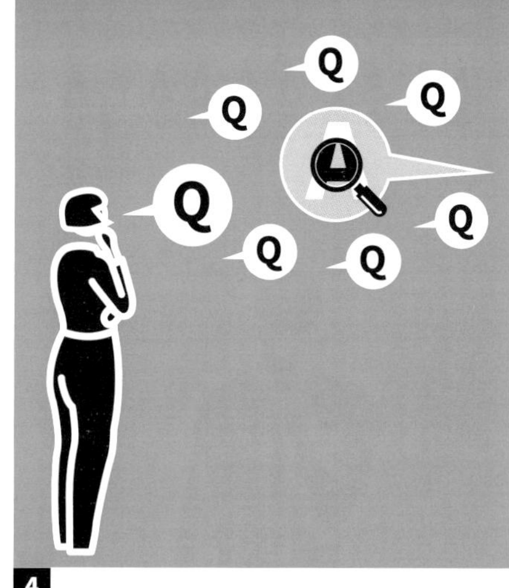

4

ASK THE SELECTED STUDENT AND PROBE

Invite the student to respond with their answer. Try to prevent this being a major '*gotcha*' – as if it's something to avoid. Make it as matter of fact as you can to normalise it. Listen to the response and probe for further understanding.

5

REPEAT THE PROCESS

Re-run the randomising process to select another student. This could be for the same question – to gain a range of responses. If you have more questions, be sure to ask everyone and give thinking time before you select.

Blend this approach with **Cold Calling**. Randomising is explicitly impersonal – you did not choose the student. That's the point. But **Cold Calling** explicitly is your choice – and it is also very powerful for students to know that you personally wanted to hear from them.

NORMALISE ERROR & UNCERTAINTY

Imagine a student in your lesson who is struggling with the work. How do you want them to feel? Ideally you want a climate where they could express doubts, uncertainties, confusion. If that climate is not present, not only will this make them anxious but it will also lead them to engage in masking behaviours for fear of being exposed: pretending to know; borrowing answers from others; hiding back in the group. Far better to normalise uncertainty and make the business of tackling errors and misunderstandings an everyday low-threat part of classroom life.

WALKTHRUs IN THIS SERIES

QUESTIONING & FEEDBACK

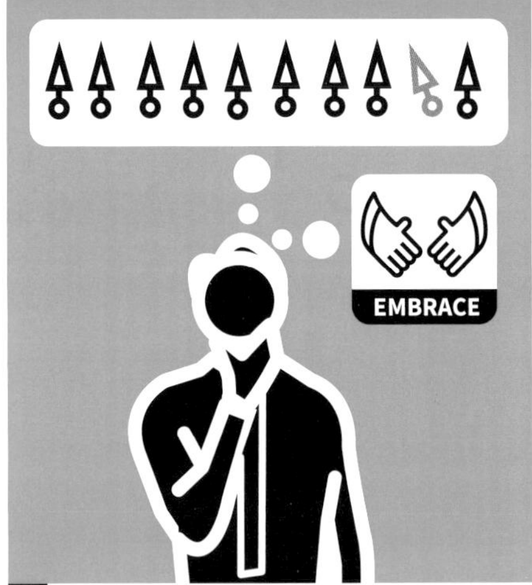

1

ASSUME AND EMBRACE UNCERTAINTY

Adopt a mindset in which you always assume that some students in your class are harbouring uncertainties – it's just a case of allowing them to surface so you can deal with them.

This may sound obvious but it's easy to slip into a pattern where you continually emphasise correctness or perhaps take a few strong responses to represent the class as a whole. Assume uncertainty is present and that errors have been made and try to seek them out. Anticipate and welcome it.

2

EXPLORE MISCONCEPTIONS AND ERRORS WHILE EXPLAINING

During instructional phases of a lesson, make a point to highlight common misconceptions. Explore the reasons behind them. Use errors and misconceptions as teaching points.

'What mistake has this student made in this example?'

'What could the student have done to make this more accurate?'

'Some people believe this is true. Why is that actually a false interpretation?'

3

EMBRACE ERROR DURING QUESTIONING

Avoid over-stressing correctness to the point that incomplete or incorrect answers appear unwelcome; something to hide. During questioning exchanges, use **Probing Questions**, **No Opt Out**, or **Say It Again Better** to help students explore their understanding, leading to improved responses. Anticipate what you will say if a student makes a mistake. Help them turn it around, re-teaching as needed, without making them feel foolish.

'That's not quite right; I see what you've done but let's have another think.'

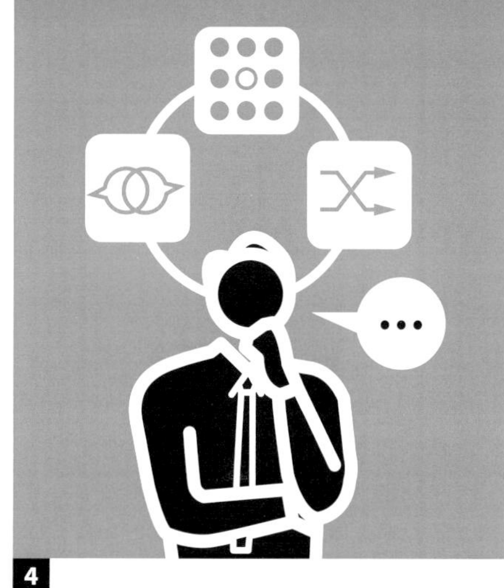

4

EMPHASISE UNCERTAINTY WITHIN METACOGNITIVE TALK

When modelling writing or problem-solving, as you narrate your thinking, emphasise the points where decisions are intrinsically uncertain or arbitrary.

'My instinct might be to think that the car must be accelerating because it's going so fast – but then I remember at a steady speed, the acceleration must be zero; so the total force must also be zero.'

'I tried "gloomy sky" but then felt "grey monotonous sky" was more interesting.'

5

EXPLORE ERRORS IN TEST FEEDBACK

When going over a quiz or test, place an emphasis on where students make mistakes alongside your celebration of the correct answers. For example, rather than focusing on a student with full marks, find students who achieved 7 out of 10. They will be reasonably pleased and will comfortably volunteer the three questions they got wrong. This then models to others that going over incorrect answers is normal and unthreatening. The whole point of a test is to identify gaps in knowledge; make this explicit and reward students for volunteering their own errors.

REDRAFTING

As described in Volume 1, in Ron Berger's *An Ethic of Excellence*, he asks: *What could you produce of quality in a single draft?*

Giving students opportunities to produce multiple drafts of some pieces of work is a key strategy that he recommends, supporting students to gain experience of producing excellent work. This supports building their esteem through their accomplishments, setting standards and teaching them the process of self-directed improvement. Planning feedback and redrafting cycles is important in many subject contexts.

1

ESTABLISH THE STANDARDS WITH EXEMPLARS

Invest time in setting the standards in advance. There might be situations where you want to see what students do independently from the beginning, but in most cases, with new learning, if they can see what excellence might look like in advance, they will be better able to pitch high. Use **Exemplars** that show a variety of outcomes to encourage diverse responses. Compare exemplars of a middle and high standard so students can see the difference for themselves.

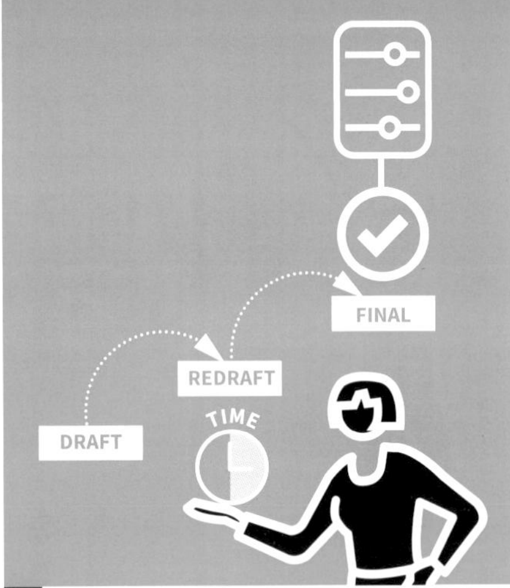

2

SET THE TASK, WITH SUCCESS CRITERIA

Set students off to complete the task. It can make a big difference if they know in advance that they will get opportunities for redrafting. Use your knowledge of your students to decide whether this will stimulate a more experimental approach or, perhaps, lead to under-pitching in the first instance. Where appropriate, devising success criteria can help to provide a structure for the task ahead. Agreeing *what excellence will look like* through discussion is often very fruitful.

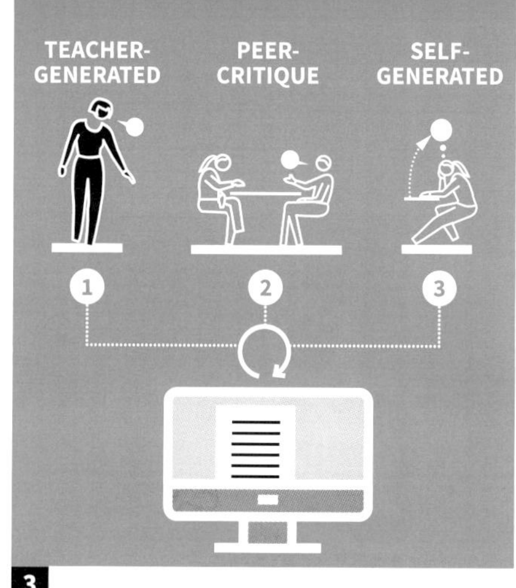

3

PROVIDE OR GENERATE FEEDBACK

After the first draft, generate feedback through one or more processes:

Teacher generated: Giving verbal or written feedback on the first draft, suggesting improvements that could be made or providing prompts and clues.

Peer-critique: Students using success criteria provide positive, specific feedback for each other.

Self-generated: Giving students time to review their work and identify improvements they could make for themselves.

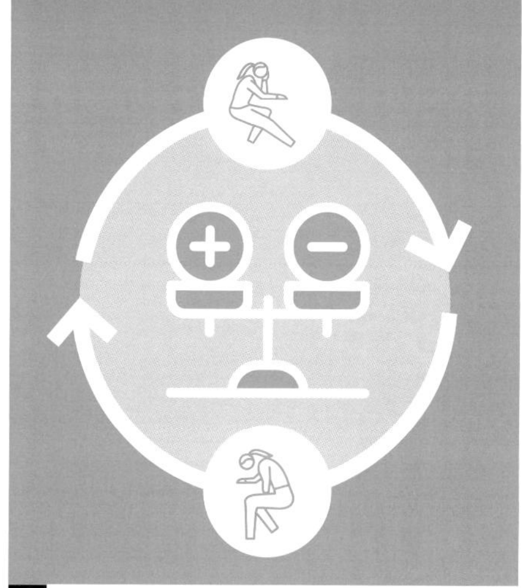

4

GIVE TIME TO REPEAT THE TASK

Re-run the task, with the full amount of time needed to produce an improved draft, with students acting on the feedback.

5

REPEAT MULTIPLE FEEDBACK AND IMPROVEMENT CYCLES

Review the second draft in the same way as before, generating feedback for a student to act on. This could feed into another full cycle leading to a third draft. At all stages, keep the feedback as specific and actionable as possible, referencing the exemplars and the success criteria.

Feedback on the final draft is still valuable but this will need to serve as an end-point evaluation to inform future work, rather than another draft.

SELECTIVE MARKING

Marking is a useful form of feedback. A teacher makes written comments on students' work in the expectation that they will respond with improved work either during an immediate re-drafting or a correcting process at some later time. However, this can only be effective if the student understands what the teacher's comments mean and can absorb them in a way that moves them forward in their performance or understanding. Often this effect can be best achieved by marking only a portion of a whole piece of work; it's easier for students to absorb and reduces teacher workload.

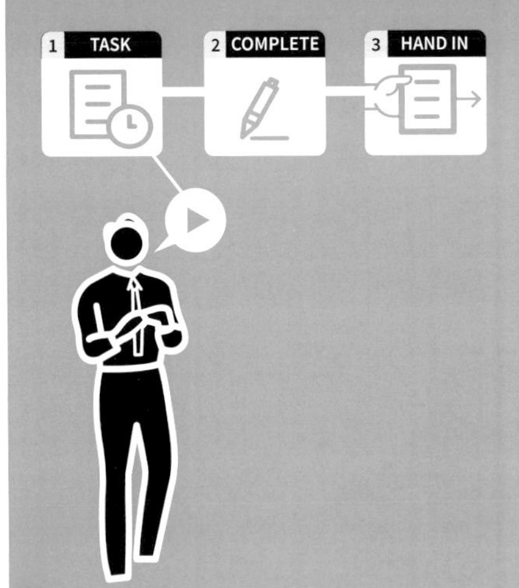

1

SET AN EXTENDED TASK AND COLLECT THE WORK

Give students a task in the usual way, engaging the **Set the Standards** process, establishing **Success Criteria** and referencing exemplars as appropriate.

Make it clear to students that you will collect the work in and evaluate it – so that they have that in mind as they do the work. However, be explicit that they will receive feedback on a selected portion, to manage expectations. Don't tell them which portion in advance, so they apply effort equally to all aspects of the work they produce.

2

SELECT A SPECIFIC SECTION TO FOCUS ON

After reading or scanning over each student's work, select a section to focus on for providing detailed feedback. This could be an equivalent section for all students or it could be selected more individually, depending on the teacher's judgement regarding which would be the most effective, given the quality of work and the location of errors and areas for improvement.

It can be useful to highlight the section with a box or other demarcation – although this is not essential.

WALKTHRUs IN THIS SERIES

QUESTIONING & FEEDBACK

NO OPT OUT 98 | HANDS UP FOR ASKING OR IDEAS 100 | RANDOMISED QUESTIONING 102 | NORMALISE ERROR & UNCERTAINTY 104 | REDRAFTING 106 | **SELECTIVE MARKING 108** | SPOT YOUR MISTAKES 110 | SUCCESS CRITERIA 112

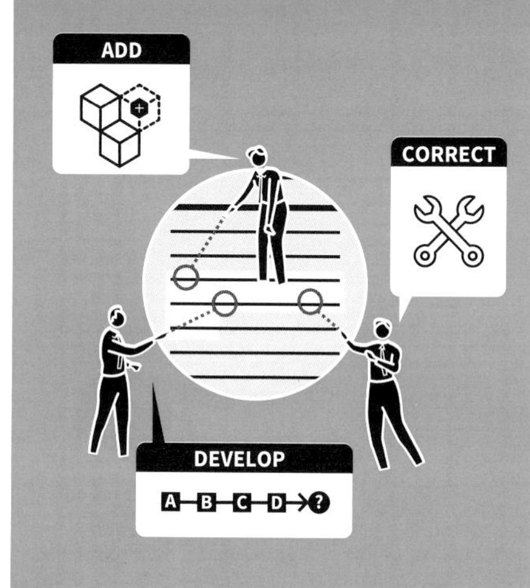

PROVIDE ACTIONABLE FEEDBACK

Focusing on the selected section, identify errors and/or areas for improvement. Provide feedback that students can respond to with specific actions, correcting errors, adding more precise details, developing arguments, using more effective language for the context and so on.

The key value of this approach is that teachers can give very detailed feedback on the selected section – rather than the more general feedback they might have given across the whole piece.

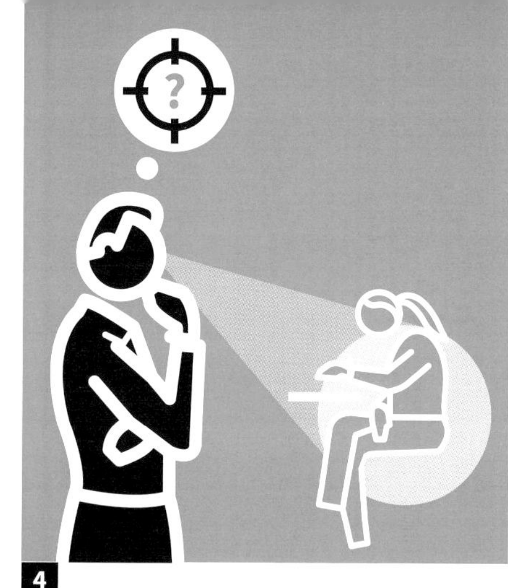

4

INITIATE REDRAFTING OF SELECTED SECTION

After returning the work, ask students to look at the selected section and give them time to respond to the feedback, ideally there and then in the lesson.

Supervise the process to ensure that students are responding in the way you had intended, dealing with queries as they arise. The goal is to produce an improved version of the selected section during the time allocated. Responding to marking in your absence is only effective if you are confident that students will not need further clarification regarding your feedback comments.

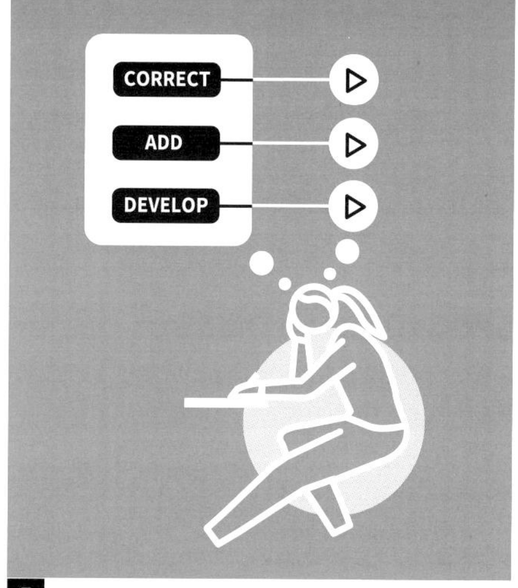

5

TRANSLATE IDEAS TO REMAINDER OF THE TASK

To complete the process, invite students to apply lessons they have learned from the selected marking to the rest of their work. This links to **Spot Your Mistakes** and **Success Criteria**. They should now be better able to self-assess the quality of their work, looking for similar areas to improve or any repeated errors beyond the selected section.

SPOT YOUR MISTAKES

An important principle in providing feedback is that, even if a teacher shows exactly where errors have been made or where students could make improvements, the students still have to absorb this feedback, make sense of it and act on it. If real learning has taken place, they would also be able to apply this feedback at a later time – not merely in direct response at the time, as with responding to a satnav system. If students can generate their own feedback, spotting their own errors and identifying their own areas for improvement, they are more likely to understand it, act on it and apply it at a later time.

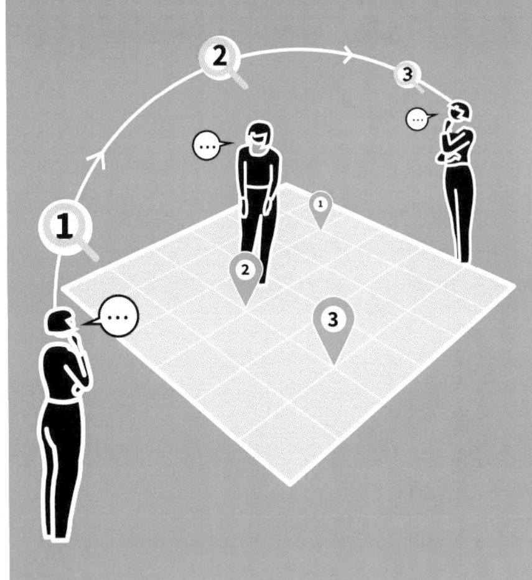

1

EVALUATE STUDENTS' WORK

The goal with this technique is to guide students through the process of finding their own mistakes and omissions so they can learn to self-edit as they go along. So, when evaluating students' work, look for areas where easily definable improvements could be made or where there are clear mistakes. Identify a few key areas rather than trying to critique and correct every detail.

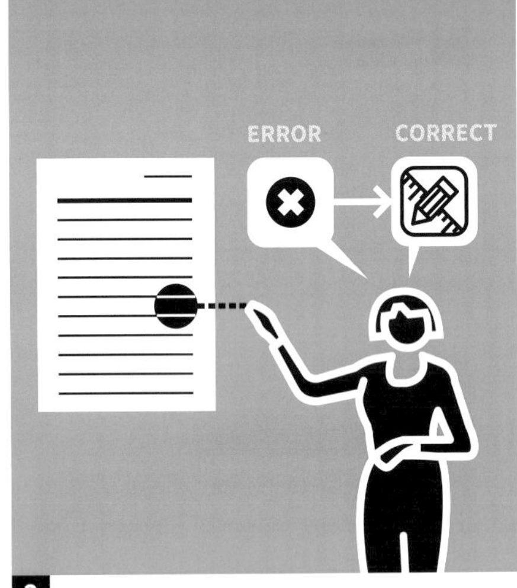

2

GUIDE THE PROCESS

Rather than pinpointing the errors and areas for improvement, mark the general area where they lie. This could be a circle drawn around the location in a piece of writing, placing a sticky note on the general area of the product or underlining a whole sentence that needs to be worked on, without saying why. It can sometimes help to prompt students by saying how many errors they should be able to find or giving a clue about the type of mistake they could be looking for – such as a spelling error.

3

INVITE STUDENTS TO FIND THE MISTAKES

Return the work and invite students to think about the quality of the work in the highlighted areas. Can they spot any obvious errors? Can they find the number or type of errors identified? Can they think of a way to make improvements? This is more open-ended than when the teacher highlights all the errors, so students will need to think hard about what might constitute a better response.

4

PROVIDE SCAFFOLDED SUPPORT

Where needed, provide supports that help students to engage in the error-spotting. This could be keyword lists, success criteria, exemplar work, mark schemes. With these resources, students can evaluate their work more readily, learning how to do so in a scaffolded way. Eventually, as with all scaffolding, the support should be reduced so students become more independent, learning to spot errors themselves with greater success and confidence.

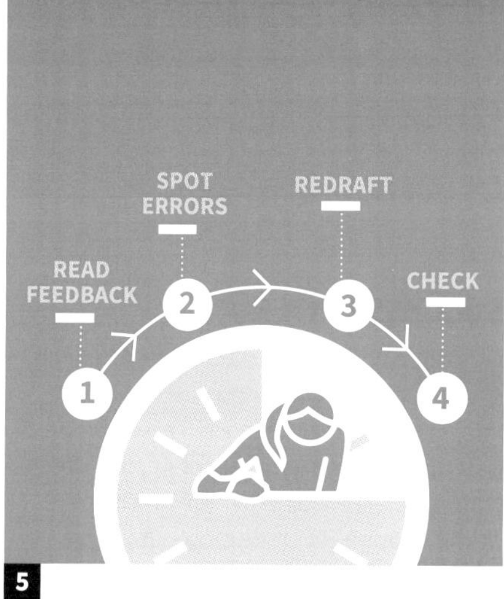

5

GIVE TIME FOR CORRECTIONS AND RE-EVALUATE

Students need time to engage with the guided feedback to spot their errors and areas for improvement and then to act on them, redrafting, improving or correcting their work. This is usefully done immediately after the work is returned so the teacher can use it as a form of **Guided Practice**, supervising the process actively, providing support and adjusting the level of scaffolding for individual students as required.

SUCCESS CRITERIA

Very often, in seeking to achieve excellence, it is helpful to know in advance what might constitute excellence. This could be described using a list of absolute, objective features of a task or piece of work; it could be descriptions of some more subjective quality judgements based on a shared understanding of standards for that particular area of learning. If criteria for success can de defined, sharing them in advance can provide a form of scaffolded support and can lead to students aiming higher than they might have done otherwise.

1

EXAMINE EXEMPLARS AT DIFFERENT STANDARDS

Start by evaluating examples of the work of the type students are aiming to produce. Show and/or discuss examples that are considered excellent. Next to that, consider work that is not quite as good. Perhaps include some work that is considered below an accepted standard. Explain and discuss the features of the examples.

Why is this one better than this one?

What must you definitely include?

How will you know if you've achieved the standard?

2

ESTABLISH THE SUCCESS CRITERIA FOR A TASK

This can be done by recording the class discussion – to reinforce their agency in shaping ideas about excellence. It could be presented to them via a pre-prepared slide or sheet.

List anything obviously objective: the length, the timing, definable elements that must be included in a performance or written product.

Referencing the exemplars, list quality descriptors that students will understand in the context of the task they're about to undertake.

CHECK FOR UNDERSTANDING

As with many other areas of instructional teaching, it is important to ensure all students know and understand what the success criteria are. It is not enough to engage just one or two students in generating the ideas or to simply present the criteria, assuming they'll make sense. Use the **Check for Understanding** routine, asking a sample of students to tell you what they understand the criteria to be. Re-explain or show more examples in advance if needed.

4

ASSESS WORK AGAINST THE CRITERIA

After collecting finished work – or watching performances – use the criteria you established to evaluate the work: *Have the criteria been fully or partially met?* This can sometimes usefully be done using a grid containing the list of criteria.

You might do this as a form of teacher marking.

You could invite the students to self-assess their own work against the criteria.

You could engage students in peer-assessment using the criteria to form the basis of their critique.

5

INITIATE AN IMPROVEMENT CYCLE

Give students an opportunity to respond to the feedback, seeking to meet more of the criteria or meet them more fully. This can be linked to **Rehearsal and Performance, Whole Class Feedback** and **Feedback as Actions**.

It also links to **Scaffolding**. The long-term goal is for students to self-generate success criteria and self-evaluate their own work, aiming for an idea of excellence they are generating. Build towards this explicitly with increasing emphasis on self-assessment.

WALKTHRU SERIES

PRACTICE & RETRIEVAL

This selection of WalkThrus explores various strategies overlapping strongly with Rosenshine's 'Principles of Instruction' and Willingham's ideas about fluency and drilling as explored in Volume 1. Students can improve their confidence and fluency with a wide range of knowledge and physical skills through engaging guided practice before moving on to practise more independently. An aspect of this is the connection between thinking and memory and the role that retrieval practice plays in securing students' fluency, storing and retrieving information from their long-term memory. Here, in Volume 2, we've included further ideas for engaging students in retrieval activities alongside strategies for managing classes where students are making progress at different rates.

MAKE EVERYONE THINK
PAGE 116
Routines to engage all students in thinking

FLASH CARDS
PAGE 120
A classic retrieval practice strategy

PRACTISE EXPLAINING
PAGE 124
Repeating and improving the quality of explanations

A LADDER OF DIFFICULTY
PAGE 128
Increasing the level of challenge systematically

MULTIPLE-CHOICE QUESTIONS
PAGE 118
A powerful method for checking understanding

DUAL CODING: MAPPING
PAGE 122
Supporting learning with graphic organisation

THRESHOLDS & PATHWAYS
PAGE 126
Managing students progressing at different rates

F|A|C|E|I|T REVISION MODEL
PAGE 130
A strategy for structuring revision

MAKE EVERYONE THINK

A central idea about learning, explained in Dan Willingham's *Why Don't Students Like School?*, is that memory is the residue of thought. He suggests that teachers should review lessons by considering what students will think about – because this is what they will be learning. Teachers need to apply this to everyone in the class. Making everyone think about the material in hand is crucial – and not as easy as it sounds. It requires routine practices that involve all students, requiring them to think in ways that activate their prior knowledge, deliberately connecting new ideas to what they already know.

WALKTHRUs IN THIS SERIES

PRACTICE & RETRIEVAL

1

ACTIVATE PRIOR KNOWLEDGE

Begin a learning sequence or lesson by engaging all students in activating their prior knowledge. Rather than asking *Can anyone remember what we did last lesson?* (which allows a volunteer to respond), give everyone a question or problem or task that stimulates thinking about prior knowledge. This could be:

- A question exactly like those covered in the previous lesson.
- A generative task – e.g. to recall the main advantages and disadvantages or summarise the key learning points from the previous topic.

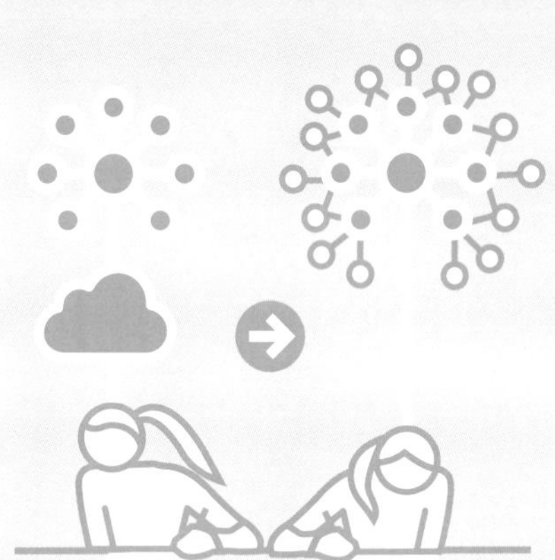

2

STIMULATE SCHEMA-BUILDING

Design tasks and questions that require students to bridge from what they know to new knowledge. Tasks should embed some element of generative recall so that students cannot simply follow instructions blindly or copy from templates, prompts or information provided.

Inject levels of complexity to deepen thinking by requiring students to use the 3Cs or to generate patterns, give explanations, justify choices, rehearse language elements, use explanatory mental models or give further examples.

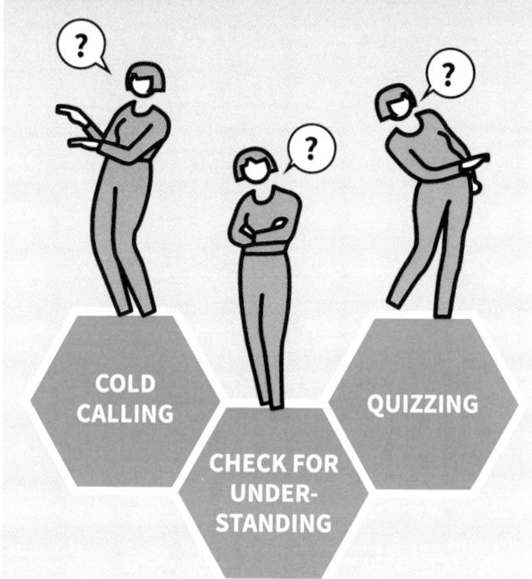

3

SYSTEMATICALLY INVOLVE ALL STUDENTS

Ensure classroom routines always involve every student:

- Use **Cold Calling** as a default so that every student expects to think of an answer to the questions.
- Ensure **Checking for Understanding** is routine so that students learn to expect to explain their thinking on request.
- Ensure any group task requires each student to demonstrate their understanding as part of the activity.
- Conduct retrieval activities so that all students answer all the questions using their own knowledge, without relying on others.

4

USE NARRATIVES AND CONFLICTS

Use structures that invite students to engage with the material, thinking about connections and sequences.

Narrative structures are well understood and can promote effective thinking patterns: *What happened next? Why did it happen? What might change if X happens to Y? What different possible outcomes are there in this scenario?*

Conflicts also provide a focus for thinking: *Which argument is stronger? These examples are both good but which is better? What is wrong in this example? How could you make this work?*

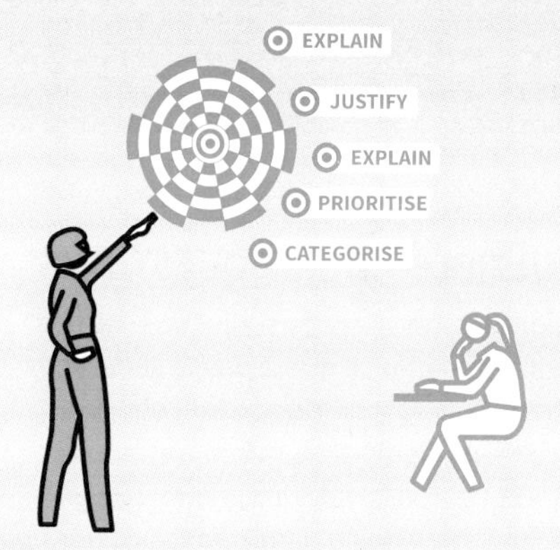

5

EMBED THINKING GOALS WITHIN TASK GOALS

If students can perform a task without having to think hard, they might consider themselves to have succeeded without learning very much. Alternatively, if the goal is explicitly for them to be able to explain, justify, categorise, prioritise, rank, or apply their new knowledge, perhaps without reference to their books and notes, then their level of thinking and engagement will be a lot higher all along. This might take the form of predicting the end of the story, explaining something to the class or tackling a new, related question or problem.

MULTIPLE-CHOICE QUESTIONS

A popular tool in many subjects is the use of multiple-choice questions to generate feedback to teachers and students about recall, understanding, misconceptions or interpretations. Well-designed MCQs go beyond providing a right/wrong answer check; they can provide diagnostic feedback as to the misconceptions and difficulties students are experiencing. They are very easy to implement in lessons but can take time to design well to serve the diagnostic function of hinge questions: questions that reveal whether fundamental ideas have been successfully learned.

(* denotes question from diagnosticquestions.com)

1

DESIGN DIAGNOSTIC QUESTIONS

Create or curate sets of questions designed to reveal key aspects of students' knowledge at the required level of difficulty.

*What is the electron configuration of calcium?**

A: 2, 18, 2

B: 2, 8, 8, 2

C: 2, 8, 6, 4

D: 2, 8, 18, 2

Answering correctly (B) requires the student to know the pattern of full electron shells and that total must be 20 – as calcium's atomic number is 20.

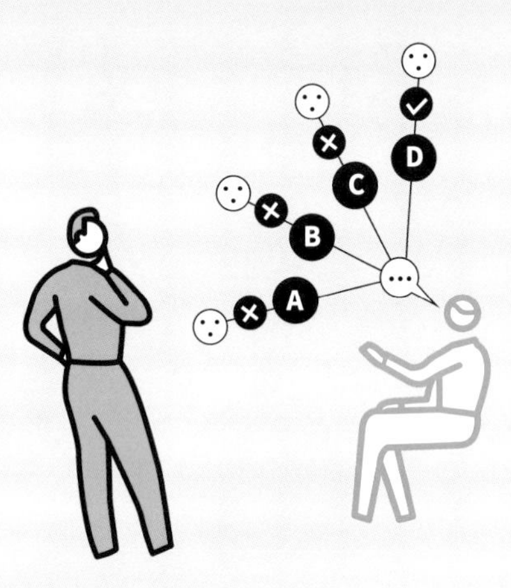

2

CREATE DIAGNOSTIC DETRACTORS

*Which is accurate French?**

A: Il y a pas de une église

B: Il n'y a pas une église

C: Il y a ne pas d'église

D: Il n'y a pas d'église

The correct answer is D. However, the detractors will tell the teacher which specific errors students are making in terms of word order and their understanding of how to deploy the *ne...pas* structure.

Detractors need to be plausible and contain specific common errors to provide useful diagnostic feedback.

WALKTHRUs IN THIS SERIES

3

USE A RANGE OF FORMATS

Examples of formats include:

- Which of the following **does not** contain ionic bonds?
- **Combinations**: From options 1,2,3,4:
  A: 1 only. B: 1,2 and 3 only
  C: 2 and 4 only. D: 4 only.
- Which of the following gives **the best explanation** for why a substance does not conduct electricity?
- In which case is the first statement correct and the second statement a **correct explanation** of the first?

4

ENACT THE ANSWER ROUTINES

Establish routines for answering questions: via a quiz sheet; via PowerPoint slides; asked verbally with answers on **Show Me Boards**; online quizzing tools giving immediate feedback to students and collating answers for teachers. Where possible, invite students to rate their confidence in the answers and/or to give reasons for their answers. This can deepen the learning. Establish routines so students know how to mark/evaluate their answers, noting the correct answer wherever they have not selected the best response.

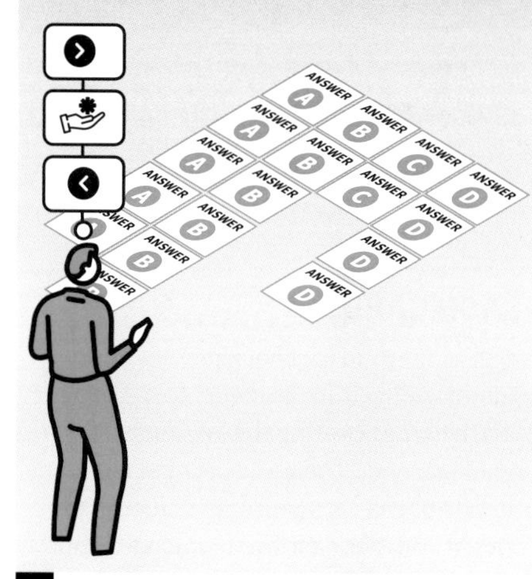

5

RESPOND TO THE RESPONSES

Follow through with the purpose of the diagnostic questions: evaluate the range of responses to the questions to determine which errors are coming up. This could mean that specific students need support with specific knowledge areas. It could mean that the whole class would benefit from revisiting key ideas.

Where students have submitted reasoning for their choices, engage with their ideas during post-quiz feedback. Explore wrong answers: Why might someone choose A? How would you explain why it is wrong?

FLASH CARDS

A classic method for checking recall and understanding is for students to make a set of flash cards covering the key aspects of a unit of learning. The basic premise is that one side of the card prompts students to retrieve knowledge from their long-term memory in the appropriate form. They then turn the card over to where the information is recorded as a way to check the accuracy of their recall. A set of cards allows students to sequence or shuffle the cards as needed and the simple recall-check method can be repeated multiple times to improve fluency.

WALKTHRUs IN THIS SERIES

PRACTICE & RETRIEVAL

To be, or not to be, that is the question:
Whether 'tis nobler in the mind to suffer
The slings and arrows of outrageous fortune,
Or to take arms against a sea of troubles
And by opposing end them.

ESTABLISH QUIZZABLE KNOWLEDGE ELEMENTS

Flash cards work best for knowledge that is easily quizzable, where there is factual knowledge that students can recall and check for accuracy and completeness themselves. This might include:

- Quotations from literature alongside their meaning and significance.
- Equations, formulae, definitions.
- Key lists of factors, defining features.
- Advantages and disadvantages.
- The meaning of graphs and symbols.

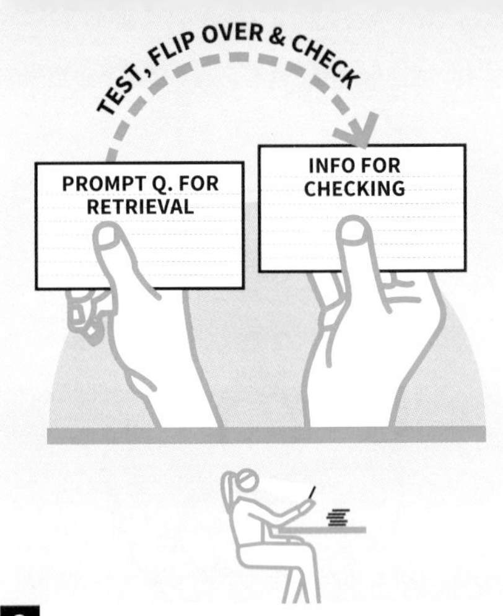

2

CREATE TWO-SIDED FLASH CARDS

One side is for the key information: lists of prompts and cues; summaries of a wider knowledge set; accurate definitions, formulae and quotations. The other side is for a prompt question.

- Define *negative externality*.
- Macbeth's guilt. Quotation and scene?

Teachers might create flash cards to issue, ensuring they are well designed and accurate. However, teaching students to create their own is itself a useful learning process, provided they make accurate, complete summaries. Initiate a quality check if in doubt.

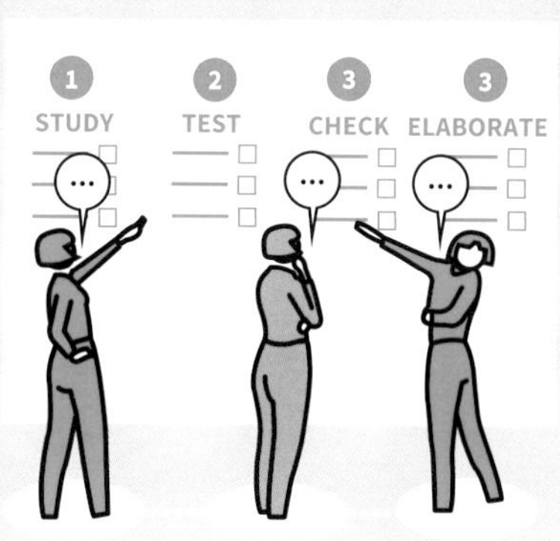

3

ESTABLISH THE CHECKING PROCESS

As with **Using a Knowledge Organiser**, the tool only works if used effectively. Train students to use flash cards properly in class. Model the process. Study the information. Use the *answer* side to engage in **Elaborative Interrogation**, ensuring that the information makes sense in a wider schema. Later, start a study session looking only at the prompt side. Answer the question or respond to the cue. Then turn the card over to check for completeness and accuracy. Focus on errors and omissions and try to reinforce the correct information with further mental rehearsal.

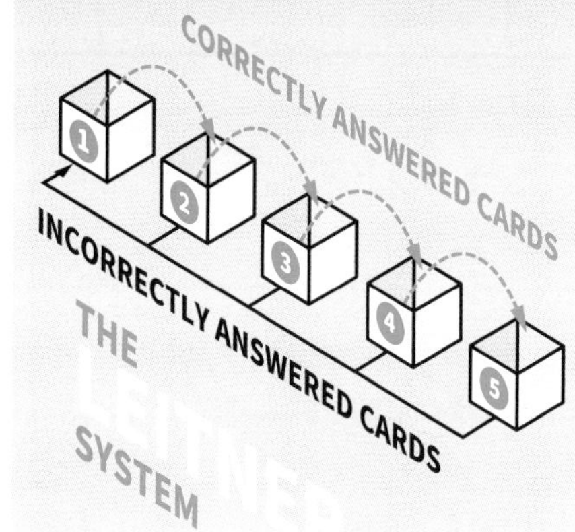

4

BUILD FLUENCY THROUGH REPETITION

The power of flash cards is realised when used repeatedly. Train students to revisit the information in a set of flash cards regularly in their study sessions, spaced over time. The more often students succeed in retrieving the information on cue, the more fluent they become, provided that time has passed since they last studied.

The Leitner System is worth exploring here: a defined method where cards are sorted and reviewed each day over a week on the basis of which knowledge is secure and which is less secure.

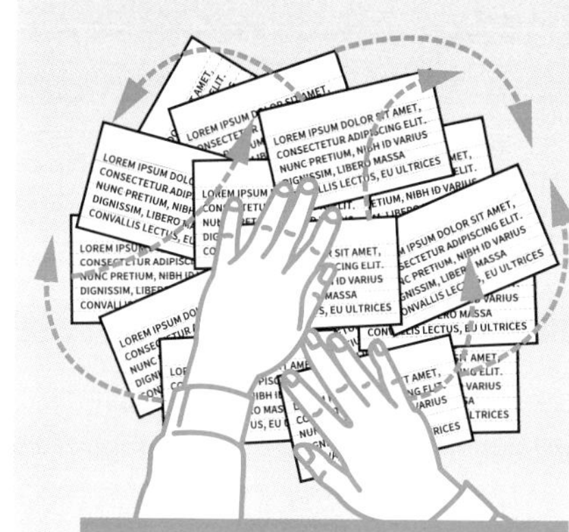

5

VARY THE CARDS AND CHECKS

Organise cards in a sequence according to curriculum content; test, check, re-test.

Shuffle cards and repeat: test, check, re-test. Filter *hard-to-remember* cards for further study prior to re-testing. Use cards for **Peer-Supported Retrieval** in pairs so students quiz each other on flash card content.

Ultimately the knowledge on flash cards needs to be transferred to more synoptic tasks and new contexts. Ensure students have opportunities to apply their retrieval of flash card knowledge in richer contexts.

DUAL CODING: MAPPING

There are two main ways dual coding can be used. One is simply to match single words with images for retrieval of, for example, lists of words. But when the content to be learned is more complex, mapping comes into its own.

Often inaccurately termed 'mind mapping', these *word diagrams* make the connections that constitute a concept both explicit and meaningful. A mind map is a legitimate tool but is just one among many – think of flow chart, concept map, fishbone diagram, relations map, Venn diagram and so on.

Choosing the appropriate type of mapping tool is key to its success – as is using it in a cluster of other strategies.

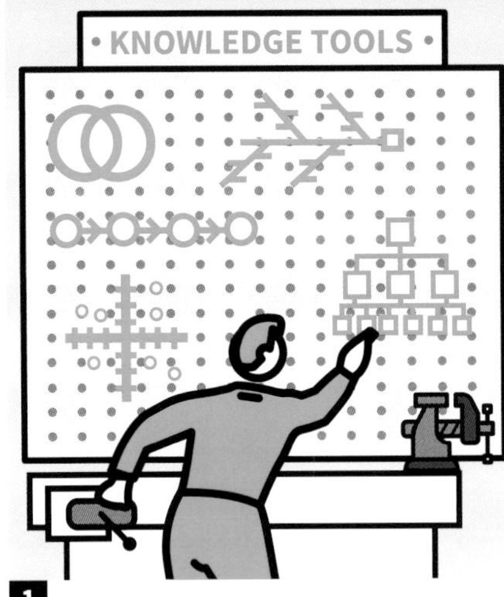

1

ESTABLISH KNOWLEDGE RELATIONSHIPS

Where it helps to connect ideas, organise the key elements in your curriculum using an appropriate form of graphic organiser:

- Hierarchies and classification diagrams
- Timelines and sequences; narratives
- Possibility trees; if this, then that
- Comparisons and contrasts: for/against; advantages and disadvantages
- **Big Picture, Small Picture**
- Spatial arrangements and models

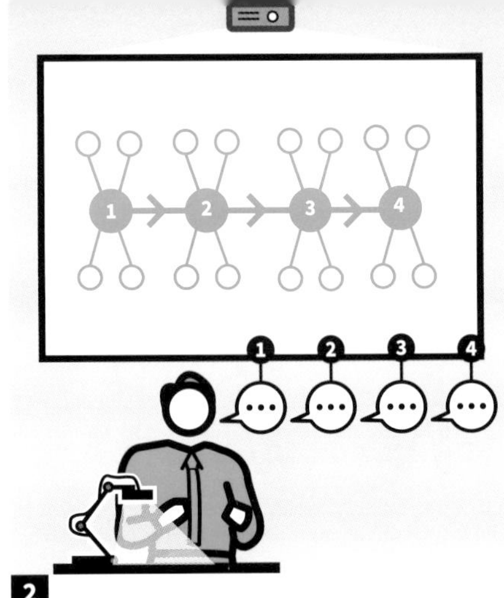

2

EXPLORE AND CREATE EXEMPLAR VISUAL MAPS

Introduce a map **Exemplar** that successfully captures the information at hand. Alternatively, create one step by step as a form of **Live Modelling**.

Take time to walk through it, highlighting how the visual representation reinforces the organisation of the ideas – beyond merely being a list.

Where possible and time efficient, show a range of exemplars so that students see a variety of possibilities. Compare the merits of different representations.

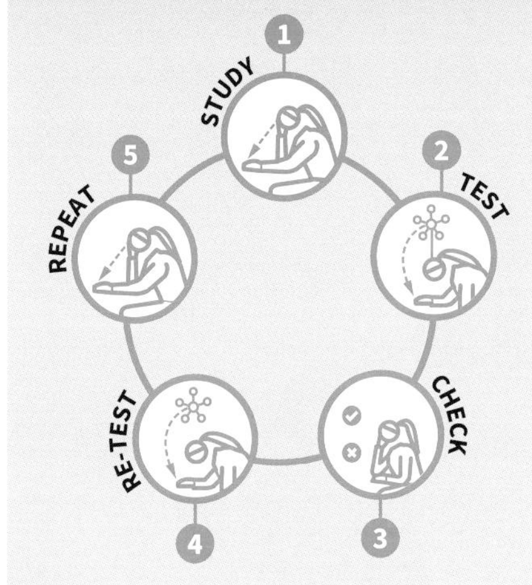

3

MODEL THE GENERATIVE RECALL PROCESS

Referring to the exemplars, model the process of generative mapping, narrating the thinking as you go along:

- *What's the best way to visualise this topic?*
- *Where do I begin? What subsections do I need?*
- *How should I organise those elements on the page?*
- *How can I show the relationships, the flow of time, cause and effect?*
- *Does it make sense?*
- *Can I follow the logic in the flow arrows?*
- *Is it complete?*

4

MAP AS A RETRIEVAL PRACTICE ROUTINE

Make the connection to **Using a Knowledge Organiser** or **Flash Cards**.

The test-check-re-test process is essentially the same. Here it is:

- Study the information from accurate sources.
- After time has passed, test generatively, producing a map organising the information in as much detail as possible.
- Check for accuracy, referring back to the sources.
- Re-test: develop a more detailed map.
- Let time pass and repeat.

5

CHECK FOR UNDERSTANDING, ERROR, AND OMISSIONS

It is important that knowledge represented in maps is then reintegrated and applied in a range of contexts. After a mapping retrieval activity, engage students in further tasks such as **Practise Explaining** or extended writing and problem-solving activities where the knowledge is applied. As ever, **Check for Understanding** through questioning. Use a visualiser to showcase good examples for discussion with the class, considering further improvements or spotting errors and omissions.

PRACTISE EXPLAINING

A powerful way for a student to develop their understanding of a concept, a phenomenon or a series of events is to formulate and communicate a coherent extended explanation. Doing this from memory requires them to have developed a secure schema for the key ideas and the capacity to sequence the ideas in a way that makes sense when relayed as an explanation. For any given concept, it's unlikely that students can do this well without practice; they need the opportunity to repeat the process, with feedback cycles built in, to strengthen the depth and fluency of their explanations.

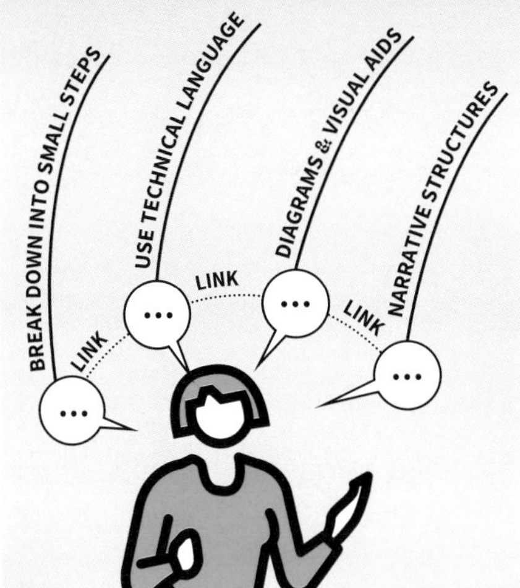

1

MODEL HIGH-QUALITY EXPLANATIONS

Explaining is the key to effective instructional teaching. In addition to the central purpose of supporting students to make sense of the material in hand, teachers' explanations also model the process itself:

- Breaking ideas down into small steps.
- Using key technical language.
- Using diagrams and visual aids.
- Linking one idea to another with narrative structures and clear cause-and-effect relationships.
- Using explanatory terms: When X happens, it causes a positive change in Y which, in turn, creates Z.

2

ENGAGE ALL STUDENTS IN EXPLAINING REHEARSAL

Either:

Invite students to practise privately, imagining explaining a concept to someone else, making notes of what they would say and the order they would say it.

And/Or:

Engage students in a **Think Pair Share** activity where they take turns to give their explanation to the other person. The advantage of the Pair Share model is that students gain practice with verbalising ideas and can receive feedback from their talk partner as part of the process.

3

SAMPLE WITH COLD CALLING

After the rehearsal activity, use **Cold Calling** to sample a range of student explanations from around the class.

It is important for students to know this will happen so that, during their rehearsal, they fully commit to the process and treat it as genuine preparation for giving an explanation, attending to the details.

4

PROVIDE OR GENERATE FEEDBACK

As part of the improvement process, identify areas for improvement in students' explanations using one of several routines:

- Give the feedback directly: highlight strengths, gaps, errors.
- Invite students to engage in a peer critique process.
- Ask students to reflect on their own explanations having heard each other's or re-studied from accurate sources, generating their own feedback.

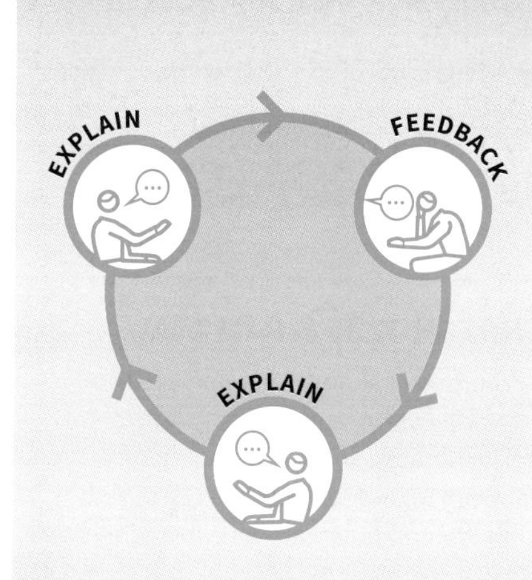

5

REPEAT FEEDBACK & IMPROVEMENT CYCLES

A crucial step (often missed out) is to give students another opportunity to deliver an improved version of the explanation.

Ask students to repeat their explanation, correcting errors, adding details, attempting to be more precise, more succinct, to connect words and images more fluently.

Then repeat the feedback and improvement cycle. Students will get better at explaining things if they have the opportunity to rehearse and improve in this way.

THRESHOLDS & PATHWAYS

A common challenge is to manage the scenario where students progress at different rates, some developing the capacity for independent practice with more demanding material while others still require more guided practice, perhaps with smaller steps and more scaffolding. It's problematic to set different learning goals for groups of students, giving them easier tasks or projecting lower expectations. It's better to frame this in terms of different levels of support and guidance. Establishing the thresholds for following different practice pathways is a practical way to achieve this in a mixed class.

WALKTHRUs IN THIS SERIES

PRACTICE & RETRIEVAL

1

ESTABLISH AMBITIOUS GOALS FOR ALL

Keep the ideas in **Teach to the Top** firmly in mind. Thresholds are intended to serve as markers along an ambitious path, not ceilings on ambition or limits to what is possible.

Use the language of pathway thresholds like this:

- *We're all aiming for Z. Firstly, get to X; then, aim for Y; after Y, Z is in reach.*
- *If you can get to X by yourself, go on ahead. Once you pass X, let me check but then head straight for Y.*
- *If you need help getting to X, here's what to do.*

2

ESTABLISH THE THRESHOLD

Thresholds need to be communicated in terms of knowledge and task goals. This can be as simple as:

- *Complete Exercise 3.2 and check you've got the answers right.*
- *Make the circuits exactly as shown in the textbook, making sure you can explain what happens when the switch is closed.*
- *Just write the opening paragraph of your speech, with the rhetorical question at the start.*
- *Play the first four bars fluently.*
- *Match the diagrams/sources to the descriptions.*

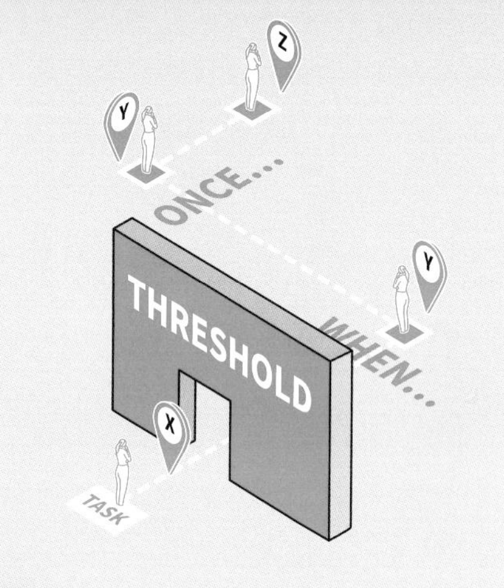

3

MAP OUT THE PATHWAYS

Beyond the thresholds, develop one or more pathways to follow, depending on students' confidence and success in reaching this point. One central pathway is the most manageable: *When you reach X, go to Y:*

- *Once you've made the three set circuits work, add a voltmeter and ammeter and take readings.*
- *Once I've checked your first paragraph, add the anaphora effect in your speech, reinforcing your argument.*

Alternatively, introduce an element of student choice in the pathways.

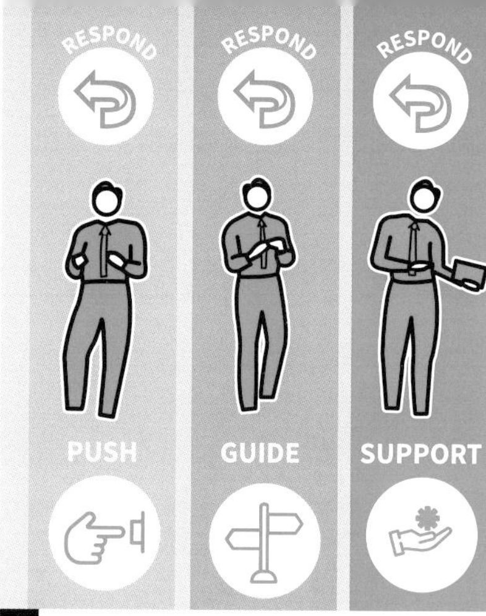

4

GUIDE PRACTICE RESPONSIVELY

This process needs careful guidance so that students are on the optimum pathway:

- If students pass through the threshold easily, push them on even further.
- If students are struggling to reach the threshold, give them more instructional guidance or feedback.
- If students need support to choose appropriate next steps, point them in a sensible direction – not one that is too hard or too easy.

Be vigilant in checking students are reaching the threshold point securely, circulating, checking for understanding.

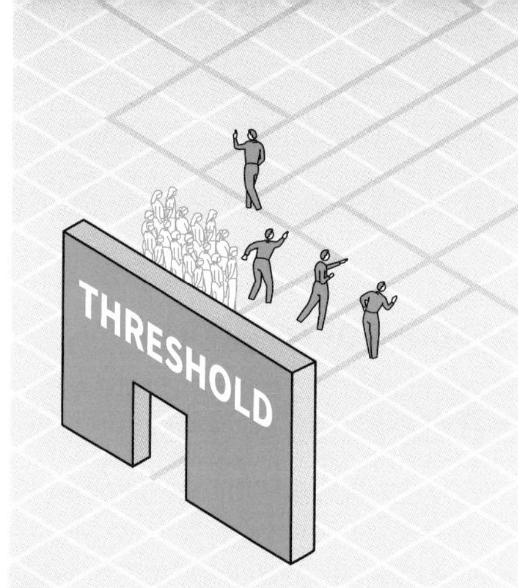

5

REGROUP & DIRECT INDEPENDENT PRACTICE

After a period of independent work, regroup and check on progress. This could be after 5, 10 or 20 minutes depending on the context. Regrouping maintains the important sense of the whole class pursuing common goals without individuals streaking on ahead or being left behind. Review progress: *Where are we? Where do we need to go next?* Invite students to showcase responses or provide an account of their progress along the pathway. Discuss error and confusion safely and openly. Then push people on with further practice.

A LADDER OF DIFFICULTY

As part of a planned approach to practice, it helps to have ways of increasing the level of difficulty without increasing the range of content being covered. This allows students to consolidate what they know, learning to apply it rather than adding more and more. A ladder of difficulty is a notional concept, making learning more challenging, less straightforward, demanding great fluency or making more connections to other areas of knowledge. If teachers are conscious of the next level of difficulty at any stage, it helps to support students to step up the ladder. Mark McCourt uses ideas about recency and cue in his mastery approach.

1

MAP OUT THE LADDER OF DIFFICULTY

Within a given area of knowledge, it is helpful to formulate a mental model of difficulty. This will include: conceptual complexity; use of language; moving from concrete to abstract; the range of interacting elements in a problem or task; needing to think several steps ahead; observing patterns and causal links.

Assessment information will be useful in identifying questions and tasks that students are typically less likely to perform well on – this is effectively what difficulty means (it's easy if everyone can do it.)

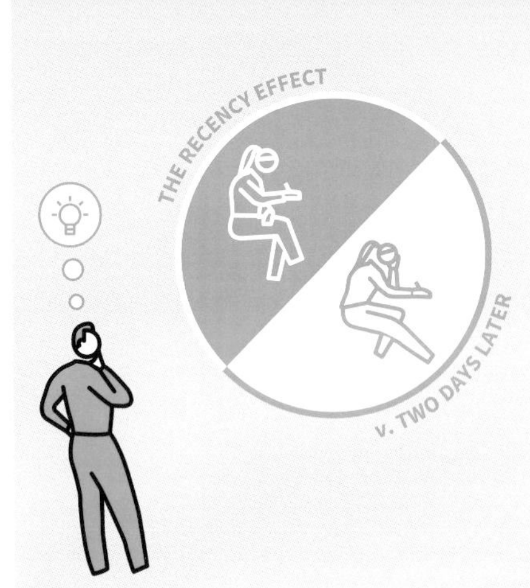

2

REMOVE RECENCY: ALLOW TIME TO PASS

Problems can be made more difficult simply by increasing the time since the material was introduced or studied. It is likely that students will be able to perform a task that you have only just shown them how to do. However, in removing the element of recency by revisiting the same material a few days later, you introduce another level of difficulty. After the initial phase of instruction and practice, allow time to pass and then check that students can still demonstrate their knowledge and understanding.

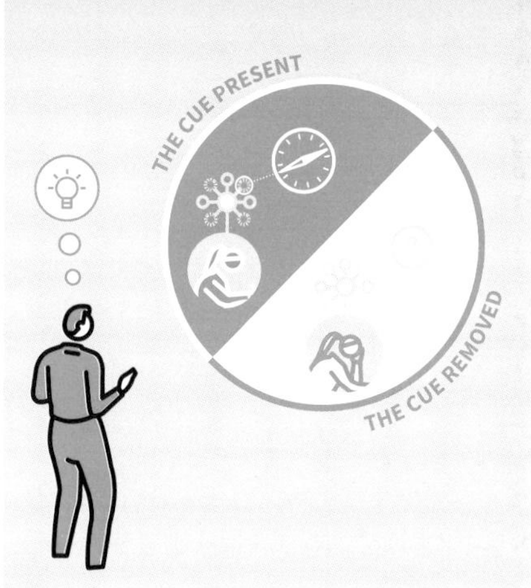

3

REMOVE CUE: SPOT THE PROBLEM TYPE

If presented with a set of problems labelled *Displacement Reactions* in science or *Using Pythagoras* in maths, students are given a cue to retrieve information relevant for these problem types. The same problems can be more difficult if the cue is removed. Problems presented without the knowledge cue or heading – e.g. to identify the products in a reaction or to solve a geometric puzzle – require students to explore a wider range of prior knowledge to establish the problem type. This is more challenging and helps students to deepen their schema connections.

4

REDUCE FEEDBACK AND SCAFFOLDING

An obvious way to increase difficulty is to give students less help; to create conditions where they have to draw more on their own resources, thinking harder and using their own metacognitive strategies.

Reduce feedback by asking students to generate their own. *How could you improve your work? Can you identify the errors you have made?*

Reduce scaffolding, giving fewer prompts, less structured guidance, less access to exemplars.

5

MAKE QUESTIONS MORE SYNOPTIC

Increase difficulty by setting questions that draw on knowledge from a wider range of topics covered. If questions about angle facts also include elements of algebra and rules about parallel lines and circles, they are likely to be more difficult than questions that cover one of those topics alone, especially if the topics are not cued.

If a writing task requires students to compare two poems, using quotations and a range of language techniques, it becomes more difficult than focusing on any one of those areas.

THE FACE IT REVISION MODEL

It's common for students, faced with a large amount of material to revise ahead of examinations and assessments, to feel overwhelmed, not knowing where to begin.

Deputy headteacher Deborah O'Connor has introduced an approach to her London comprehensive school that they call FACE It. The neat double meaning in the acronym is designed to provide encouragement as well as structured guidance. This is supported by good home study resources and in-class retrieval practice techniques.

DEBORAH O'CONNOR

WALKTHRUs IN THIS SERIES

PRACTICE & RETRIEVAL

LEARN THE FACTS

The simplest place to begin is to learn the core factual content in a topic: terminology, definitions, equations, dates, names, places, quotations, labels, sequences, units, events, people.

This is the quizzable knowledge that students might have on their Flash Cards or Knowledge Organisers. Students focus on retrieval practice techniques like self-quizzing.

For example, the equation for photosynthesis; the role of chlorophyll; the starch test; the concept of limiting conditions; the concept of gas concentration.

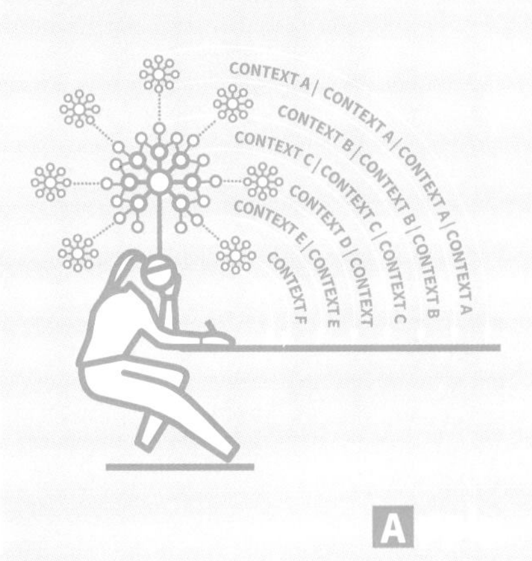

2

APPLY IN CONTEXT

With facts secure, tackle questions where the knowledge is tested in a context – beyond straightforward recall. It's not enough to know isolated facts; that knowledge needs to be used in a range of contexts. Often previous examination questions and textbooks will be a good source of questions of this type.

For example, how a graph of crop yields vs CO_2 concentration relates to the equation for photosynthesis; how results of covered leaf or variegated leaf experiments can be explained.

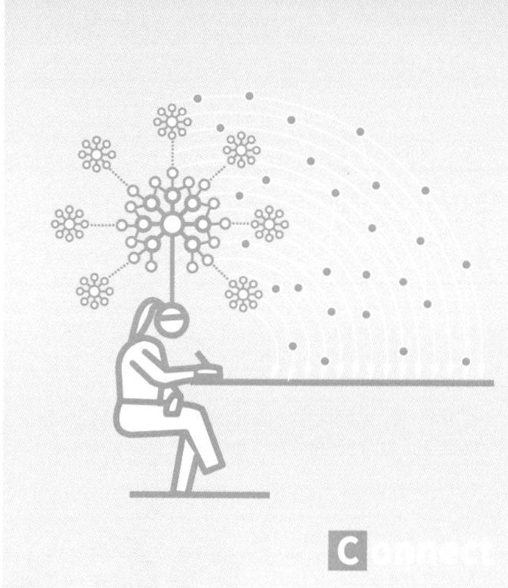

CONNECT IDEAS

Attempt questions that require students to draw on knowledge from more than one topic area or to apply knowledge to previously unseen ideas. They might need to identify patterns and causal links that would not have been explicitly taught before. Sometimes they need to connect detailed ideas into a much wider schema of interconnected topics.

Link work on crop yields to the nitrogen cycle, nitrogen-fixing bacteria and use of nitrate-providing fertilisers.

TEST IN EXAM CONDITIONS

Use past exam questions to rehearse the process of responding under time pressure, demonstrating students' knowledge and understanding, taking account of the marks available. This needs to be introduced once the other aspects are more secure. There's no point asking students to remember a lot of factual knowledge under time pressure if this hasn't previously been secured in a more low-stakes situation.

For example, a CO_2 *graph needs to be analysed for 4 marks; leaf starch test results need to be explained for 3 marks.*

5

REVISION TROUBLE? FACE IT

Teach students to use FACE It to support their revision planning and as a diagnostic tool:

Have you learned your **F**acts?

Have you practised **A**pplying your knowledge in context questions?

Have you started to **C**onnect ideas with more synoptic questions?

Have you tested yourself in timed **E**xam conditions?

This also works away from formal exam settings where E means Express your knowledge.

MODE B TEACHING

In Tom's book *The Learning Rainforest*, he introduces the concept of Mode A and Mode B teaching to reflect the reality that many teachers typically balance different modes of teaching over time to add depth and variety of practice opportunities. Mode A teaching refers to the staple of teacher-led instructional teaching that forms the context for most of our WalkThrus. Mode B teaching is a broad collection of activities where, typically, students are given choices, engage in more extended oral contributions and work collaboratively. This selection is just a small sample of the possibilities. The challenge for teachers is to weave Mode A and Mode B teaching into a cohesive whole, as discussed in the Mode A : Mode B WalkThru on page 56.

HANDS ON

Numerous elements of a great knowledge-rich curriculum require students to gain knowledge first hand, through *hands-on* experiences: doing things, feeling things, experiencing things, seeing things for themselves. In terms of schema-building, there is plenty of knowledge that cannot be delivered by instruction; certain phenomena or activities must be experienced before the related vocabulary, conceptual model or abstract representation make sense. Hands-on curriculum elements need to be planned so that they are universal entitlements.

1

IDENTIFY THE EXPERIENCES

Use the ideas in **Blend Knowledge and Experience** to identify where hands-on experiences are essential or, at least, very powerful:

- Handling tools and materials in art, technology, cooking.
- Experiencing moods, atmospheres, feelings in drama, literature, music.
- Behaviours of magnets; texture, density of materials; ice melting on skin; insects moving in a jar.
- Organising tessellating shapes into patterns.

See **Museum/Gallery visits**.

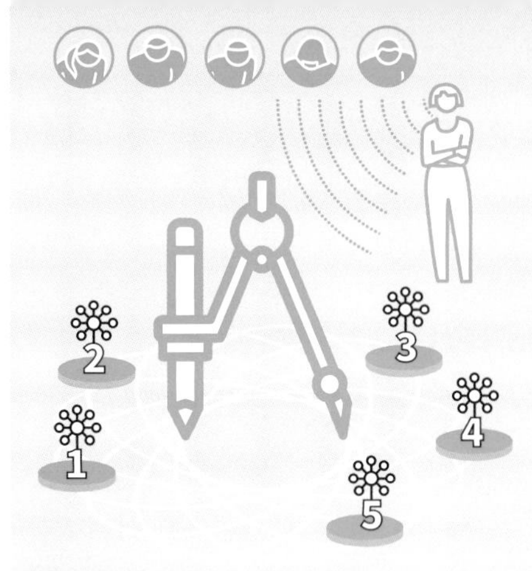

2

HANDS ON *FOR EVERYONE*

If these experiences are vital for secure schema-building in the particular curriculum area, then this is likely to be the case for all students. Plan activities so that students will all gain the required experiences.

This might include:

- Providing all students with their own tools and materials to handle.
- Taking turns, one by one, while other work is done by the others.
- Creating a circus of activities, where students rotate from one to the next.

WALKTHRUs IN THIS SERIES

MODE B TEACHING

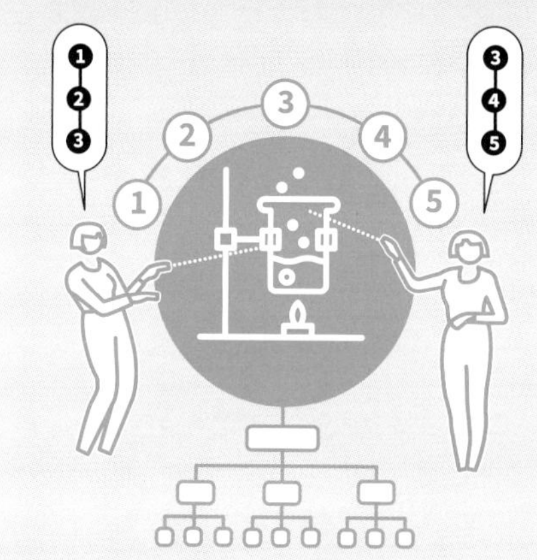

3

PREPARE THE GROUND

Explain the purpose of the hands-on experience, putting it into the context of the flow of ideas in the topic in hand. This helps students to make connections. Where appropriate, pre-teach the key vocabulary that students will need to describe the phenomenon or experience. This could be done using a preliminary demonstration or diagram.

Where helpful, pre-teach conceptual models e.g. a particle model for matter or explaining the concept of symmetry before students explore it in a hands-on fashion.

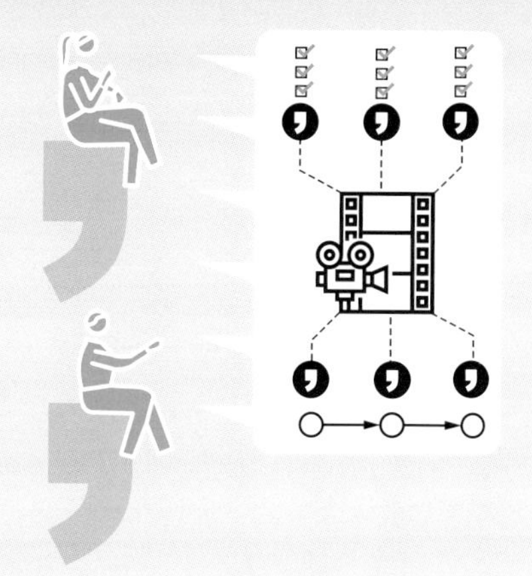

4

SHARE REACTIONS, RESPONSES & REASONING

Design tasks or questioning routines that require students to connect their experiential knowledge to their prior knowledge. This could include:

- **Think, Pair, Share**: students explaining a phenomenon or experience to each other.
- **Cold Call** and **Check for Understanding**: soliciting responses in a dialogue with the class.
- **Open Response Tasks**: inviting students to produce a response that demonstrates their understanding from their hands-on experience.

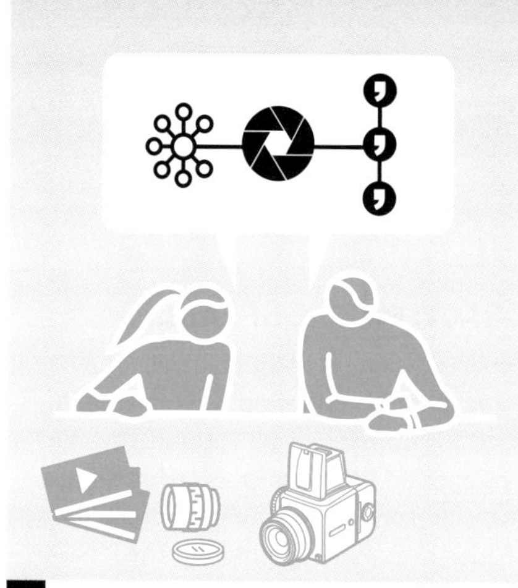

5

LINK BACK TO THE RELATED CURRICULUM

Hands-on experiences have value in their own right, but also lay foundations for subsequent learning. Build on the students' shared experience to link hands-on knowledge to more conceptual ideas.

Can they now explain the behaviour of materials in different contexts, having explored them manually themselves?

Can they now articulate the effect of language features in the play, having experienced those effects in the performance?

ORACY: PUBLIC SPEAKING

Public speaking is a valuable skill for all young people to develop. This can mean anything from making an address to an audience on a formal occasion to telling a story, presenting an argument or pitching an idea in a smaller gathering. The ideal scenario is where these opportunities are genuine, allowing students to make a planned presentation or speech for a real purpose and real audience. The level of authenticity will depend on the opportunities in any given context and can always be simulated in a classroom context as a back-up option.

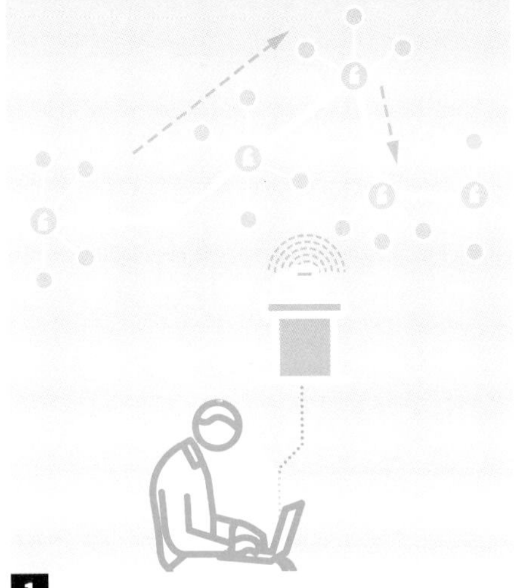

1

PREPARE THE SUBJECT CONTENT

Ask students to consider the substance of what they want to say. What is the main message? What are the key arguments? What information do they want to share?

Establishing the content of what needs to be communicated is an essential first step. This applies to telling a personal story, making an argument for or against a motion, pitching an idea.

Support students to organise their ideas into a sequence, creating a narrative structure for their speech.

2

TEACH THE LANGUAGE TECHNIQUES

Model a range of techniques to engage and persuade the audience. Give examples and invite students to emulate them, selecting from a repertoire that might include:

Rhetorical opener: Can you imagine what it's like to sleep rough?

Rule of 3: Our solution is cheap, popular, exciting!

Repetition: Einstein was a genius. An incredible genius.

Anaphora: Three clauses starting with the same phrase: 'How dare you … How dare you … How dare you…' (Greta Thunberg).

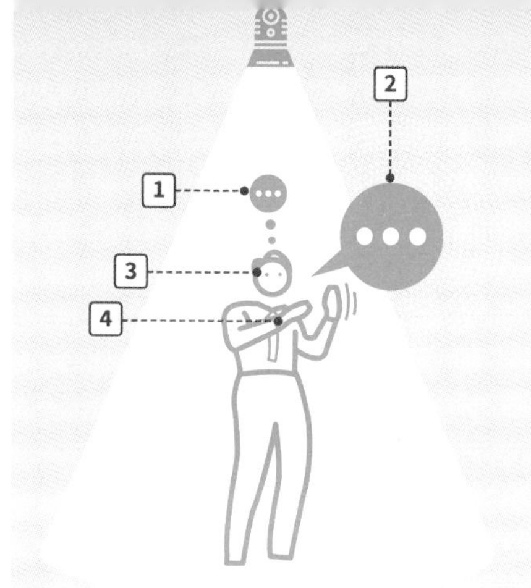

TEACH THE DELIVERY TECHNIQUES

Model a range of techniques for students to deliver their speech in a confident, engaging manner.

Using the text: Consider whether students will speak from memory, use cue cards or read from a script.

Voice projection: Support speakers to reach everyone in the room, in an audible, clear tone, varying the rhythm and dynamics for emphasis and impact.

Eye contact: Holding attention, making a personal connection.

Hand gestures: Adding emphasis – but avoiding distractions.

GUIDE THE REHEARSAL

With speeches planned, give students an opportunity to rehearse in a low-stakes setting. Use the ideas from **Rehearsal & Performance**, generating feedback cycles for students to hone their speeches.

Use pairs or small group audiences: students take turns to present to their peers for practice.

Practise in the same space to experience the acoustics.

Where required, rehearse for recall so that lines and performance cues are delivered from memory with confidence.

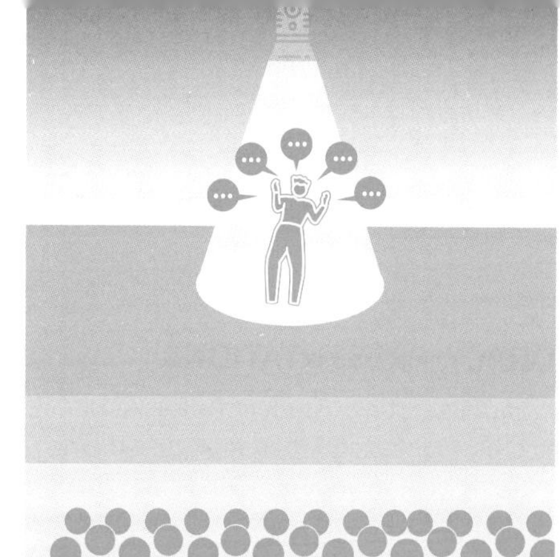

RUN AN AUTHENTIC EVENT

Give students the experience of delivering their speech in the type of event they had planned for – or a simulated version if necessary.

The experience and confidence gained from delivering to a real audience is significant. Be ready to step in to support with nerves or forgotten lines to make the experience as positive as possible.

Celebrate successes, affirming all the positive elements of the speech that students manage to deliver, with some key pointers to consider on the next occasion.

ORACY: PRESENTATIONS

In various settings, students are asked to present information to showcase their learning on a given topic. This allows them to consolidate a body of knowledge into a coherent schema, communicating key ideas in a clear sequence. This might be linked to **Oracy: Instructional Inputs**, where students are essentially teaching something to their peers. More commonly, it is an opportunity for all students to share the results of some independent research. The key is to design lessons so all students gain from each other's presentations, exploring a wider range of examples or perspectives than they could do by themselves.

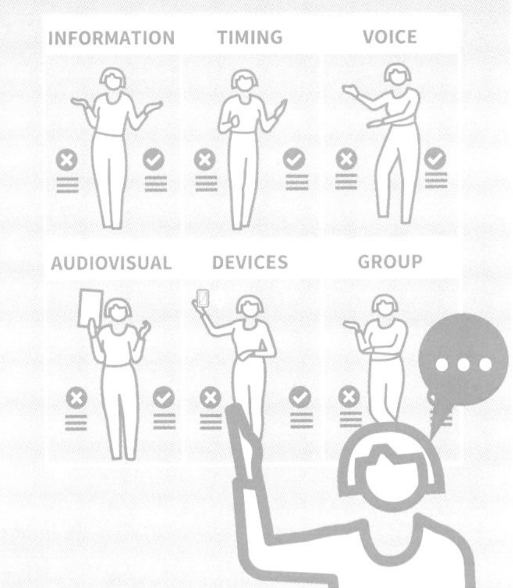

1

ESTABLISH SUCCESS CRITERIA

Engage students in a discussion about the elements of a successful presentation. Model examples and non-examples to illustrate why these elements are important. Include a range of content and presentational aspects:

- Quality, depth, range, accuracy of information presented
- Timing and pace
- Voice projection
- Appropriate use of audio-visual aids
- Use of devices to inform, engage and persuade
- Contribution of each member in a group

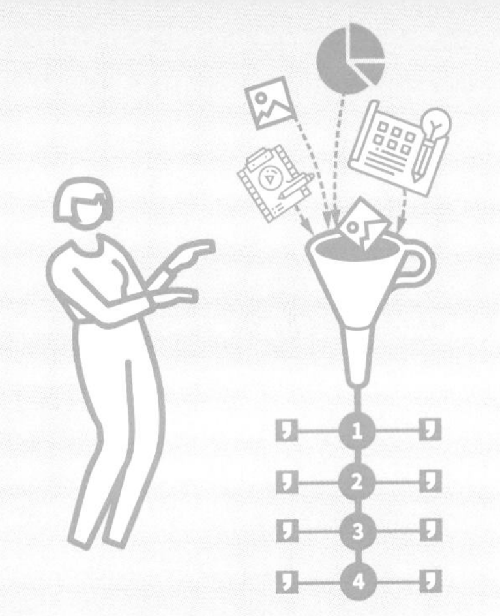

2

MAKE THE CONTENT THE MAIN FOCUS

Ensure students focus most time on thinking about the content of their presentation, relative to the mechanics of delivering it. The students' goal is to make sense of a topic, compiling factual elements and images to formulate a coherent exposition with a logical sequence. The need to summarise information is challenging in itself and might need modelling and scaffolding, generating headings, bullet points and the main message. Encourage divergent, creative examples and viewpoints to add to the range of ideas the class is exposed to.

WALKTHRUs IN THIS SERIES

MODE B TEACHING

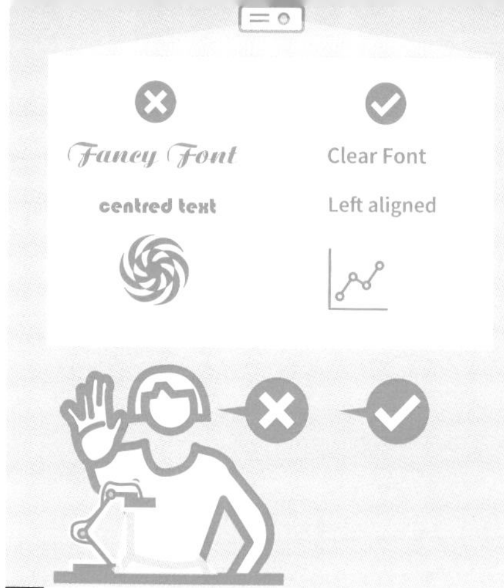

3 EMBED THE TECHNOLOGY

Where technology is new – for example, the first time students use PowerPoint or other similar presentation applications – it is necessary to teach students explicitly how to use the key features.

However, when part of a curriculum-focused presentation, the technology should sit in the background. Discourage overuse of animation, fussy fonts and image manipulation unless they directly reinforce meaning in the content. Encourage the use of images and diagrams to accompany the spoken input, following **Dual Coding** principles.

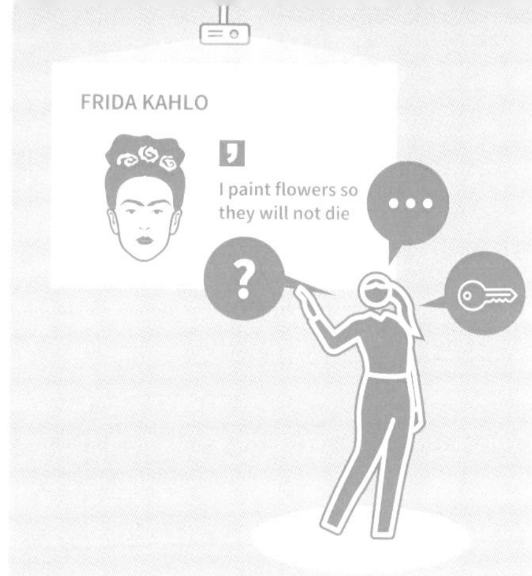

4 ADDRESS AND INVOLVE THE AUDIENCE

Establish a set of principles:

- Make eye contact; face the audience, not the slides.
- Do not read text from slides – talk to images and bullet points; show you know and understand the material; don't simply read it out.
- Include questions for the audience.
- Explain the structure of the talk at the beginning and conclude with a summary of key points.
- Invite questions from the audience.

Teachers can chip in to **Check for Understanding**.

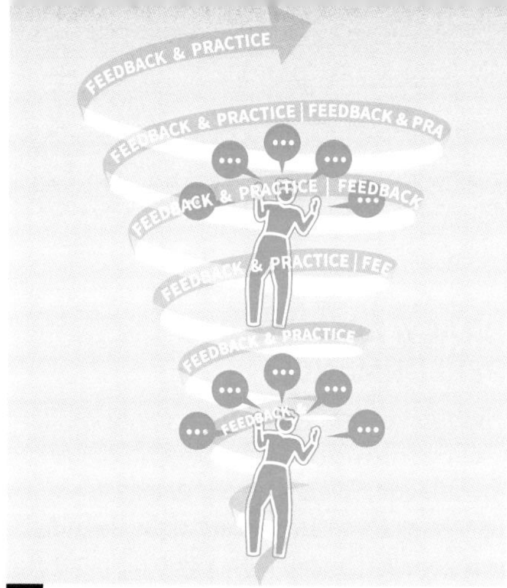

5 REVIEW AND REPEAT

As with any other type of performance or piece of work, it is rare for anyone to deliver excellence on their first attempt. Students benefit from having the opportunity to gain feedback and then repeat their presentations having made improvements, reaching a higher standard. This will be especially important if they have included factual errors.

It may be more time efficient to do this where only some students are presenting in any one lesson, taking their turn as part of a more extended programme.

ORACY: RECITATION & PERFORMANCE

This form of oracy is typically found in association with drama or English where monologues, dialogues or poems are recited or acted out as part of the learning experience. The principle value is in the experience of communicating the meaning of the script through an expressive recitation or performance. There is intrinsic value in having the ability to recite poems or dramatic monologues from memory and the often challenging process of memorisation should be seen in that context: a demanding challenge with joyful outcomes. Of course, this WalkThru could be readily adapted for choral recitation, but here we are looking more at individuals.

WALKTHRUs IN THIS SERIES

MODE B TEACHING

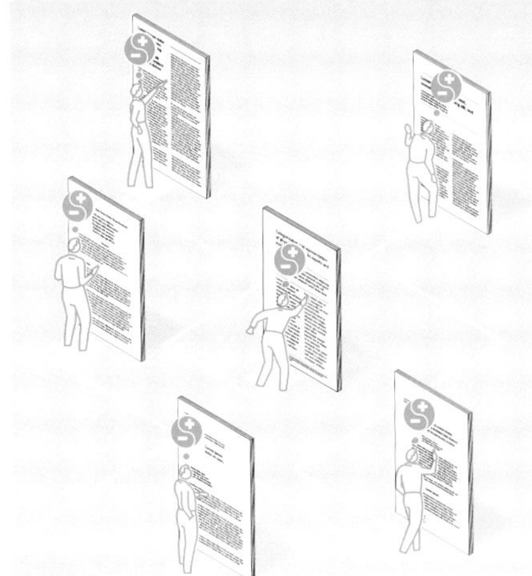

1

SELECT THE TEXT AND FORM

Identify texts that make a valuable contribution to students' knowledge and experience, based on the significance in the wider curriculum or particular features that make the performance interesting, rewarding or supportive of other aspects of the curriculum (e.g. knowledge of rhyming schemes, rhetorical devices).

Select individual, small group or larger choral forms.

Adjust the length of the text relative to students' capacity for memorisation and the rehearsal time available.

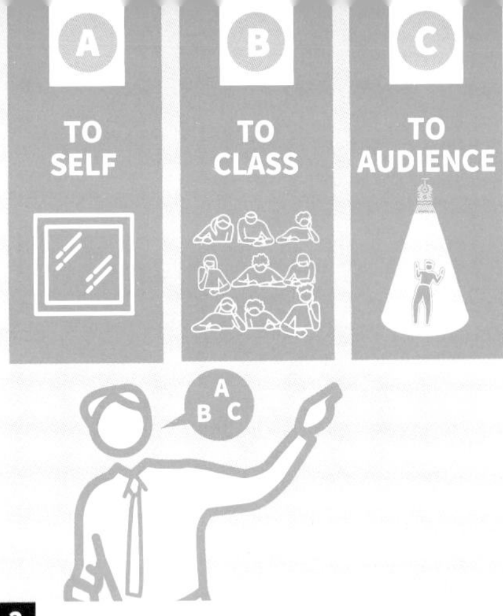

2

IDENTIFY THE AUDIENCE

Make it explicit in the planning whether students will be performing to the class, to a more formal audience or perhaps just for themselves. This will influence the nature of performance that is needed.

Recitation for personal fulfilment might be the end point but the device of performing to the class may be the means by which students engage with the text, finding the motivation to embrace the memorisation aspect.

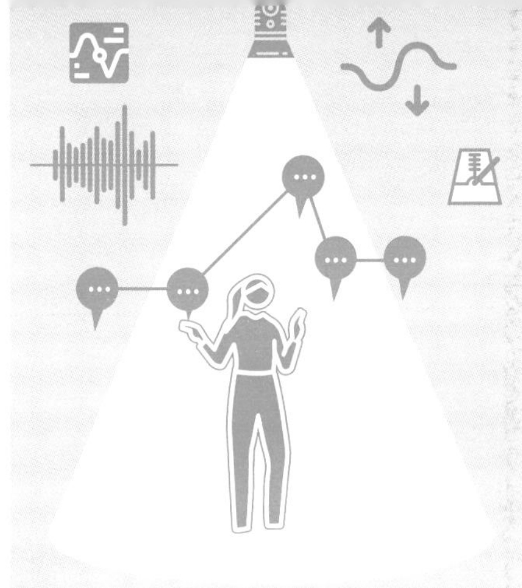

3

CREATE DRAMA

Follow step 3 in **Oracy: Public Speaking**, placing an emphasis on delivery techniques that connect the audience to the text:

- Pauses
- Changes of pace
- Loud/soft dynamics
- Rhythm and rhyme

Wherever appropriate, link aspects of the performance to the meaning of the text. Use this process as a way to support students' understanding of the text.

4

REHEARSE AND MEMORISE

Memorising a text typically follows a pattern:

- Part A: read, cover, recite from memory; check. Practise.
- Part B: read, cover, recite from memory; check. Practise.
- Then recite A and B together; check. Practise.
- Part C: read, cover, recite from memory; check. Practise.
- Recite A, B, C together; check. Practise.
- Add more parts of the text, gaining fluency with each section.

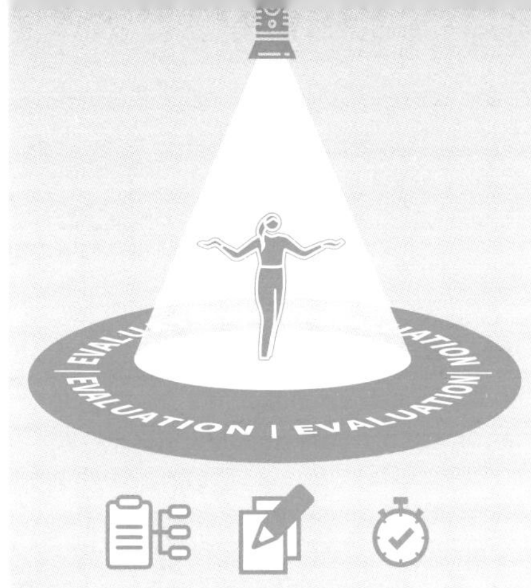

5

PERFORM AND EVALUATE

Follow the steps in **Rehearsal & Performance**.

Give students a chance to evaluate their recitations and, if at all possible, to repeat them, embedding some improvements.

Focus on the overall quality and drama of the performance rather than the precision of the recall – even if the latter needs further work. Keep the main purpose in mind.

OFF-PISTE

This is as much a mindset as a strategy. In the context of a coherent, knowledge-rich curriculum, it is important to retain a degree of flexibility to allow for spontaneity and responsiveness. The metaphor of going off-piste suggests that, for the most part, the curriculum is planned and carefully sequenced. However, there is often rich learning to be gained when teachers deviate from the plan, capitalising on unforeseen events in the community or in the wider world to widen or deepen students' learning. This only happens if teachers embrace these opportunities and harness their potential in a positive manner.

WALKTHRUs IN THIS SERIES

MODE B TEACHING

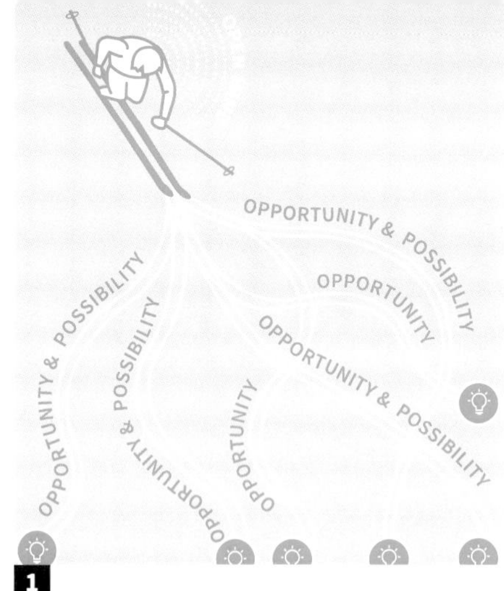

1

ADOPT A MINDSET OPEN TO POSSIBILITIES

Recognise that learning takes many forms and many routes and, provided that secure foundations are being laid in the mainstay of the curriculum, some opportunities can provide knowledge and experiences even as one-off events and moments. These can relate to specific areas of knowledge, hands-on experiences or opportunities to respond in particular ways. Linking to *Trivium 21c*, it is possible to support all three elements – Grammar, Dialectic and Rhetoric – in off-piste moments.

2

CAPITALISE ON EVENTS & CIRCUMSTANCES

Respond to local events: a weather event, a visit from a significant person, a power cut, a new arrival to the community.

Respond to global or cosmic events: an election, a protest, an eclipse, an environmental or political incident, a space mission.

Respond to a new book, a discovery, a family issue or festival, a new art installation or TV show.

3

PITCH IT UP: DEEPEN AND ENRICH

Use off-piste diversions to add depth and rigour to the curriculum; to explore the hinterland a little further. Use them to create a motivational, knowledge-seeking dimension as the curriculum is brought closer to home, made more concrete, more tangible, more current.

Be aware of the opportunity costs. Time spent off-piste is time taken away from other planned curriculum activities, so it has to add value. Make that evaluation before pressing ahead.

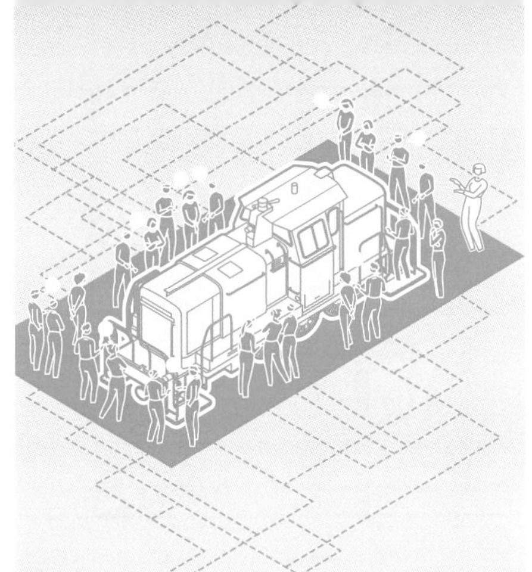

4

MAKE SPECIAL EVENTS COUNT FOR EVERYONE

Ensure that all students are able to gain experience or knowledge from your off-piste exploration. If there are opportunities to handle artefacts, make sure everyone can participate or get as close as possible.

If some students have opportunities to meet people or go on small-scale excursions, make sure they report back to everyone else in some detail. If the weather inspires you to go out into the long grass on a summer day armed with pooters, try to give every student the chance to capture and observe some insects of their own.

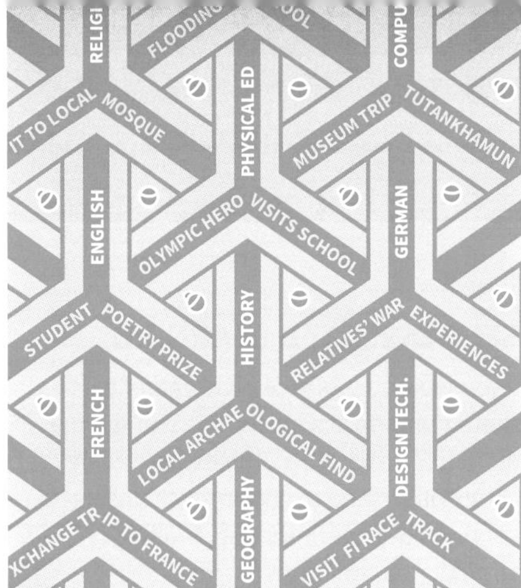

5

WEAVE THE LEARNING INTO THE CURRICULUM

Rather than off-piste learning remaining disconnected, separate from students' main curriculum, try to weave it back in. For example, if, during a power cut, you have to sit in the dark and tell stories, use this as stimulus for a piece of creative writing. If a new object is discovered in the solar system, link it back to the space and forces curriculum, next time it comes around. If archaeologists unearth a newsworthy find, take time to connect the find or the process of archaeology to the areas of study students are engaging in that year.

Attempt | Develop | Adapt | Practise | Test

SELF-DIRECTED LEARNING

If you watch a group of young people skateboarding at a skatepark, you see that there is a wonderful culture where each person is striving to challenge themselves continually, experimenting, trialling approaches and receiving quick self-generated feedback about their success. It's both challenging and motivating. As part of a strong Mode B curriculum, setting up self-directed learning with this spirit as part of the overall diet can yield wonderful outcomes, provided that key factors are in place.

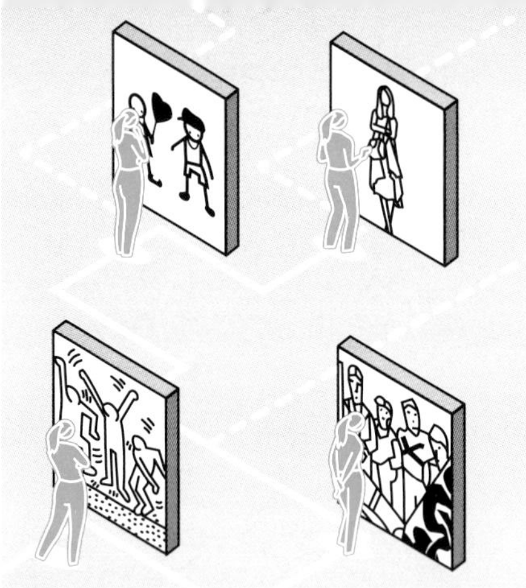

1

DESIGN SELECTED OPPORTUNITIES

In the context of a strong knowledge-rich curriculum, there are often opportunities to weave in elements of self-direction. This might include:

- Creative journeys in art or writing: students explore personal directions, selecting influences and media.
- Experiments with forces or simple circuits in science, with students following systematic lines of enquiry.
- Research tasks where students select and pursue areas of study.

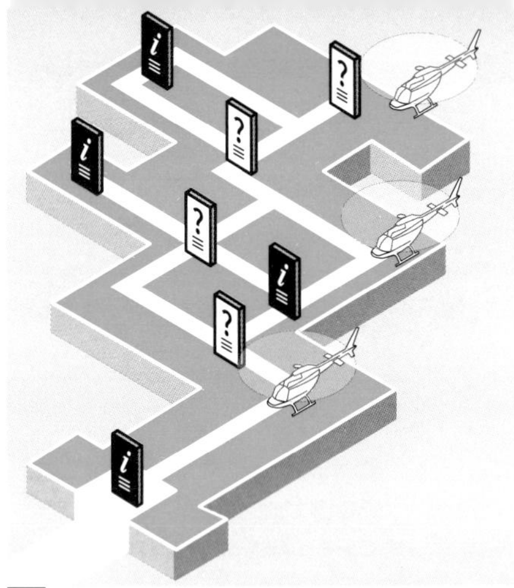

2

ESTABLISH THE TERRITORY

Until students are fully confident in learning this way, it helps to set out a knowledge area for them to explore. Self-directed learning needs to follow subject-specific disciplinary routines that might need prior modelling. Before they set off, ensure they understand the process: where to begin, the questions to ask, the places to look, forms of expressing ideas, how to review their success. In knowledge terms, establish the areas that might be most fruitful in the context of the wider curriculum.

WALKTHRUs IN THIS SERIES

3

ESTABLISH THE STANDARDS

Compile a set of exemplar pieces of work that you or previous students produced to illustrate the general standards that might be achieved. Skateboarders can see each other's runs and tricks; artists can view each other's work; writers can read others' poetry or stories.

Without seeking to confine or overly direct, show students examples that constitute excellence in the terms of the discipline: creative, thorough, imaginative, precise, persuasive – as appropriate.

4

CREATE FEEDBACK LOOPS

The key to self-directed learning is that students receive timely feedback about their success within the process of undertaking the tasks. This links to the Goal-Free effect reported by Sweller in *Cognitive Load Theory*. Ensure that students are able to self-check, self-evaluate, self-edit, self-correct using a mechanism relevant to the subject. This could involve referencing certain patterns of data; a process of self-testing; a judgement against some criteria; comparison with the exemplars.

5

GUIDE, CHALLENGE & SUPPORT

As with other forms of **Independent Practice**, it's important to balance challenge and support, building confidence while also allowing students to learn to make mistakes or fail and then persevere. Monitor students as required so that they are not left floundering; model key processes to push them forward and offer feedback if they struggle to generate it themselves. Celebrate success in overcoming obstacles as well as the quality of the outcomes themselves.

MUSEUM/GALLERY VISITS

One of the most rewarding learning experiences students can have is to visit a museum or an art gallery. Inevitably, these will be occasional opportunities that take time to organise, so it is important to make the most of them. Of course, a visit to a museum or gallery is an experience of value in itself – simply sampling the atmosphere, the awe and wonder of casting an eye over the array of exhibits. However, the depth of learning can be significantly enhanced and the experience enriched if the visit is linked directly to the curriculum in a planned manner.

WALKTHRUs IN THIS SERIES

MODE B TEACHING

1

LAY THE CURRICULUM GROUND

Before students make the visit, engage them in preparatory contextual work. Pre-teach the content needed: some key narratives and vocabulary. For example, seeing the Rosetta Stone in the British Museum is a very powerful experience if you know about it in advance: '*Wow, this is the actual Rosetta Stone, right here!*' Similarly for works of art: the power of seeing an actual, real painting by Picasso or Van Gogh is significantly enhanced if you have a sense of the significance of their work in a wider context.

2

EMBRACE THE WHOLE EXPERIENCE

Even if the visit has a central focus, the overall experience can provide an excellent opportunity to reference the curriculum hinterland. Students will see that, although certain exhibits are where they need to spend most time, there are all these other rooms to explore; their area of study sits in a much wider frame. Allowing some time to explore freely can be extremely rewarding, especially if they are asked to report back on what they find. This expectation gives their explorations a depth and purpose.

3

MAP OUT POINTS OF FOCUS

Most museums and galleries are far too big to explore in full to any great depth on a single visit and any pressure to do so can be overwhelming. On an educational visit, it's usually far better to map out some key exhibits to focus on for the main part of the trip. Using your knowledge of the exhibits, curate a selection that you want all students to see – the exhibits that link to your wider curriculum and that you will reference explicitly. Knowing the layout in advance can help to plan the route, which can be crucial in a large building.

4

SET SCAFFOLDED RESPONSE TASKS

Left to wander, students may not necessarily know how to engage with the artefacts; meaning and significance are not necessarily self-evident. To give structure to the visit and the learning, produce some prompts, questions or tasks requiring students to look at each of your chosen exhibits in the way you intend from a curriculum perspective. Draw their attention to features, facts, details. Ask them to explore their emotional responses and make connections from one artefact to another, linked to the curriculum theme.

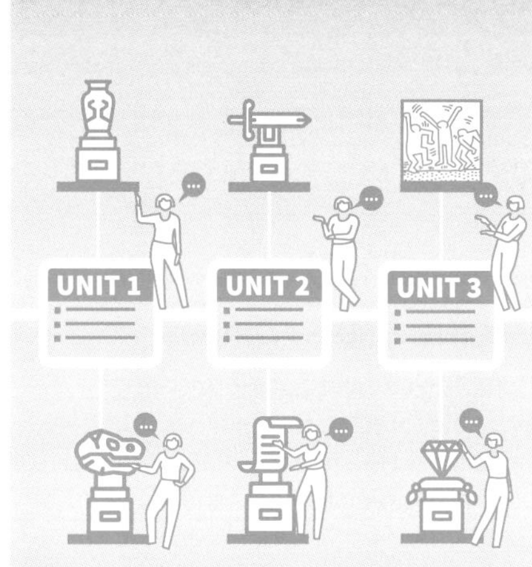

5

HARNESS THE LEARNING

Fold the learning from the visit back into the flow of the curriculum. The timing of the visit will influence how you do this but, where possible, consolidate factual and tacit experiential knowledge gained from seeing the exhibits: animal skeletons and dinosaur fossils; war documents and armaments; costumes and armour; buildings and ruins; formal statues and sculptures; artefacts of daily life. Refer to them explicitly in subsequent activities so that the key knowledge is integrated with instructional inputs and classroom tasks.

ONLINE CLASS FORUMS

Multiple web-based platforms are available for schools with the appropriate safeguards and data protection protocols built in, allowing teachers and students to communicate online, between their face-to-face contact in lessons. If this opportunity is harnessed effectively, it can provide significant additional learning opportunities for students, supporting them with their independent studies and creating a culture of learning sustained beyond the space and time constraints of classroom contact.

A class forum, where teachers and students can meet virtually, is a good way to use these tools.

WALKTHRUs IN THIS SERIES

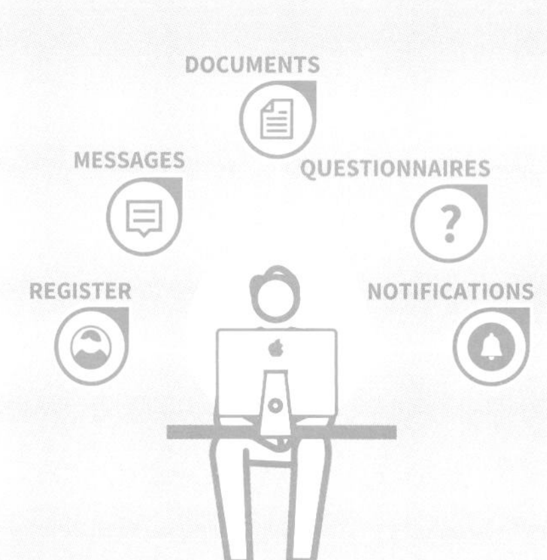

SORT THE TECHNICALITIES

Select a platform all your students can access online; part of a school-wide system or standalone. Key features needed for a forum include the facility to:

- Register and group users defined by your individual teaching class list.
- Post and moderate messages to and from students.
- Post links and documents.
- Post interactive elements such as questionnaires.
- Activate/deactivate notifications via email.

If possible, enrol a class *tech team* to maintain the content.

2

ESTABLISH COMMUNICATION ROUTINES & PROTOCOLS

These should include:

- Appropriate use of language, to minimise the need for moderation.
- Who has comment and sharing rights over certain areas of content, such as with co-creation of documents.
- Frequency and timing of posting materials so that students know when to expect updates and understand the limitations of teacher time when seeking help.
- Expectations around task-setting and document sharing, especially if this is the main route for setting homework or providing study-support resources.

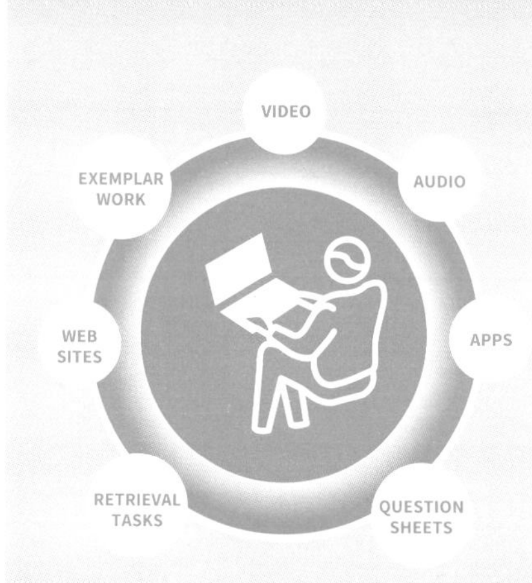

CAPTURE & SHARE MULTIMEDIA RESOURCES

Use the forum to curate resources that allow students to gain access to selected, trusted sources of information. This might include materials generated within the class:

- Exemplar work
- Video or audio recordings of discussions, demonstrations or performances
- Question sheets, study materials
- Self-checking retrieval practice tasks

It might include external resources such as curated websites, video clips and software tools.

CULTIVATE STUDENT OWNERSHIP

When students have the maturity and confidence, it can be extremely powerful to give them a degree of ownership and control over the content on the forum. Once students start to share useful information with each other and learn to give constructive feedback on each other's work, a forum can become genuinely dynamic; a tool students value highly. This needs to be fostered by the teacher in a planned way. If you never create the opportunity, students never learn to use it well. Your student *tech team* sidekicks can be a major asset and it's a role they enjoy immensely.

5

INTEGRATE INTO LESSON FLOW

At its most useful, an online forum sits in the background as a well-understood, well-used tool that supports the normal flow of learning from lesson to lesson. Students know that resources and tasks will be posted there; they know they can use it to ask for help between lessons; they know it is a go-to place to find out more about the subject. Teachers can rely on students using it to access material they post or to make their difficulties known. It takes some time and commitment to establish this culture but it is well worth the investment.

WALKTHRU SECTIONS

HOW?

WALKTHRUs FOR DEVELOPMENT

03

The How? section provides guides for teachers and leaders to support them in the implementation of WalkThrus as a tool for teacher development. This includes our ‘5Es’ implementation plan and guides to Instructional Coaching and Teaching Sprints as processes for securing effective professional learning. We have also included guides for online training and the use of video for self-evaluation. Given its importance in our thinking, we’ve repeated the ADAPT WalkThru from Volume 1, emphasising the need for teachers to develop each strategy for use in their specific context.

5Es WALKTHRUs IMPLEMENTATION PLAN

Our 5Es describe the stages schools and colleges need to go through to embrace WalkThrus fully, leading to them forming an embedded feature of their continuing professional development (CPD) culture and processes.

The question we are asked more than any other is 'Where do we start?' This is clearly an important consideration. However, perhaps most important is to plan the whole process for the long term; our 5Es Implementation Plan is intended to give some guidance to achieve that, recognising that institutions will be different in their starting points.

1

ENGAGE

Set up a launch event introducing teachers to WalkThrus and the process that lies ahead. Include:

- Pre-reading of the books or selected WalkThrus, with a follow-up discussion at a staff training session.
- A sample slide and video presentation focusing on one or two WalkThrus in detail.
- A demonstration of a sample of techniques by a member of staff.
- Discussion around which WalkThrus to focus on at a school, team or individual level.
- Sharing a calendar of the CPD cycle.

2

EXPLORE

Establish the key mechanism for teachers to follow the **Practice with Purpose** process. This might focus on:

- Regular team meetings where everyone focuses on the same set of WalkThrus.
- Individual **Instructional Coaching** sessions, spread across the year.
- Small groups such as peer-coaching pairs or triads meeting regularly to implement WalkThrus with time for reflection.
- Additional whole-staff training events at set points in the year, reinforcing key ideas, alongside the team/peer structures.

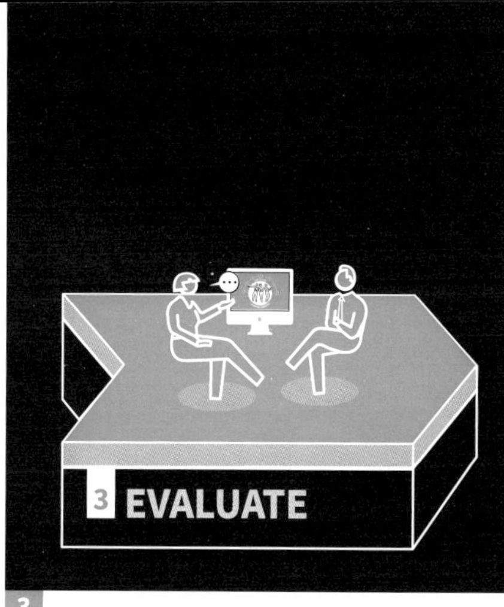

3

4

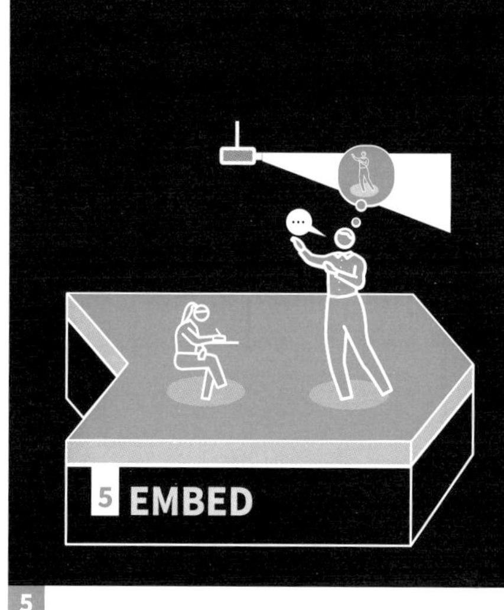

5

EVALUATE

Set up a key evaluation point towards the end of the academic year to provide an end-point to aim at within the year. This helps to drive the intensity of the Explore process, with every teacher knowing they need to share their findings and reflections from the year's CPD work. This could include publication of team reports or a staff journal; a whole-staff showcase event with a series of short presentations; a market-stall event where teachers present their work to colleagues via displays and small presentations, in an informal environment.

EXTEND

It's sensible for the first year to be regarded as something of a trial run – as teachers get used to using WalkThrus to support CPD Cycles, Shared Understanding, Three Point Communication and **Lesson Observation** processes. However, it's crucial to see this as a long-term improvement journey.

In the second year, key learning from the Evaluate process needs to feed into the next iteration. This needs to include induction of new staff and new leaders of CPD. Review the calendar and the Explore process to make sure every teacher is engaging, practising with purpose.

EMBED

Ultimately, the goal is for WalkThrus to be utilised as an embedded feature of professional learning. This requires the systems for Explore and Evaluate to happen on a continuous annual cycle, with appropriate adjustments made along the way. This might involve introducing new WalkThrus to **Solve the Learning Problems** more successfully; intensification of the instructional coaching for some or all staff; more modelling of strategies and planned CPD events. At all stages, it's vital to deepen the shared understanding, referring to WalkThrus directly in every process.

PRACTICE WITH PURPOSE

A succinct exposition of the elements of effective professional learning is presented in the *Practice with Purpose* paper by Texas-based Deans for Impact, subtitled 'The Emerging Science of Teacher Expertise'. Highlighting research from a range of fields, they suggest that teacher training *'cannot produce experts immediately'*. However, *'novice teachers who have had the opportunity to practice deliberately are on the path to being ready to teach as they begin their careers, and to develop deeper expertise over time'*. Here we explore how these five steps link to WalkThrus' underpinning principles.

BENJAMIN RILEY, FOUNDER

1

PUSH BEYOND

Deans for Impact highlight the need for novice teachers to embark on a 'purposeful developmental trajectory', guided through their early challenges and supported to push 'just beyond' their current capabilities. We'd also suggest that more experienced teachers need to continue pushing beyond, evaluating their default habits, making an intentional commitment to improve their practice. School and college cultures need to foster that spirit.

2

SPECIFIC GOALS

A **Practice with Purpose** recommendation is that 'practice activities focus on improving a particular aspect of teaching rather than working toward broad, general improvement'. Essentially, defining specific aspects of teaching is the basis of our WalkThrus concept. The trick is to identify the things that have greatest impact on students' learning and can, in time, become embedded habits. Ideally, goals will be sequenced, starting with the basics, and will be measurable in some way.

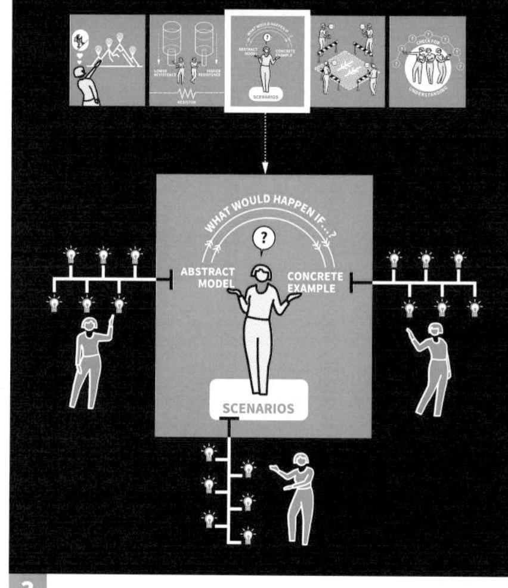

3

FOCUS

We don't improve by flitting from one thing to another. CPD and professional review systems need to motivate teachers to sustain a focus on a few areas of practice so that they give themselves a chance to really improve. Deans for Impact suggest that teachers may also need opportunities to intensify this focus in simulated situations outside the classroom or a *decomposition* of teaching – breaking strategies down into specific steps and practising those. This is why our five-step guides provide a helpful framework.

4

HIGH QUALITY FEEDBACK

Even the most self-evaluative teachers can benefit from feedback. Deans for Impact suggest this needs to be given as soon as possible after the practice and teachers need opportunities to repeat the practice soon after that. In our view, teachers absolutely must be involved in the generation of this feedback, but **Instructional Coaching** also embeds the role of observer-coach expertise. Aspects of assessment information also feed into this area – as highlighted in the T for Test from our A|D|A|P|T process.

5

MENTAL MODEL

All along the way, teachers should be formulating and deepening a model for why things work and don't work. A strong basis in a conceptual model for how learning happens is part of this. We shouldn't be doing things because we're told to or because we always have – we should do them because of the way they secure learning. **Practice with Purpose** emphasises the vital role of the model-building embedded in teachers' developmental process. Our Why? section helps teachers to do this.

INSTRUCTIONAL COACHING

Instructional coaching is firmly based on technical knowledge of specific spheres of performance. As such, an instructional coach must have a large repertoire of methods to share with teachers. Leading light Jim Knight emphasises that this information is best summarised as pithy, step-by-step guides. This is the role of the WalkThrus.

If resources allow, it's most effective when instructional coaching is adopted throughout the organisation and applied over a sustained period of time. At its core is an understanding of how knowledge, practice, time and feedback are necessary for grounded and sustained teacher development.

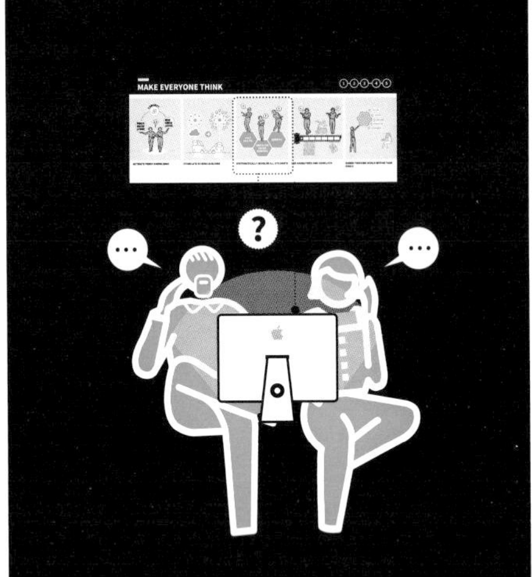

1

INVITE, SELECT & APPLY THE A|D|A|P|T PROCESS

Instructional coaching is based on personal agency and propelled by invitation. Teacher and coach explore the teacher's needs (and the needs of their students) and the most probable solutions within the WalkThrus repertoire.

Once selected, the WalkThru is analysed in terms of the A|D|A|P|T process to place it firmly in the teacher's classroom context.

By doing this, the teacher's theory of action begins to surface.

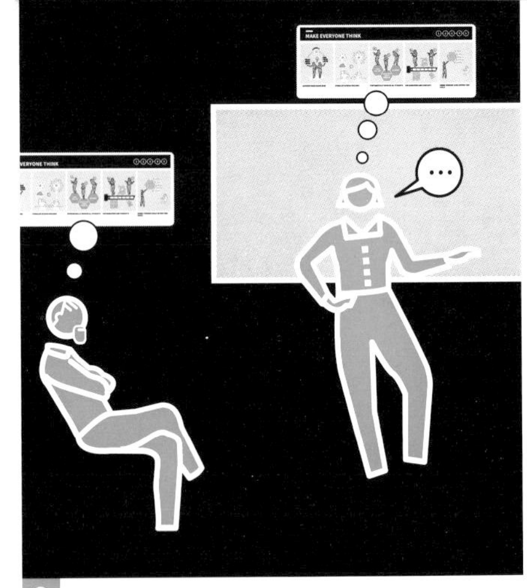

2

COACH MODELS THE WALKTHRU IN ACTION

As part of the dialogue, the coach might draw on their expertise to model how the WalkThru looks in practice in the teacher's classroom. Coaches explore how examples of the strategy might work alongside non-examples to illustrate the technique, including adaptations agreed in Step 1.

During a coaching demonstration, the teacher observes through the lens of the adapted WalkThru. It is critical that the plan and its execution are perceived together, to better compare them later.

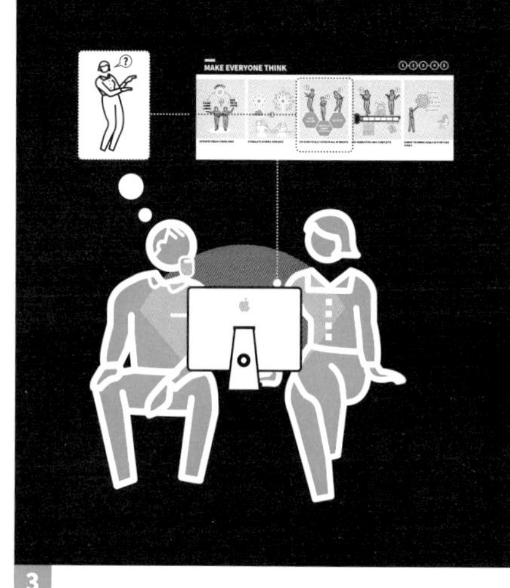

3

REVIEW THE DEMONSTRATION

As Matt O'Leary states in his book *Classroom Observation*, it's all about the teacher's perception. So this step is essential in surfacing ideas about the effectiveness of the different steps involved in the WalkThru.

By explaining their observations and the thinking behind them, the teacher reveals both their theory of action and their consequent perceptions – what they noticed.

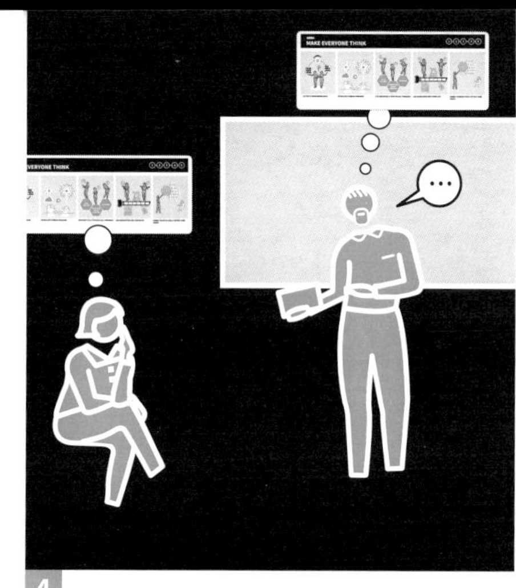

4

COACH OBSERVES THE TEACHER'S WALKTHRU

Soon after the preparatory discussion in Steps 1–3, the teacher uses the WalkThru in a specific lesson, observed by their coach. The shared understanding achieved in the previous steps builds the teacher's trust in the coach's observations. They know that what the coach sees will be through the lens of the adapted WalkThru.

It's this shared and agreed lens of the WalkThru that provides clarity and precision about the method and builds trust through the common perception.

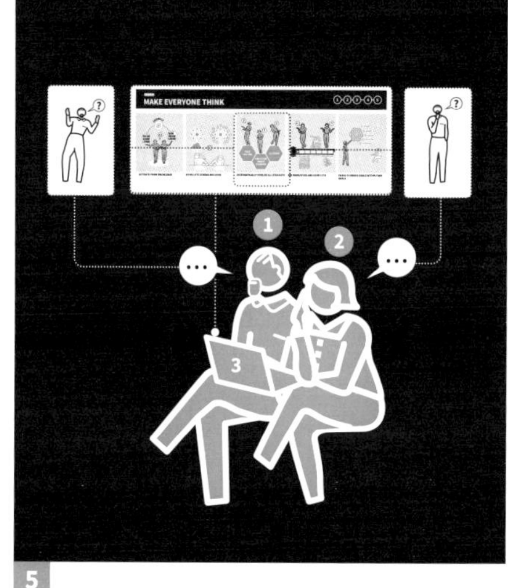

5

MEET FOR REVIEW, FEEDBACK & PLANNING

When back together, either directly after the observation or some time later, teacher and coach discuss what they saw in relation to the period under observation. The joint planning process helps shape a more equal relationship.

This partnership is reinforced with the dynamic of Three Point Communication, stimulating openness in the feedback and engagement in new plans for the next cycle.

FEEDBACK IN INSTRUCTIONAL COACHING

Leverage Leadership by Paul Bambrick-Santoyo covers several areas of school leadership, with Chapter 3 focusing specifically on Observation & Feedback. The ideal scenario envisaged is where a teacher and their coach meet regularly to discuss and agree new action steps in a cycle with regular short observations. The emphasis is on supporting the teacher to identify their own precise action steps through discussion, with a time-specific plan for implementing them. The nature of the feedback from the coach is vital to the success of the process.

PAUL BAMBRICK-SANTOYO

1

PROVIDE PRECISE PRAISE

It's important to avoid vague language of judgement or the nebulous idea that practice is general and non-specific. Saying *'Hey, that was a great lesson'* might sound encouraging but isn't helpful. Instead, we should say objective things like *'The way you engaged Michael seemed very effective; you got him to respond well to your modelling of the writing task'* – because modelling was the area the teacher was working on. Precise praise keeps the focus on the teacher's action steps.

2

PROBE

Leading up to the next step, with action steps identified, probing feedback questions help to focus a teacher's attention on the key area of their practice.

'How do you think Jennifer was doing with those harder problems?'

'Do you think Mo understood why his answer was weak?'

We avoid more open questions – *'How do you think the lesson went?'* – because that widens out the scope for the evaluation when we're trying to foster a more focused approach.

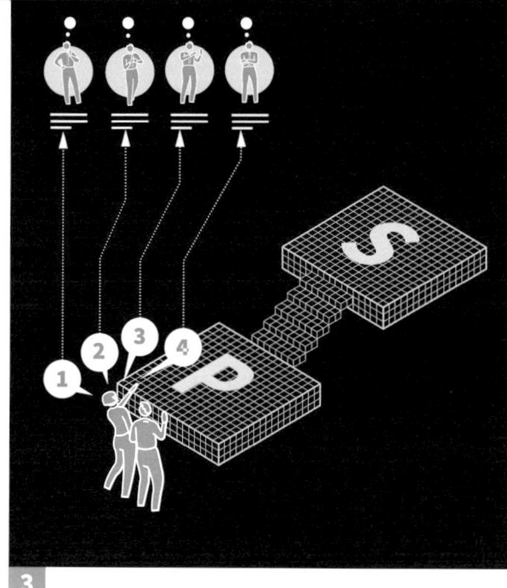

3

IDENTIFY PROBLEM & CONCRETE ACTION STEP

This is the central part of the process. There are four possible *levels* of engagement. First is the ideal where the teacher identifies both the problem they're trying to address and the action steps they need to take. Each subsequent level increases the level of direction or guidance from the observer-coach. It's vital that specific action steps are identified and linked to specific issues. Even the most effective, confident teachers have problems to address, so this isn't and shouldn't be a judgemental process.

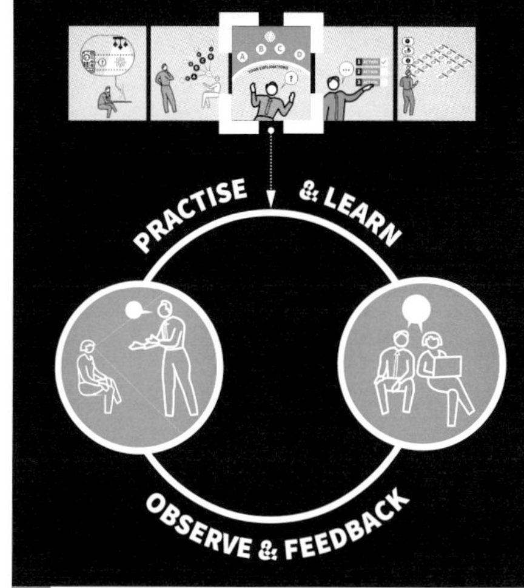

4

PRACTISE

Bambrick-Santoyo suggests: *'Great teaching is not learned through discussion. It's learned by doing … by practising doing things well. Supervised practice is the fastest way to make sure all teachers are doing the right things.'* The coach and teacher should explore how the action step should be taken. Our A|D|A|P|T model suggests people *attempt* each WalkThru either in a CPD session or via an active mental rehearsal with coaches modelling it too. It's crucial to secure shared understanding of what that action step will look like in practice.

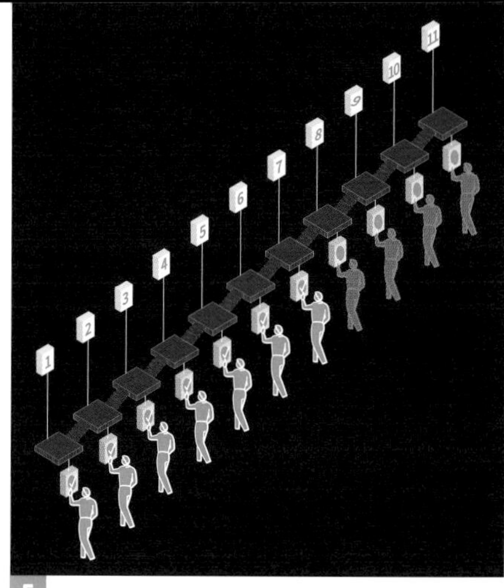

5

PLAN AHEAD; SET THE TIMELINE

We need to plan actively for improvement to happen. Action steps need to be recorded for future reference so we can be very intentional and later ask *'Did you do the things you said you were going to do?'* The final step in the feedback discussion is to agree a timescale appropriate to the issue in hand, ideally in days and weeks, not months.

Bambrick-Santoyo describes processes where teachers and their coaches have lots of very light, lean, short interactions rather than a few heavy-duty interactions.

TEACHING SPRINTS

Drawing together big ideas from research on effective teacher learning, Teaching Sprints is a simple process which supports teachers to learn about, practise and review a small slice of their teaching over a short period of time. The intensity of this collaborative process is a powerful catalyst, injecting energy and generating focused commitment from teachers to move their practice forward.

Here, the originators of the Teaching Sprints process, Simon Breakspear and Bronwyn Ryrie Jones, describe how it works in practice.

SIMON BREAKSPEAR

BRONWYN RYRIE JONES

GUEST AUTHORS

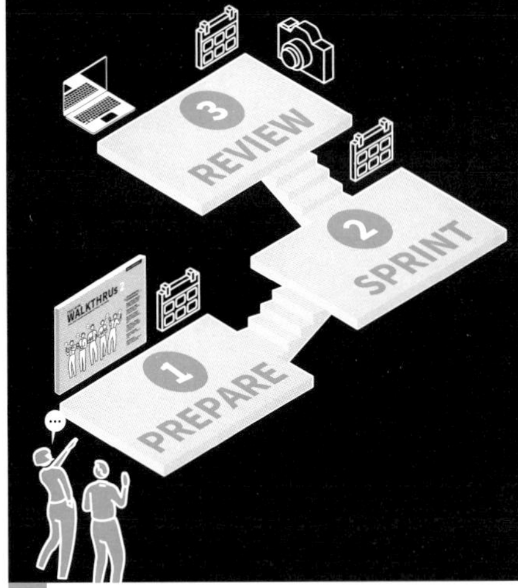

1

SET UP FOR SUCCESS

Before your team starts a Teaching Sprint, it's a good idea to map out the time and resources you'll need to move through the three phases – Prepare, Sprint, Review.

Make sure all the sessions you need are fully calendared and protected from other activities.

2

PHASE 1: PREPARE

In the Prepare Phase, your team gets clarity on an aspect of instruction you want to improve. This involves engaging with the *best bets* from the evidence base and agreeing on intended practice improvements. The Prepare Phase ends when all members of the team commit to practising a specific evidence-based technique or strategy in the Sprint Phase. This could be one WalkThru or a small cluster of techniques. It's vital to establish absolute clarity about what the technique will look like when practised with fidelity.

3

4

5

PHASE 2: SPRINT

The Sprint Phase is all about bridging theory and practice; here, the mode of learning shifts to intentional practice. Over two to four weeks, as part of their everyday teaching, every team member practises the agreed technique in classrooms. Throughout the Sprint, the team monitors the impact of new approaches, and teachers adapt the strategies based on impact. Supported by a simple protocol, the group meets for a quick, focused check-in to monitor progress and sustain momentum.

The Attempt, Develop and Adapt elements of A|D|A|P|T come into play here.

PHASE 3: REVIEW

After two to four weeks in the Sprint Phase, your team comes together again to close out the Teaching Sprint. During the Review Phase, you reflect on learning as practitioners.

The team discusses changes to practice, considers the impact evidence, and decides how new learning might be transferred into future practice.

THINK AHEAD

Forming new instructional habits is hard, and all professional learning takes time. At the end of the Sprint, teachers may well want to continue trialling and refining the new instructional technique. The team may equally decide that they'd like to revisit the research literature, or think more deeply about the broader possibilities for further improvement in this area of instruction.

The Practice and Test elements of A|D|A|P|T come into play as teachers continue to develop fluency with new instructional habits.

ONLINE TRAINING

While in-person training is our traditional mode, there are many aspects of online training that better suit both new patterns of work and the growing evidence around professional development. WalkThru resources are integrated to form a highly effective online strategy.

By everyone having access to the same WalkThru resources, a shared understanding is maintained and a collegiate culture fostered. At the same time, teachers follow their individualised approaches to learning and customise the WalkThrus to match their contexts.

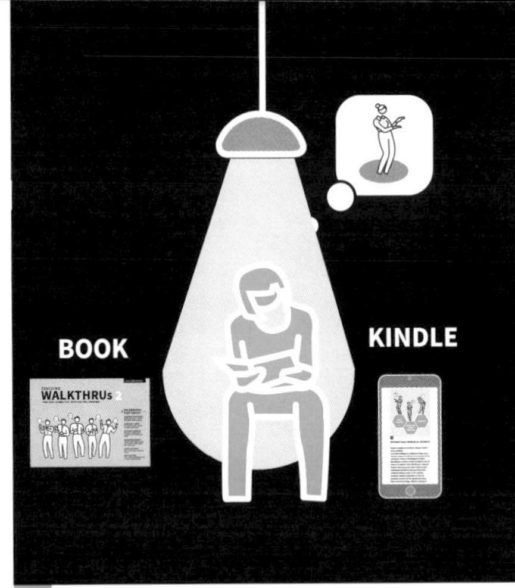

1

PRIME LEARNING BY PRE-READING THE WALKTHRUs

When teachers read up about the content of their training session beforehand, they later make more connections and strengthen the learning. They can read from the book or from a digital device.

With the WalkThrus, reading takes on another dimension. There is a visceral quality to reading text and seeing images about actions – a type of mental rehearsal for later performances.

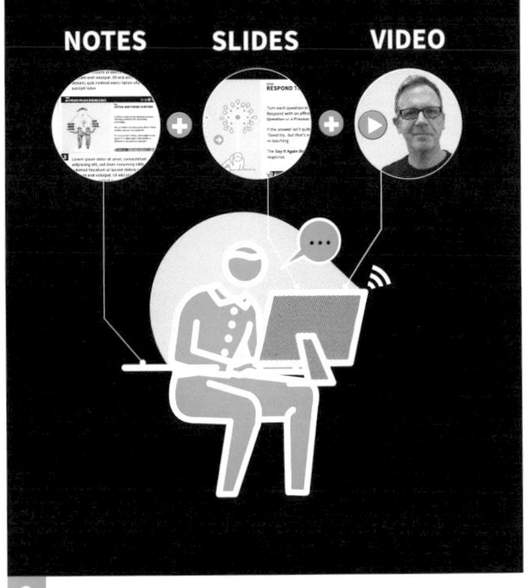

2

PRESENT THE SLIDES WITH TRAINER NOTES & VIDEOS

Online learning can be more targeted than whole-staff training. Consequently, it is often delivered in smaller groups.

Teachers presenting for the first time – with the added challenge of making the experience interesting – are supported with a mix of highly graphic slides, full trainer notes and video summaries. The notes have key concepts, research links and directions for activities.

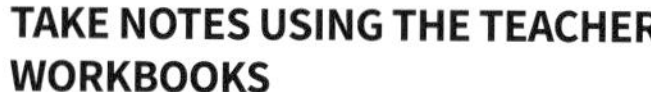

3

TAKE NOTES USING THE TEACHER WORKBOOKS

During the presentation, teachers are invited to take notes in their workbooks. This entails being clear about key terms and the underlying concepts. It will also offer opportunities to link the research points to the actual WalkThrus themselves.

By working hard at meshing evidence with personal experiences, teachers will be primed to look at the next step: adapting the WalkThrus.

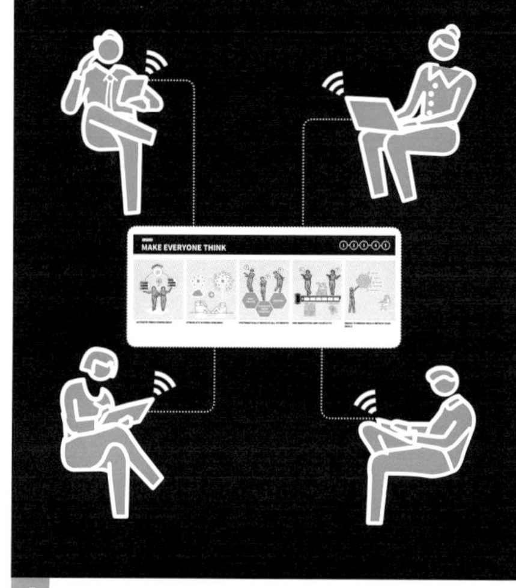

4

DISCUSS AND WORK ON THE A|D|A|P|T MODEL

In digital break-out rooms, or discussing with an assigned partner on WhatsApp mobile conversation, teachers will add their classroom context to the WalkThrus by using the A|D|A|P|T model:

Attempt | walk it through

Develop | add your details

Adapt | tweak as you see fit

Practise | try it out

Test | what's the impact?

This personalisation is key to fruitful deliberate practice.

5

SHARE PLANS, SCHEDULE PRACTICE & FEEDBACK

Either in the smaller groups, assigned pairs or back together in the larger group, teachers now share their plans for practice.

Schedules are agreed for the possible coaching sequences of practice, observation and feedback, in accordance with the organisation's culture and policies. Throughout this progression, the WalkThrus remain a consistent and shared point of reference.

VIDEO SELF-OBSERVATION

When you're not able to have a coach observe you, video can provide a powerful alternative that some may prefer.

A video record allows you to review your teaching at your own pace and as frequently as you wish. This way, nothing is missed, as often happens in the unpunctuated rush of live observations.

The WalkThrus equip you with a framework through which to view and analyse your execution of the technique. Their precision helps sharpen what to look for, providing a basis for a review of the potential gap between plan and performance.

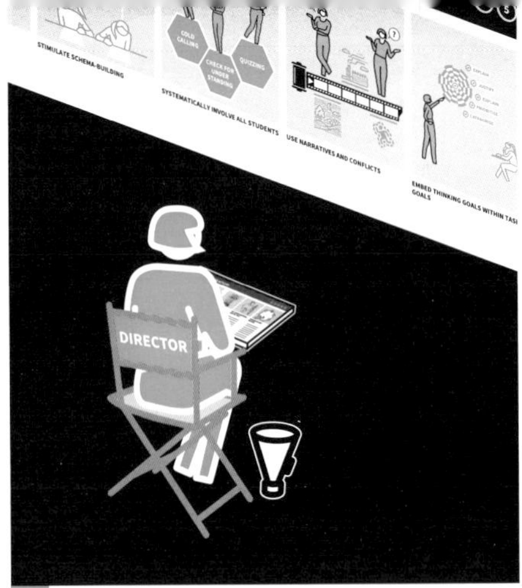

1

READ THE WALKTHRU SCRIPT & A|D|A|P|T IT

Be in the director's chair for your own movie. Select your WalkThru and then ensure it fits your classroom scene, applying the same ADAPT process as usual:

Attempt | walk it through

Develop | add your details

Adapt | tweak as you see fit

Practise | try it out

Test | what's the impact?

This preparation really helps make your movie successful. It's a mental rehearsal that builds a fluent performance.

2

LIGHTS, CAMERA, ACTION! EXECUTE THE WALKTHRU

With the camera set on you, go through your moves, step by step.

Keep the WalkThru firmly in mind, as you execute what you had imagined earlier.

You can use expensive camera systems or a simple addition to your phone set to track you as you move. This filmed episode needn't be long. Just sufficient to capture your WalkThru.

3

JOT DOWN NOTES AS YOU VIEW THE RUSHES

As you first watch yourself, notice how your attention can easily be distracted by surface, irrelevant details.

Take note of your emotional response to watching the video. It's natural to experience initial embarrassment in some form, but try to filter this out.

Instead, only focus on your actions and their direct impact on the students. Don't worry about your notes being neat. You'll deal with organisation in the next step.

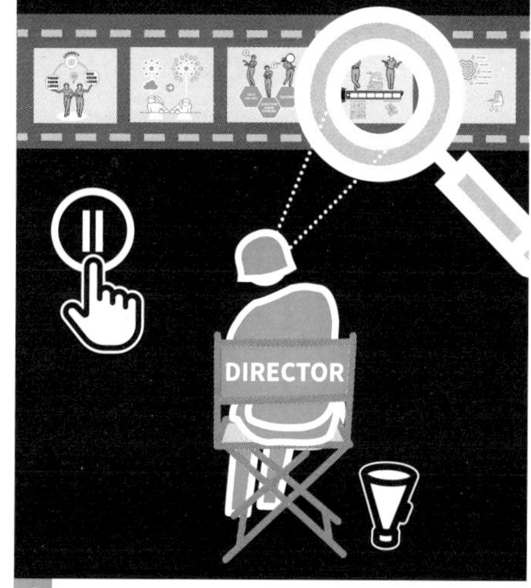

4

PRESS PAUSE, ZOOM IN ON A FRAME & REFLECT

A major advantage of video is not relying on memory. Another is being able to pause the action, giving time to really look and analyse.

Use this ability to segment your performance into separate steps, by aligning your reflection with the five sequences of the WalkThrus. Make your notes link with the adaptations you invented earlier in the process.

5

PLAN THE RESHOOT OF THE REMAKE

Work on the gaps between your WalkThru plan and what your video revealed.

What was the impact on the students? Were your timings accurate? Is there a need to establish a reinforcing loop within the steps?

These and similar questions will shape the extent to which you change your WalkThru plans.

THE A|D|A|P|T PROCESS

A key part of our thinking behind WalkThrus is that they are deliberately generic and context free. We are committed to the idea that a WalkThru is a not a rigid recipe or checklist that must be adhered to. It is only ever a reference point for reflection or to support coaching and feedback discussions.

At the bottom-right of every WalkThru page you will find the same message repeated: Attempt, Develop, Adapt, Practise, Test – spelling out ADAPT. It is essential that teachers ADAPT the WalkThrus so that they take form in their very specific contexts – with their subject; their students; their classroom.

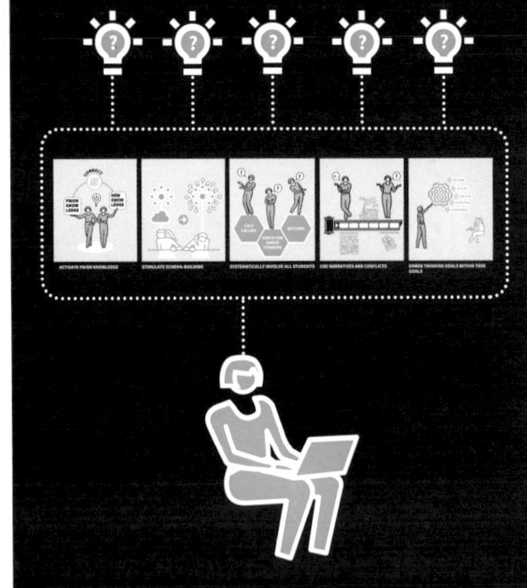

1

ATTEMPT

Take one WalkThru at a time. Run through the five steps and attempt to apply them to your context. You might do this as a mental WalkThru process; you might try it out in a real classroom context to establish whether the steps make sense. Evaluate the success of your attempt. *Do the steps work? Are they in the right sequence? Is anything missing? Would you do it differently?*

2

DEVELOP

Add additional details to the steps so that they are more fine-grained; more precise; more detailed in relation to your subject content or the make-up of a specific class.

HELEN TIMPERLEY

Learning is not a one-off event, but rather a process of learning and change over time.

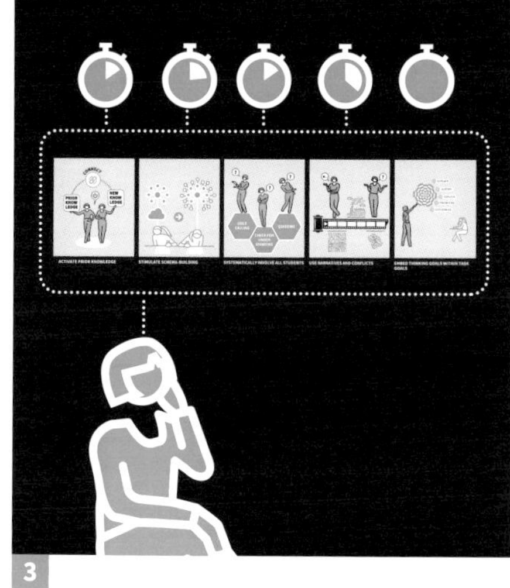

3

ADAPT

Change the WalkThru so that it works better for you. You might want to change the order; spend longer on certain steps than others; create more loops back to the beginning; link to other strategies more directly; or call them different names.

> When the theory behind a strategy is poorly understood, these adaptations are likely to be inconsistent with the theory underpinning them and, therefore, less effective.

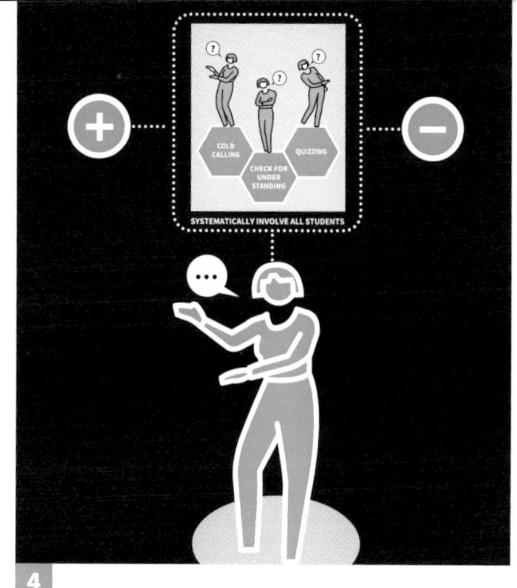

4

PRACTISE

Put your adapted WalkThru into action. If you are going embed it into your routine practice, you will need to practise the steps, evaluating their success as you go, making small adjustments of emphasis and timing until you feel that the strategies are working well.

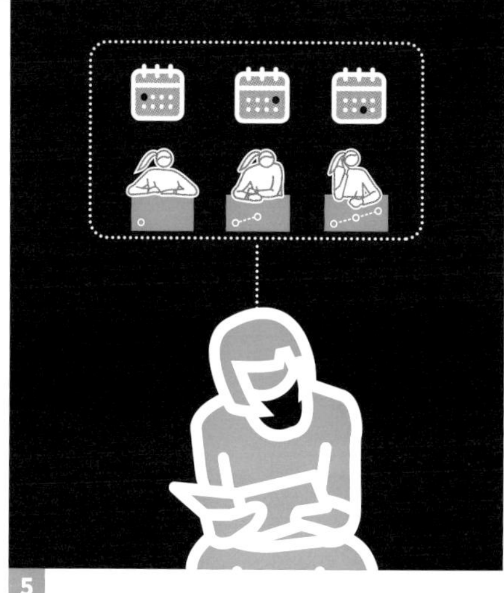

5

TEST

The effectiveness of a strategy is really measured by the impact it has on student learning. To evaluate your impact, you may gain insights from your subjective sense of how things feel; but for a more rigorous analysis, you will also need to test it in a systematic, objective manner. This might include examining the quality of student work and the outcomes of various formative assessments. Continue to ADAPT the WalkThru in light of the insights you gain.

Bambrick-Santoyo, P.	**2012**	**Leverage Leadership**	Jossey-Bass, San Francisco, US
Breakspear, S. & Ryrie Jones, B.	**2021**	**Teaching Sprints: How Overloaded Educators Can Keep Getting Better**	Corwin, Thousand Oaks, California, US
Center for Education Policy Research, Harvard University		**Leveraging Video for Learning**	https://cepr.harvard.edu/files/cepr/files/1._leveraging_video_for_learning.pdf
Collins, A., Seeley-Brown, J. & Holum, A.	**1991**	**Cognitive Apprenticeship: Making Thinking Visible**	American Educator, vol 15
Deans For Impact		**Practice With Purpose: The Emerging Science of Teacher Expertise**	https://deansforimpact.org/wp-content/uploads/2016/12/Practice-with-Purpose_FOR-PRINT_113016.pdf
Eisenberg, E., B., Eisenberg, B.,P., Medrich, E., A. & Charner, I.	**2017**	**Instructional Coaching In Action**	ASCD, Alexandria, US
Enser, Z. & Enser, M.	**2020**	**Fiorella & Mayer's Generative Learning In Action**	John Catt, Woodbridge, UK
Fiorella, L. & Mayer, R. E.	**2015**	**Learning As a Generative Activity**	Cambridge University Press, New York, US
Gregory, A. et al	**2017**	**My Teaching Partner-Secondary: A video-based coaching model**	Theory Pract. 2017 ; 56(1): 38–45. doi:10.1080/00405841.2016.1260402
Kennedy, M.	**2016**	**Parsing the Practice of Teaching**	Journal of Teacher Education, 2016, Vol. 67(1) 6–17 © 2015 American Association of Colleges for Teacher Education
Knight, J.		**Instructional Coaching: A Partnership Approach to Improving Instruction**	Corwin Press, Thousand Oaks, California, US
Knight, J. (ed)	**2009**	**Coaching: Approaches and Perspectives**	Corwin Press, Thousand Oaks, California, US
Knight, J.	**2016**	**Better Conversations: Coaching Ourselves and Each Other To Be More Credible, Caring and Connected**	Corwin Press, Thousand Oaks, California, US

Knight, J.	**2018**	**The Impact Cycle**	Corwin Press, Thousand Oaks, California, US
Lang-Raad, N., D.	**2018**	**Everyday Instructional Coaching**	Solution Tree, Bloomington, US
Lemov, D.	**2010**	**Teach Like a Champion**	Jossey-Bass, San Francisco, US
Lemov, D., Woolway, E. & Yezzi. K.	**2012**	**Practice Perfect**	Jossey-Bass, San Francisco, US
Lovell, O.	**2020**	**Cognitive Load Theory In Action**	John Catt, Woodbridge, UK
McCourt, M.	**2019**	**Teaching for Mastery**	John Catt, Woodbridge, UK
Nuthall. G.	**2007**	**The Hidden Lives of Learners**	NVCER Press, Wellington, NZ
Robinson, M.	**2013**	**Trivium 21c**	Crown House, Camarthen, UK
Shimamura, A.	**2018**	**MARGE A Whole-Brain Learning Approach for Students and Teachers**	https://shimamurapubs.wordpress.com/marge-a-whole-brain-learning-approach-for-students-and-teachers/
Sims, S. & Fletcher-Wood, H.	**2020**	**Characteristics of Effective Teacher Professional Development**	https://improvingteaching.co.uk/wp-content/uploads/2020/04/pdreview_apr20revision.pdf
Stone, D. & Heen, S.	**2014**	**Thanks for the Feedback: the Science and Art of Receiving Feedback Well**	Viking, New York, US
Strober, D., R. & Grant, A. M. (eds)	**2006**	**Evidence Based Coaching Handbook**	John Wiley & Sons, New Jersey, US
Sweller, J., Ayres, P. & Kalyuga, S.	**2011**	**Cognitive Load Theory**	Springer, New York, US
Timperley, H.	**2011**	**Realizing the Power of Professional Learning**	Open University/McGraw Hill, Maidenhead, UK
Weinstein, Y. & Sumeracki, M.	**2019**	**Understanding How We Learn**	Routledge, Abingdon, UK
Willingham, D. T.	**2009**	**Why don't students like school?**	Jossey-Bass, San Francisco, US

BOOKS

When every teacher has their own copy of the WalkThrus – paper or digital – you establish shared understanding across the whole organisation. For training events, this means the projected slides and teacher worksheets all coordinate for effective learning.

TRAINER MATERIALS

Fully re-formattable PowerPoint and Google Slide decks, coordinating with the audience's WalkThru books

Trainer notes for every WalkThru, containing ideas for activities, links to related WalkThrus and summary notes

VIDEOS

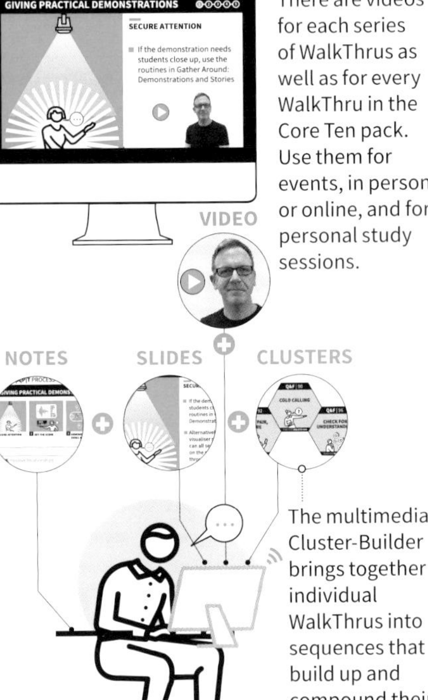

There are videos for each series of WalkThrus as well as for every WalkThru in the Core Ten pack. Use them for events, in person or online, and for personal study sessions.

The multimedia Cluster-Builder brings together individual WalkThrus into sequences that build up and compound their impact.

TEACHER WORKBOOKS

Printed or in digital format, each teacher has access to the full range of materials. Or they can be curated into smaller, more bespoke packages to suit different groups and individuals.

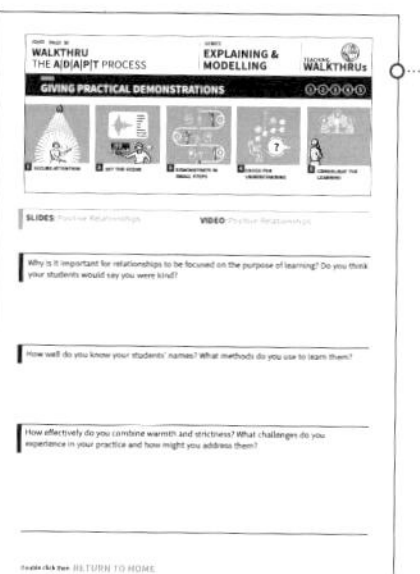

The worksheets give teachers immediate access to related multimedia content, making switching from slides, notes and video a cinch.

LEARNING ONLINE

Collaborate and coach using all this potential.

WEBINARS & SUPPORT

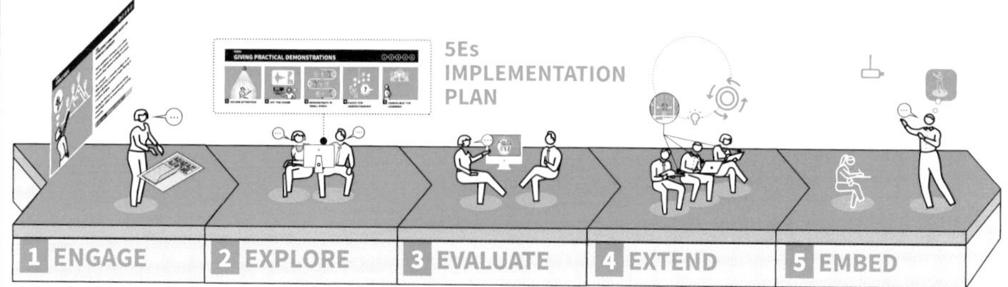

The purpose of our webinars is to help your organisations apply the WalkThrus to accelerate and strengthen your development strategies. Practical strategies are explained for each stage of the implementation process.

Taking place every month, the webinars are followed up by a Q&A session to address individual responses.

TOPICS COVERED

GET STARTED

Start planning your CPD programme

Get going with Instructional Coaching

Visit our website

Email us for a discussion

Visit the John Catt website for bulk book orders